'BLERWYTIRHWNG?'
THE PLACE OF WELSH POP MUSIC

i Jon, wrth gwrs

'Blerwytirhwng?'
The Place of Welsh Pop Music

SARAH HILL
Cardiff University, Wales, UK

ASHGATE

Published by
Ashgate Publishing Limited
Gower House
Croft Road
Aldershot
Hampshire GU11 3HR
England

Ashgate Publishing Company
Suite 420
101 Cherry Street
Burlington, VT 05401-4405
USA

Ashgate website: http://www.ashgate.com

British Library Cataloguing in Publication Data
Hill, Sarah
  'Blerwytirhwng?' : the place of Welsh pop music. – (Ashgate popular and folk music series)
  1. Popular music – Wales – History and criticism 2. Rock music – Wales – History and criticism 3. Wales – Social life and customs – 20th century I. Title
  781.6'4'09429

Library of Congress Cataloging-in-Publication Data
Hill, Sarah, 1966–
  'Blerwytirhwng?' : The place of Welsh pop music / by Sarah Hill.
    p. cm. – (Ashgate popular and folk music series)
  Includes bibliographical references (p.   ) and index.
  ISBN-13: 978-0-7546-5898-6 (alk. paper)
  1. Popular music – Wales – History and criticism. I. Title. II. Title: Place of Welsh pop music.

  ML3492.7.W35H55 2007
  781.6409429–dc22

ISBN 978-0-7546-5898-6

2006032403

Printed and bound in Great Britain by MPG Books Ltd, Bodmin, Cornwall.

Contents

List of Illustrations

General Editor's Preface

The upheaval that occurred in musicology during the last two decades of the twentieth century has created a new urgency for the study of popular music alongside the development of new critical and theoretical models. A relativistic outlook has replaced the universal perspective of modernism (the international ambitions of the 12-note style); the grand narrative of the evolution and dissolution of tonality has been challenged, and emphasis has shifted to cultural context, reception and subject position. Together, these have conspired to eat away at the status of canonical composers and categories of high and low in music. A need has arisen, also, to recognize and address the emergence of crossovers, mixed and new genres, to engage in debates concerning the vexed problem of what constitutes authenticity in music and to offer a critique of musical practice as the product of free, individual expression.

Popular musicology is now a vital and exciting area of scholarship, and the *Ashgate Popular and Folk Music Series* aims to present the best research in the field. Authors will be concerned with locating musical practices, values and meanings in cultural context, and may draw upon methodologies and theories developed in cultural studies, semiotics, poststructuralism, psychology and sociology. The series will focus on popular musics of the twentieth and twenty-first centuries. It is designed to embrace the world's popular musics from Acid Jazz to Zydeco, whether high tech or low tech, commercial or non-commercial, contemporary or traditional.

Professor Derek B. Scott
Chair of Music
University of Leeds

Acknowledgments

Of the many people who gave generously of their time and experience I would like first to thank Ken Gloag of Cardiff University for his years of support; David Wyn Jones, Richard Middleton, and Nick Cook for their feedback on earlier versions of this book; and Jerry Hunter, Dilwyn Roberts-Young, Pwyll ap Siôn, and Dai Griffiths for their many and varied insights. A number of recordings of Welsh popular music were made available to me through the generosity of the Music Department at Cardiff University and the kind cooperation of the Sound Archive at the National Library of Wales in Aberystwyth and the Recordings Library at BBC Wales in Llandâf. For their invaluable input I would like to thank Meredydd Evans and Phyllis Kinney; Dafydd Iwan (Sain), Richard and Wyn Jones (Fflach), Rhys Mwyn (Crai), Johnny R (R-Bennig) and Emyr Glyn Williams (Ankst); Gareth Morlais, Hywel Gwynfryn and Aled Glynne Davies (BBC); Ifor ap Glyn, Myrddin ap Dafydd and Alun Llwyd; Maldyn Pate (Y Blew), Geraint Davies and Delwyn Siôn (Hergest), David R. Edwards (Datblygu), Steffan Cravos (Y Tystion), and Gruff Rhys (Super Furry Animals).

PART I

'Blerwytirhwng?'

Chapter One

Introduction

'*Blerwytirhwng?*' – 'Whereareyoubetween?' This title of a song by the Welsh band Super Furry Animals asks a complicated question about an in-between place called Wales.[1] Geographically, this small peninsular country sits on the edge of the United Kingdom; to the east of Wales is England, separated by Offa's Dyke, a long earthwork,[2] and to the west, America, separated by the North Atlantic. Politically, Wales has taken tentative steps from centralized British power to devolution. Culturally, Wales is home to two unrelated languages, Welsh and English. Temporally, it exists on a fulcrum of five hundred years of colonization and these brief, furious decades of globalization. Wales is a concertina of cultures and languages wondering what kinds of sounds it can or should make in the world. '*Blerwytirhwng?*' is a question posed as much to Super Furry Animals' Welsh audience as to Wales itself, and it is the structural question around which this book is based.

'*Blerwytirhwng*' is itself a concertina question, with the compacted words suggesting the pressures at work on the place. Super Furry Animals, a Welsh band signed to the global Sony label, represent the most recent phase in a multi-layered cultural process. Since the Second World War, Wales has undergone an extended period of self-examination, community formation, and political activism, and over the past fifty years, Welsh musicians have appropriated a variety of Anglo-American musical styles to expedite the Welsh quest for national self-definition. This process is by no means unique to Wales, but as a peripheral culture, Wales has often lagged behind the mainstream; cultural change has only shadowed, not instigated, political upheaval.

So what follows is an exploration of something called 'Welsh popular music'. Popular music could be defined generally in stylistic, class and commercial terms,[3] but 'Welsh popular music' is a relative term which challenges a fundamental assumption: that the word 'popular' is meant to signify something which is liked by a large group of people. Whatever the collection of people, the adjective 'Welsh' makes the group much smaller. The term 'popular' is one half of an historically

---

1   First released on *Llanfairpwllgwyngyllgogerychwyrndrobwllantysiliogogogochyny gofod (in space)* (Ankst 057, 1995), and subsequently re-released on *Outspaced: Selected B-Sides and Rarities* (Creation Records, 1998).

2   Offa, the King of Mersia, reigned from 757 to 796. Offa's Dyke is among the oldest built structures in Britain. There is some debate, however, as to whether the dyke was constructed from the West, to keep people out, or from the East, to keep people in.

3   For a thorough exploration of the problems associated with the definitions of 'popular music', see Richard Middleton, *Studying Popular Music* (Milton Keynes: Open University Press, 2002).

assumed opposition between 'high' and 'low' art. In the Welsh model, 'popular music' includes all musics not embraced within the 'art music' category – traditional, folk, rock, and the like. These 'popular' categories cannot, in most circumstances, be treated as interchangeable signifiers of the same music. In the Welsh example, traditional, folk and rock may be three different musics, yet they are complementary, and have historically been covered by the same umbrella term, 'popular', to denote 'of the people'.

'The people' in Wales occupy similarly hazy territory. The history of the Welsh people is not one of an indigenous, internal class system, but rather one of historical subjugation by their more powerful neighbors to the east, the English. The five hundred years of English rule which the Welsh have endured gave rise to the generic Welsh term, *gwerin*, to denote 'the people' of Wales as a populace apart from an increasingly English land-owning class.[4] This term suggests a community united in the religious ideals of Protestant Nonconformity, in the use of the Welsh language, and in the adherence to and development of popular traditions. Though *gwerin* implies a sense of the 'ordinary', the 'common', 'folk', it has been the central term around which certain musical traditions and a common cultural history have evolved. This particular Welsh 'popular' history shadows the history of the popular traditions in Anglo-British and Anglo-American life, and it is the combination of these histories, borrowed and indigenous, which has informed the evolution of that contemporary tradition to which I refer, loosely, as 'Welsh popular music'.

But it is not just the term 'popular' that is problematic; to residents of Wales, that English term 'Welsh' is inherently controversial, too. Anglophone residents of Wales might assume that a study of 'Welsh popular music' would signify exclusive interest in Anglo-Welsh musicians, while Welsh speakers would question the inclusion of Anglo-Welsh music in an otherwise unique cultural history. Because the English term 'Welsh popular music' implies all popular music performed, recorded, or produced in Wales, it is inclusive of Welsh- and English-language work. One Welsh formulation of the term, *cerddoriaeth bop Gymreig*, signifies primarily Anglophone music; another, *cerddoriaeth bop Gymraeg*, signifies exclusively Welsh-language music; the third, less satisfactory formulation, *cerddoriaeth bop Cymru*, the popular music *of Wales*, signifies an unwillingness to commit to either linguistic category – and, for all its inane inclusivity, is the only term which one can use to describe the following to those Welsh-speakers who express an interest in it. And it is, after all, primarily their cultural history which is explored in the following pages.

That there should be such difficulty describing an otherwise easily defined project is an indication of the range of problems involved. But it should be stated at the outset that there are, in Wales, three distinct identity formations – Welsh, Anglo-Welsh, and English.[5] The cultural-linguistic determination is a central

---

4   For a thorough exploration of the development of the notion of *gwerin*, see Gwyn Alf Williams, *When Was Wales?* (London: Penguin, 1985).

5   For an exploration of this idea see Denis Balsom, 'The Three-Wales Model', in John Osmond, ed., *The National Question Again: Welsh Political Identity in the 1980s* (Llandysul: Gomer Press, 1985). In it he explores the problems inherent in the relationship between the Welsh language and the concept of Welsh identity. By considering the responses, collected

component to any discussion of Welshness, for it immediately places the subject in one of the above three categories. These categories are themselves problematic, and while some may claim that they are not as distinct as they once were, others may claim that the distinctions became more apparent in the final decades of the twentieth century. The process of Welsh identity in the post-war years, like the struggles for identity in a number of other minority cultures in Europe and beyond, may be mapped in a variety of ways, but I will chart the cultural formation of 'popular' music and its touchstone role in the creation of Welshness from the end of the Second World War to the close of the twentieth century.

'Welshness', of course, is a contested construction. Because the term is invariably linked to issues of linguistic territory, it is volatile and requires clarification. Assertions of Welshness have often arisen in the face of an external threat to the Welsh identity, and one of the clearest examples of such a threat would be in the historical motion by the English to eradicate the indigenous language of Wales. In the face of this opposition, the Welsh language has been protected by certain cultural traditions. The National Eisteddfod, for example, can trace its roots back to the twelfth century. The basic traditions established in the first Eisteddfod – poets and musicians competing for a 'chair' at the host's table – were codified in the nineteenth century, and the National Eisteddfod has been held annually since then, alternating between locations in the north and the south, throughout the first week of August. The competitions around which the Eisteddfod is based celebrate Wales' unbroken bardic tradition of *cynghanedd* – strictly-metred alliterative verse – and the unique musical tradition of *cerdd dant* – impromptu singing to harp accompaniment. Most importantly, it is the one week in the year when Welsh becomes the majority language. Thousands of Welsh speakers converge at the Eisteddfod, effectively shifting the linguistic structure of the host area. Concessions are made to Anglophone visitors to the Eisteddfod field, but the underlying belief is that the Eisteddfod represents a protected, and protective, linguistic environment. The cultural traditions celebrated at the Eisteddfod are not translateable; admission to the inordinately powerful community formed during Eisteddfod week requires the acquisition of the Welsh language. For one week a year, the minority becomes the majority.[6]

---

in 1979 by the Welsh Election Study, to the question 'do you normally consider yourself to be Welsh, British, English or something else?', Balsom divided the map of Wales into three identity formations: Welsh-speaking Wales, *Y Fro Gymraeg*; the 'Welsh-identifying, non-Welsh-speaking group', *Welsh Wales*; and 'the British identifying non-Welsh-speaking group', *British Wales*. As a result, Balsom states that 'contemporary Wales reveals an interesting pattern of cross-cutting cleavages: language and a subjective sense of identity define three primary social groupings; ethnic identity unites the Welsh and distinguishes the British; but ethnicity is itself of variable intensity where only the most well-founded is likely to be of political consequence. The critical variable defining the intensity of ethnic identity remains language' (p. 9). The relationship between these groups is of particular importance to the discussion of linguistic borders and dispersed communities; and the alliances cultivated amongst the Welsh-identifying groups in opposition to 'others' are a common theme underlying the development of Welsh (and Anglo-Welsh) popular music.

6   This notion of minority cultural community formation is echoed in the case studies presented in Mark Mattern, *Acting In Concert: Music, Community, and Political Action* (New

A second example, *Urdd Gobaith Cymru*, the Welsh League of Youth, was founded in 1922. Intended as a means of ensuring a future for the Welsh language, the *Urdd*'s activities include summer camps, magazines, sporting competitions, and annual Eisteddfods. Its fifty thousand members pledge their allegiance to 'Christ, our fellow-men, and Wales', thereby establishing from the age of eight a commitment to a Welsh-speaking Wales, founded in a common religious ideal. The *Urdd* Eisteddfod similarly instills in young Welsh persons an understanding of a shared cultural history – and also a familiarity with a system of public competition and performance in poetic and musical arts which had an enormous effect on the development of an indigenous popular culture in the Welsh language.

The Eisteddfod and the *Urdd* may seem able to ensure the health of the Welsh language, but it is important to remember that they are isolated within the larger political construct of the United Kingdom. When the status of the Welsh language reached crisis point in the early 1960s, the Welsh-speaking population fought for their linguistic rights and the assurance of governmental acceptance of the language, which would lead to its ultimate survival.[7] This period of language activism was instigated by Saunders Lewis, the author and former president of *Plaid Cymru*, the National Party of Wales. On 13 February 1962 Lewis delivered his radio lecture, *Tynged yr Iaith* (The Fate of the Language),[8] in which he stated:

Nid dim llai na chwyldroad yw adfer yr iaith Gymraeg yng Nghymru heddiw. Trwy ddulliau chwyldro yn unig mae llwyddo. Efallai y dygai'r iaith hunan-lywodraeth yn ei sgil; 'wn i ddim. Mae'r iaith yn bwysicach na hunan-lywodraeth. Yn fy marn i, pe ceid unrhyw fath o hunan-lywodraeth i Gymru cyn arddel ac arfer yr iaith Gymraeg yn iaith swyddogol yn holl weinyddiad yr awdurdodau lleol a gwladol yn y rhanbarthau Cymraeg o'n gwlad, ni cheid mohoni'n iaith swyddogol o gwbl, a byddai tranc yr iaith yn gynt nag y bydd ei thranc hi dan Lywodraeth Lloegr.

[Restoring the Welsh language in Wales today would be nothing less than a revolution. Success is only possible through revolutionary means. Maybe the language would bring self-government in its wake; I don't know. The language is more important than

---

Brunswick: Rutgers University Press, 1998). In particular, Chapter 7, 'Entering the Circle: Powwow Music in Minnesota and Western Wisconsin' provides interesting parallels to the issues of cultural inclusion and exclusion in the Eisteddfod. While the spiritual dimension to powwow traditions is not reflected in Eisteddfodic traditions, Mattern's discussion of the powwow circle works very well as a metaphor for the Welsh case: the bardic circle, *Gorsedd y Beirdd*, is open for admittance to those who have made a contribution to Welsh culture or the Welsh nation.

7   For a comprehensive look at the rise of the Welsh language movement, see Dylan Phillips' account of the first twenty-five years of the Welsh Language Society, *Trwy Ddulliau Chwyldro...? Hanes Cymdeithas yr Iaith Gymraeg, 1962–1992* (Llandysul: Gwasg Gomer, 1998).

8   The full text of *Tynged yr Iaith* has been published a number of times since its broadcast, and is available online at www.cymdeithas.com; English translations are available in *Planet* 4 (1971), in Trevor Herbert and Gareth Elwyn Jones, eds., *Post-War Wales* (Cardiff: University of Wales Press, 1995), and in Alun R. Jones and Gwyn Thomas, eds., *Presenting Saunders Lewis* (Cardiff: University of Wales Press, 1973).

self-government. In my opinion, if Wales gained any kind of self-government before the Welsh language was accepted and used as an official language in all local and state administration in the Welsh-speaking areas of our country, the language would never be an official language at all, and the death of the language would come more quickly than it will under English rule.[9]]

Tynged yr Iaith heralded an extended period of civil disobedience in Wales, and led directly to the creation of *Cymdeithas yr Iaith Gymraeg*, the Welsh Language Society. The *Cymdeithas* was the central force for language activism from the 1960s onwards, and was responsible for organizing rallies, campaigns and protests throughout Wales in an effort to establish linguistic rights for Welsh speakers and to secure the future of the Welsh language. The demands for linguistic survival in the early days of the *Cymdeithas* included the publication of bilingual government-issued forms, bilingual road signs throughout Wales, the establishment of Welsh-medium schools, and an increased presence of the Welsh language in all areas of public life. Because these demands required a mobilization of forces and the unification of a community, the notion of 'Welshness' fostered under these circumstances is a very powerful one. It is not, however, a 'Welshness' shared unilaterally by the entire Welsh population, for it is based on linguistic territory, and in the last century the number of Welsh speakers in the country has wavered only slightly on either side of the twenty per cent mark.

To define an identity based solely on the linguistic struggles of a minority community within an historically subjugated society is not without its problems. Struggles for community survival in Wales, on the local and the national levels, have also been centered around rising unemployment, miners' strikes, governmental neglect, and chapel closures; the history of Welsh-speaking Wales merely provides one pathway through those moments when the notion of a Welsh identity was destroyed, debated, and defended. Because these moments signify points of dissent or rebellion, points of societal fracture, they are the most vivid indicators of the development of a common identity, of a community. The music which emerged at these moments of fracture is indicative of the ways in which contemporary Welshness was articulated, and it is these moments which serve to illuminate the present study, for they show the negotiation of new traditions, of new ways of understanding selfhood and nationhood, new ways of understanding cultural identity. Language assumes the central symbolic power of identity negotiation; as a result, this study considers music in a context formed by language, rather than for its own, 'purely musical', qualities. While there is much to be gained from the detailed analysis of musical form and content, issues of style and culture are of greater significance here.

While it would be absurd to suggest an absolute inception of any tradition, musical or otherwise, a study of this type can only begin at a clear point of crisis, and conclude at another moment of crisis or resolution. This of course creates a further set of problems. The history of Anglo-American popular music provides its own evolutionary map onto which the development of a Welsh identity in the latter half of the twentieth century may be superimposed. The political and social motivations

---

9   Saunders Lewis, *Tynged yr Iaith*; translation mine.

behind Anglo-American popular music led to the emergence of communities, subcultures and countercultures in Britain and the United States; the political and social motivations behind the emergence of Welsh popular music led to the creation of a community which was by its very nature a subculture of the larger British model.[10] Because Wales is located culturally within Anglo-America, her contributions to this larger history are occasionally noted in more general studies. Anglophone Wales has as much ownership of this common history as does any other Anglophone culture on the Celtic fringe; but the adoption of this Anglophone tradition into the Welsh-language culture is a telling phenomenon. In this way points of intersection can be identified between Welsh popular music and Anglo-American culture, and points of fracture examined as evidence of crises in the process of a Welsh identity. More importantly, these serve as a gauge of changing perceptions of Welshness.

Welsh-language popular music follows the same trajectory as Anglophone popular music, but at a different chronological pace. It follows the pace of a culture in the process of defining itself, of developing a sense of self-confidence, of providing for itself that which the dominant culture fails to provide for it. Because Welsh-language culture exists within the larger Anglo-American culture, many of its points of enunciation are the same as those of the wider model, but the musical symbols of those moments often betray its relative youth and inexperience. Those are the moments which are of particular importance in the following pages, for they provide a grounding rhythm to the process of Welshness at issue: slow and tentative at first, accelerating through its development, and climaxing in a bilingual cacophony toward the end of the century.

---

10 'British' is used to designate the Anglophone cultures of England, Scotland and Wales. The problematic concept of 'Britishness' is an issue which is addressed in later chapters.

Chapter Two

Theories of Culture

Welsh popular music may be a minority concern, but it symbolizes a much larger pattern of resistance. In a global marketplace, asserting local identity is crucial to cultural survival. By using Wales as an example, it is possible to understand more clearly the formation of peripheral communities in general, to locate Welsh culture in a geographic and linguistic space on the margins of the Anglo-American world, and to relate the development of Welsh popular music to the musics of other communities involved in similar struggles. These 'families of resemblance'[1] exist to challenge the dominant paradigm, whether cultural, linguistic, or musical; in Welsh popular music, it is all three.

Before mapping the emergence and development of Welsh popular music, there are several key words to define: culture, place, community and identity. Each of these words has its complications. 'Culture' alone is 'one of the two or three most complicated words in the English language'.[2] There are a number of approaches to take in order to theorize the word 'culture',[3] two of the primary approaches being 'culture as civilization',[4] and 'culturalism'.[5] The primary distinction between these two approaches is in the treatment of the rise of 'popular culture'. In the first approach, culture represents 'the best that has been thought and said in the world', and invests in men and women of 'culture' the responsibility for perpetuating a set of ideals understood as embodying the best in human endeavor. The cultivated middle classes are pitted in opposition to the uncultivated masses, and the development of a lived working class culture poses a threat to 'high' culture, tantamount to anarchy. For Arnold, popular culture is therefore working class culture, representative of social and cultural decline; (high) culture is available only to the educated middle classes. This is the binary opposition at the base of his theory, and has served as the

---

1   Families of resemblance' is a term used by George Lipsitz in his study of Hispanic musicians in Los Angeles, 'Cruising Around the Historical Bloc – Postmodernism and Popular Music in East Los Angeles', *Cultural Critique* 5 (1986–87): 157–77.

2   Raymond Williams, 'Culture', in *Keywords* (London: Fontana Press, 1988), p. 87.

3   A helpful summary of the different approaches to the theory of culture may be found in John Storey, ed., *Cultural Theory and Popular Culture: A Reader* (Edinburgh: Edinburgh University Press, 1996).

4   See in particular Matthew Arnold, *Culture and Anarchy* (London: Cambridge University Press, 1932) and F.R. Leavis, *Mass Civilisation and Minority Culture* (Cambridge: Minority Press, 1930).

5   Primary texts of interest here are Raymond Williams, *The Long Revolution* (London: Chatto & Windus, 1961) and *Culture and Society: 1780–1950* (New York: Columbia University Press, 1983); Richard Hoggart, *The Uses of Literacy* (Oxford: Oxford University Press, 1958); and Stuart Hall and Paddy Whannel, *The Popular Arts* (London: Pantheon Books, 1964).

argument with which culturalism has been engaged in critical dialogue. Culturalism, by contrast, is a theory which stresses production over consumption, and which offers tools for the deeper understanding of a culture through its artefacts, or documented practices. It is in the work of Hoggart, Hall and Williams that mass or popular culture is treated without hierarchical language. The stress in the work of culturalists on human agency values cultural production as expression of a particular society's way of life. It is for this reason that the work of Raymond Williams is of particular importance to the understanding of Welsh popular music as the symbolic expression of an evolving culture.[6]

Culture as Process

In his seminal work on cultural studies[7] Williams identifies three general categories of culture: ideal, 'in which culture is a state or process of human perfection, in terms of certain absolute or universal values'; documentary, 'in which culture is the body of intellectual and imaginative work, in which, in a detailed way, human thought and experience are variously recorded'; and social, 'in which culture is a description of a particular way of life, which expresses certain meanings and values not only in art and learning but also in institutions and ordinary behaviour'.[8] The description 'Welsh popular music' therefore refers to a body of work created within a specific time frame; there are historical elements of Welshness which will have affected our understanding of the 'ideal' and 'documentary' culture, which must be taken into account when considering the development of Welsh popular music as a living culture. Welsh popular music of the last four decades of the twentieth century may serve as documentary evidence of a previous moment on the temporal scale, but the significance of these moments is still felt in Welsh popular culture as it is lived today.

---

6   Raymond Williams (1921–88) was born in Pandy, South Wales, to an Anglophone family. His roots lay in the border of England and Wales; his place at the centre of English academia – he was elected Fellow of Jesus College, Cambridge in 1961 and appointed Professor of Drama in 1974, where he remained until his retirement in 1983 – is itself evocative of the processes of and struggles for Welshness outlined in these pages. For more on Raymond Williams' relationship with Wales and his thoughts on Welsh culture, see Daniel Williams, ed., *Who Speaks for Wales? Nation, Culture, Identity* (Cardiff: University of Wales Press, 2003).

7   The academic field of Cultural Studies was founded largely on the works of Raymond Williams, F.R. Leavis and Richard Hoggart. For a general introduction to the discipline see Lawrence Grossberg, Cary Nelson and Paula Treichler, eds., *Cultural Studies* (New York: Routledge, 1992) and John Storey, *Cultural Studies and the Study of Popular Culture* (Edinburgh: Edinburgh University Press, 1996). Significant collections of papers based in this tradition and produced at the Birmingham Centre for Contemporary Cultural Studies include Stuart Hall, Dorothy Hobson, Andrew Lowe and Paul Willis, eds., *Culture, Media, Language: Working Papers in Cultural Studies, 1972–79* (London: Routledge, 1980) and Stuart Hall and Tony Jefferson, eds., *Resistance Through Rituals: Youth Subcultures in Post-War Britain* (London: Routledge, 1976).

8   Williams, *The Long Revolution*, p. 57.

In *Culture and Society* Williams states that

[t]he word, culture, cannot automatically be pressed into service as any kind of social or personal directive. Its emergence, in its modern meanings, marks the effort at total qualitative assessment, but what it indicates is a process, not a conclusion.[9]

This notion of process, of continual motion, is central to the understanding of any creative culture. There is similarly an implication of processual cycles in popular culture, determined by political and social factors. The interplay between political struggle and social change was reflected in the music created by the Welsh-speaking community, and as the need for political action changed, so did the music.

The idea of 'community' is similarly bound to the idea of 'culture', and it is one which Raymond Williams illuminates in terms of 'communication'. This raises the central argument in any discussion of Welsh popular music: language. Without language, there can be no communication; without communication there can be no culture.[10] But it is the exclusive nature of a minority language which complicates the understanding of a popular culture based on that language. There is a contradiction inherent in the term 'Welsh popular music': it is a music popular to a minority of the population of Wales, itself a minority culture situated in the larger political construction of the United Kingdom, itself a small network of islands located on the fringes of the European continent. Any discussion of such a 'popular' culture is by nature relative; yet the network of communication established in the Welsh-speaking community has developed into a microcosm of the larger British model. The relationships between the Welsh and British models determine our understanding of Wales as a separate culture, and inform discussions of the 'micro' level in terms of dominant and subordinate cultures, hegemony and counter-hegemony.

Theorizing Welsh Popular Culture

Cultural history must be more than the sum of the particular histories, for it is with the relations between them, the particular forms of the whole organization, that it is especially concerned. I would then define the theory of culture as the study of relationships between elements in a whole way of life. The analysis of culture is the attempt to discover the nature of the organization which is the complex of these relationships. Analysis of particular works or institutions is, in this context, analysis of their essential kind of organization, the relationships which works or institutions embody as parts of the organization as a whole. A key-word, in such analysis, is pattern: it is with the discovery of patterns of a characteristic kind that any useful cultural analysis begins, and it is with the relationships between these patterns, which sometimes reveal unexpected identities and correspondences in hitherto separately considered activities, sometimes again reveal discontinuities of an unexpected kind, that general cultural analysis is concerned.[11]

---

9 Williams, *Culture and Society: 1780–1950*, p. 295.

10 This is not to suggest that music, even without words, does not communicate as a series of codes. This is an issue to which I return in Chapter 12.

11 Williams, *The Long Revolution*, pp. 46–7.

There are a number of elements at play in the theorizing of Welsh culture in general and Welsh popular culture in particular, and they are all to some extent determined by the relationship between Wales and the Anglo-American dominant culture. First, there are political, economic and social arrangements. In its role as western component of the United Kingdom, Wales has historically been reliant on London government for political and economic matters. Even with the establishment of the National Assembly for Wales in 1999, very few matters concerning domestic political life in Wales are determined on her own soil. Although greater governmental representation is given to the people of Wales in the National Assembly than in Westminster, the political strength in Cardiff is limited by funds dispersed by London. The economic climate in Wales has changed in the years since the establishment of the Welsh Assembly, and will continue to change; but the dependence of Wales upon England has determined the relationship between the two countries, which at particular moments in history has been rife with resentment. This has in some instances been the binding element in social formations, which have produced cultural artefacts through which their resentment has been filtered.

Though Wales may have been reliant on England for political and economic stability, her social arrangements have been based on a more indigenous model. The Nonconformist chapel exerted perhaps the most significant influence on the construction of a Welsh identity. In applying a cultural theory to the history of Welsh popular music it is important to consider the extent to which this social arrangement has been reinforced and altered. That is to say, by what means, and at what points in history, has a 'traditional' configuration of 'Welshness' been determined, exploited, and refuted.

> In a society as a whole, and in all its particular activities, the cultural tradition can be seen as a continual selection and re-selection of ancestors. Particular lines will be drawn, often for as long as a century, and then suddenly, with some new stage in growth, these will be cancelled or weakened, and new lines drawn. In the analysis of contemporary culture, the existing state of the selective tradition is of vital importance, for it is often true that some change in this tradition – establishing new lines with the past, breaking or re-drawing existing lines – is a radical kind of *contemporary* change. We tend to underestimate the extent to which the cultural tradition is not only a selection but also an interpretation.[12]

The artefacts in which a culture invests historical importance provide an insight into the values of the culture, and the collection of artefacts maps a progression of the culture through different points in its history. History in the case of Wales is a concept bound equally between an indigenous history and an historical relationship between the Welsh people and the English. Popular music provides one map through the post-war years to the turn of the century, and reflects the cultural interplay between Anglo-American culture and a growing cultural self-confidence within the Welsh-speaking community. As the general history of Anglo-American popular music unfolds, it is the adoption and adaptation of this culture into the Welsh context which provides Welsh popular culture with its very structure.

---

12 Ibid., pp. 52–3.

Williams suggests that there are three levels of culture: lived culture, accessible only to those persons present at the time of cultural organization; recorded culture, preserved and available to us as the culture of a period; and the selective tradition, which serves as the link between the lived and recorded culture. What filters down through the years is a collection of those works considered to be of lasting relevance to previous generations of a cultural organization, which the current generation may choose to select or replace with another. Williams posits that the selective tradition creates 'a general human culture; ... the historical record of particular society; ... [and] a rejection of considerable areas of what was once a living culture'.[13] There seems to be some danger here that a selective tradition is merely another description for a canon. The notion that 'a general human culture' can be inferred from a documentary selection of cultural artefacts is curiously reductive; and that the historical record of a society is not an archival source of all cultural production, but only a representative cross-section, might be cause for concern to those chroniclers of contemporary culture whose investment in one particular cultural artefact or another might not be rewarded with its acceptance into a future canon. Williams' qualification that the selective tradition is by necessity 'a rejection of considerable areas of a once-lived culture' instills in the culture itself the responsibility for selecting its ancestors with caution.

As Welsh popular music developed in the post-war years, its agents had effectively two distinct yet related histories from which to choose ancestors: the dominant, or hegemonic, Anglo-American popular musical history, and the subordinate, or counter-hegemonic, Welsh popular musical history. This suggests one further categorization by Raymond Williams: residual and emergent ideologies in a 'dominant' cultural process. Williams' definitions of these terms are quoted here at length, as they suggest a subtext to the idea of a selective tradition.

Any culture includes available elements of its past, but their place in the contemporary cultural process is profoundly variable. [...] The residual, by definition, has been effectively formed in the past, but it is still active in the cultural process.... Thus certain experiences, meanings, and values which cannot be expressed or substantially verified in terms of the dominant culture, are nevertheless lived and practised on the basis of the residue – cultural as well as social – of some previous social and cultural institution or formation. It is crucial to distinguish this aspect of the residual, which may have an alternative or even oppositional relation to the dominant culture, from that active manifestation of the residual ... which has been wholly or largely incorporated into the dominant culture. [...] A residual cultural element is usually at some distance from the effective dominant culture, but some part of it, some version of it ... will in most cases have had to be incorporated if the effective dominant culture is to make sense in these areas. Moreover, at certain points the dominant culture cannot allow too much residual experience and practice outside itself, at least without risk. It is in the incorporation of the actively residual – by reinterpretation, dilution, projection, discriminating inclusion and exclusion – that the work of the selective tradition is especially relevant.[14]

---

13 Ibid., p. 46.
14 Raymond Williams, 'Dominant, Residual, and Emergent', in *Marxism and Literature* (Oxford: Oxford University Press, 1977), pp. 122–3.

Williams then contrasts the 'residual' with the 'emergent':

> By 'emergent' I mean, first, that new meanings and values, new practices, new relationships and kinds of relationship are continually being created. [...] Since we are always considering relations within a cultural process, definitions of the emergent, as of the residual, can be made only in relation to a full sense of the dominant. Yet the social location of the residual is always easier to understand, since a large part of it (though not all) relates to earlier social formations and phases of the cultural process, in which certain real meanings and values were generated. In the subsequent default of a particular phase of a dominant culture there is then a reaching back to those meanings and values which were created in actual societies and actual situations in the past, and which still seem to have significance because they represent areas of human experience, aspiration, and achievement which the dominant culture neglects, undervalues, opposes, represses, or even cannot recognize. The case of the emergent is radically different. It is true that in the structure of any actual society, and especially in its class structure, there is always a social basis for elements of the cultural process that are alternative or oppositional to the dominant elements. [...] For new practice is not, of course, an isolated process. To the degree that it emerges, and especially to the degree that it is oppositional rather than alternative, the process of attempted incorporation significantly begins.[15]

It is possible to incorporate these terms into the discussion of Welsh popular music – or indeed any 'minority popular' music – to denote various moments of stylistic change or political transition. The minority culture's opposition to, or integration into, the dominant culture reflects a negotiation of power. Furthermore, it returns us to the idea of a 'double history': the emergence and re-emergence of styles, and the stylistic homage paid to specific musicians, suggest an awareness of the development of a common history, or tradition. The importance of certain forms of musical production are discernible in the development of contemporary popular culture, and stylistic changes and cultural shifts may be mapped in terms of what Williams calls 'structures of feeling'.

Popular Music as 'Structure of Feeling'

> *[S]tructure of feeling* ... is as firm and definite as 'structure' suggests, yet it operates in the most delicate and least tangible parts of our activity. In one sense, this structure of feeling is the culture of a period: it is the particular living result of all the elements in the general organization. And it is in this respect that the arts of a period ... are of major importance. For here, if anywhere, this characteristic is likely to be expressed; often not consciously, but by the fact that here, in the only examples we have of recorded communication that outlives its bearers, the actual living sense, the deep community that makes the communication possible, is naturally drawn upon. [...] [I]t does not seem to be, in any formal sense, learned. One generation may train its successor ... in the social character or the general cultural pattern, but the new generation will have its own structure of feeling, which will not appear to have come 'from' anywhere. For here, most distinctly, the changing organization is enacted in the organism: the new generation responds in its own ways to the unique world it is inheriting, taking up many continuities, that can

---

15 Ibid., pp. 123–4.

be traced, and reproducing many aspects of the organization, which can be separately described, yet feeling its whole life in certain ways different, and shaping its creative response into a new structure of feeling.[16]

Anglo-American popular music, defined here as an art of the period from the end of the Second World War, is the expression of a living culture. It is a culture generally comprised according to generational affiliation, and as the generations have changed so has the music. This cultural pattern evolved generally from a number of previous models. One such model can be located at the emergence of rock'n'roll as a distinctly youth-oriented cultural form. From this moment each subsequent decade has seen the evolution of a distinct response to the patterns which preceded it:[17] in the 1960s a form of American 'folk' music was introduced to a new generation which appropriated it to speak for the changing needs of contemporary society; in the 1970s political and social unrest were reflected in an extreme paring-down of musical form to its basic elements; in the 1980s there was a re-urbanization of popular music as its political messages were relayed via previously marginalized communities; and in the 1990s a combination of traditions were revisited in an attempt to define a new structure of feeling. It could be argued therefore that each generation was 'trained' on an existing model, and that as discrete communities were organized around the participation in and enjoyment of a musical product, the culture of the period was defined by the music being created.

The changes in social value systems are similarly mapped in the evolution of Anglo-American popular music. With each successive generation certain dictates were addressed, and in some cases negated, by the emergence of a new structure of feeling. These may be mores inherited from a previous generation, the result of changing political patterns, or a shift in economic and social relations in the culture. One example of this would be protest music of the 1960s. The international desire for radical social change was not an inheritance from a previous generation; it was a reaction to it. Popular music of that period was free to express contemporary political views in part because certain boundaries and restrictions on popular culture had been negated with the emergence of rock'n'roll in the 1950s. This is an over-simplification, but it serves to prove the earlier point that popular music is culture in process, and as such, popular music can be interpreted as a communication from that culture.

The same points may be made with regard to Welsh popular music, with the added complication of language to consider. Wales, as a nation in the United Kingdom, is part of the Anglo-American culture; Welsh-speaking Wales is marginalized from the mainstream of that culture. As part of the dominant culture Wales had access to this 'deep community' of popular musicians; but Welsh-speaking musicians on the margins of the Anglo-American popular culture were faced with a kind of choice, either to embrace the cultural pattern, or to shape it into a different structure of feeling which prioritized language difference above commonality. Here again, there can be

---

16 Williams, *The Long Revolution*, p. 48.

17 A decade is purely a temporal, not a stylistic, marker. Though certain stylistic traits may be neatly categorized as representing the 'sound' of the 1960s, 1970s, etc., in no way does this periodicity determine style in absolute terms.

no culture without communication, and communication is dependent upon language. Language identifies community, and the Welsh language identifies a community with a particular political agenda. The structures of feeling which emerge in the social history of Welsh popular music, while reflecting to some extent those of the Anglo-American culture, were born of the cultural needs of a particular community. The articulations of those needs may be interpreted as following an ideological pattern – dominant, residual, or emergent.

Language and Culture

It is clearly of vital importance to a culture that its common language should not decline in strength, richness and flexibility; that it should, further, be adequate to express new experience, and to clarify change.[18]

The Welsh language was modernized in part through popular music, and popular music provided the vehicle by which the Welsh-speaking community could be mobilized. The idea of 'community' is explored further in the next chapter; what must be addressed now is the role of language in the shaping of a structure of feeling.

The centrality of the Welsh language to the continuing cultural struggle between Wales and England is reflected in one sentence from Gwyn Alf Williams: 'Whom the Gods wish to destroy they first afflict with a language problem'.[19] A threat to the Welsh language is a threat to Welsh culture; to eradicate a language is to eradicate a history and a people. A language's 'strength, richness and flexibility' lies in its contemporaneity. Those places in which the Welsh language has been traditionally secure mark a kind of border to which any English in-migration is seen as threatening. Though the English language may permeate daily life in those Welsh strongholds, the indigenization or translation of English culture into the Welsh language strengthens the native culture against anglicization. The moments in the twentieth century when the Welsh language faced the threat of anglicization can therefore be articulated in the emergence of an indigenized popular culture. These are moments which will be discussed individually in further detail: they represent the emergence of new structures of feeling and a regeneration of Welsh culture within its evolving relationship to the Anglo-American dominant

Anglo-American popular music of the 1960s was cited earlier as representing a structure of feeling, a moment in which political consciousness and cultural expression were fused. In Wales in the 1960s this spirit of international protest was adapted to reflect the needs of the language movement. A popular culture was nurtured in the struggle for the Welsh language, and was inter-dependent on the survival of the Welsh language. In the decades which followed, as the language crisis deepened, and as the needs of the language movement changed, so did Welsh popular music. If the 'first generation' of Welsh popular musicians emerged in the early days of the language movement, the 'second generation' were raised during a time when the language movement had already fought a number of battles. The challenges

---

18 Williams, *Culture and Society*, p. 322.
19 Gwyn Alf Williams, *When Was Wales?*, p. 294.

facing the movement during the years when the 'second generation' were active musicians, were already different from the 1960s, and similarly with the third and fourth generations of Welsh popular musicians. There was in Welsh popular music a shift in emphasis away from the language movement and toward the evolving Anglo-American popular culture. It was a procession at once further away from the roots which bred the cultural organization, and yet closer to the cultural roots which bred the music. That is to say, a movement within Welsh popular music away from its political roots was merely a symbolic motion back to its musical roots.

Politics, Social Movements and Culture

Keeping in mind the definition of culture as a process, we may begin to appreciate the relationship between social movements and structures of feeling. A social movement is also a noun of process, implying a continual motion toward change; in the history of Anglo-American popular culture the connection between music and social change is well documented.[20] Structures of feeling reflect the art of a given period, and the art of a given period is in part a reflection of contemporary political and social conditions. As social and political conditions change, so new structures of feeling may emerge; changes in political conditions are in part a reaction to, or a result of, social movements. What social movements enable are 'communities' united in political ideals.

In his volume on politics and popular culture John Street isolates a number of issues which refer back to the discussion of popular music as structure of feeling:

> Breaking convention, in itself, may not be radical. It has to constitute some notion of 'progress'. There are, of course, many problems with the idea of progress – from what? for whom? – but whatever defines it, the assumption is that something has changed for the better. Not that this change can be intended in any obvious instrumental sense; popular culture cannot form part of some Five-Year Plan. The change is a matter of feelings and of moments. Popular culture's radicalism is measured in its power to disconcert, in the way it raises questions rather than answers them, in the way it reveals feelings rather than reflections. But even if popular culture is not prescriptive, even if it cannot be 'designed', it would be a mistake to overlook the political processes that make its effects possible (and the other processes that might operate).[21]

The 'unpopular popular' is a useful phrase to apply to a definition of Welsh popular culture. It removes value judgment from the concept of 'popular', implying that a

---

20 The collection edited by R. Serge Denisoff and Richard A. Peterson, *The Sounds of Social Change: Studies in Popular Culture* (Chicago: Rand McNally, 1972), provides a useful contemporary account of the politics of popular music during a period of significant social change. For more recent studies of politics and popular music see Ron Eyerman and Andrew Jamison, *Music and Social Movements: Mobilizing Traditions in the Twentieth Century* (Cambridge: Cambridge University Press, 1998); Mark Mattern, *Acting in Concert: Music, Community, and Political Action*; and John Street, *Rebel Rock* (Oxford: Basil Blackwell, 1986) and his *Politics and Popular Culture* (Cambridge: Polity Press, 1997).

21 Street, *Politics and Popular Culture*, p. 194.

culture need not be 'popular' – liked by a large number of people – to be significant. A 'disruptive cultural effect' might suggest a challenge to the dominant cultural order, a negotiation of power; but it is Street's qualification of the term 'progress' which is of interest here. It recalls Raymond Williams' notion of selective tradition, the continuities which are carried over from one cultural generation to the next. When those continuities are broken, when the patterns are changed in the emergence of a new structure of feeling, there is a palpable sense of progress from one cultural articulation to the next. As Street suggests, the change may not be radical in and of itself; it is the reaction to change that gauges radicalism. This brings us to a central component in the identification of a culture: its boundaries.

Culture and (Linguistic) Boundaries

> For culture – the weaker, more secular version of that thing called religion – is not a 'substance' or a phenomenon in its own right, it is an objective mirage that arises out of the relationship between at least two groups. This is to say that no group 'has' a culture all by itself: culture is the nimbus perceived by one group when it comes into contact with and observes another one. It is the objectification of everything alien and strange about the contact group: in this context, it is of no little interest to observe that one of the first books on the interrelationship of groups (the constitutive role of the boundary, the way each group is defined by and defines the other), draws on Erving Goffman's *Stigma* for an account of how defining marks function for other people: in this sense, then, a 'culture' is the ensemble of stigmata one group bears on the eyes of the other group (and vice versa).[22]

One common trait among social movements and structures of feeling is the unspoken organization of community. A social movement presupposes an understood commonality amongst perhaps otherwise disparate populations, amongst persons of otherwise conflicting political, religious or sexual orientations, or even amongst persons of different ethnic origins. The spirit of radical protest in the 1960s serves to prove this point: regardless of generation, gender, or national affiliation, communities were organized around the desire for the establishment of equal civil rights for African-Americans, for the end to the war in Vietnam, for the promotion of expanded consciousness, for the legalization of homosexuality, and for a number of other issues aimed at promoting peace and tolerance. In some cases social and political concerns were common across these communities, but the structure of feeling which emerged as a result of a number of factors at this particular point in history was articulated variously by these different communities, seemingly united in a common desire for change. Commonality and community are again invoked as two elements of the same cultural process.

What separates one community from another is a difference in ideology. As the objective here is to map the development of a Welsh identity, language serves as the most obvious inherent ideological boundary separating the Welsh community from any other. Those who speak Welsh are automatically admitted into the community;

22 Fredric Jameson, 'On "Cultural Studies"', *Social Text* 34 (1993), p. 33.

those who do not speak Welsh remain on the outside. It is a fundamental 'us vs. them' construction common to any linguistic community, whether in the majority or the minority of any nation. But there is a deeper linguistic territoriality perceptible in historically marginalized communities, or those communities seeking recognition within a larger political entity. In this respect there are parallels to be drawn between the Welsh community and other Celtic minorities – Irish, Scots Gaelic, Breton – as well as with linguistic minorities located within larger European nation-states – Basque, Catalan, Galician. These are sympathetic kinship ties – 'families of resemblance' – which are commonly drawn as strategies of empowerment, and especially in discussions of minority cultures in the postmodern world. Before re-assessing the development of Welshness in these terms, it would be instructive to address the problems inherent in the construction of cultural identity based on linguistic organization.

> I would make the hypothesis that language, and particularly a fully developed language, is a fundamental attribute of self-recognition, and of the establishment of an invisible national boundary less arbitrary than territoriality, and less exclusive than ethnicity. [...] But there is also a powerful reason for the emergence of language-based nationalism in our societies. If nationalism is, most often, a reaction against a threatened autonomous identity, then, in a world submitted to cultural homogenization by the ideology of modernization and the power of global media, language, as the direct expression of culture, becomes the trench of cultural resistance, the last bastion of self-control, the refuge of identifiable meaning. Thus, after all, nations do not seem to be 'imagined communities' constructed at the service of power apparatuses. Rather, they are produced through the labors of shared history, and then spoken in the images of communal languages whose first word is *we*, the second is *us*, and, unfortunately, the third is *them*.[23]

Here again, language enables communication; communication creates community; language defines community; language unites communities divided by territorial boundaries. Linguistic memory is cultural memory, and a linguistic minority which has faced domination by a 'majority' neighbor is united in a culture with a shared history of marginalization. The 'us vs. them' opposition becomes the most concrete unifying feature of the community. The question of a Welsh cultural identity cannot be addressed without mention of linguistic association. But in remembering the 'three-Wales model', linguistic affiliation can be but one of at least three constructions of Welsh identity; exclusionary claims to Welshness based on linguistic organization are endlessly problematic.

> [The] basic drama is played out not so much between the English and the Welsh as between the two categories of Welshmen who confront the issue of language and identity face to face daily: the pro-Welsh Welsh and the Anglo-Welsh. Is Welshness possible without the Welsh language? Is a Welshman who does not speak Welsh equivalent to an Englishman who does not speak English? Because he speaks English but is not an Englishman, is the Welshman who does not speak Welsh neither psychologically British nor Welsh, that is, essentially a 'marginal man'? Such questions point to the interdependence of language

---

23 Manuel Castells, *The Power of Identity* (Oxford: Blackwell Publishers Inc., 1997), p. 52.

and identity in Wales, to issues of torn consciousness, ambivalence, self-hatred and language hatred, and split or suppressed identity that are part of the legacy of Wales' long association with England; indeed, of the post-colonial legacy everywhere. [24]

To imply that a person is more or less qualified to claim a cultural identity based solely on linguistic affiliation is to subjugate that cultural identity to internal fractures which weaken it and make it susceptible to cultural domination by outside forces. A powerful example of this problem may be found in the derivations of the two words used to describe the same group of people: 'Welsh', and '*Cymry*'. To the native people of Wales, from about the eighth century onward, '*Cymry*' signified 'fellow countrymen'; to the contemporaneous foes on the other side of Offa's Dyke they were '*weallas*', foreigners, Welsh. This, of course, poses central questions about basing the Welsh identity on linguistic belonging.

The difficulty in defining a 'Welsh identity' is inherent in the definitions of 'us' and 'them'. The general (Anglophone) Welsh 'us' might be defined on geographical terms, with 'them' signifying generally the English. But within Wales the 'us' can mean a Welsh speaking 'us' as opposed to a general Anglophone 'them'; or a non-Welsh-speaking Welsh 'us' to an English 'them'; or a non-Welsh-speaking Welsh 'us' to a Welsh-speaking 'them'; or an Anglophone English 'us' in Wales to a Welsh or Welsh-speaking 'them'. It can be a generic distinction between the construction of 'Welshness' and the construction of 'Britishness', the cultural differences within Wales becoming a cultural alliance against the larger British culture. These permutations of a relatively simple binary opposition are symptomatic of a long history of cultural mistrust between Wales and England, and they are so deeply ingrained as to be irresolvable. Yet they serve as the cultural backdrop for further explorations into issues of community and place, and suggest that the over-arching Welsh/English geographical opposition serves to unify these disparate Welsh identities into what Bourdieu terms a 'habitus'.

Culture and Habitus

The concept 'habitus' contains the meanings of habitat, habitant, the processes of habitation and habit, particularly habits of thought. A habitat is a social environment in which we live…. [In] it, the material, the symbolic, and the historical are not separate categories but interactive lines of force whose operations structure the macro-social order, the practices of those who inhabit different positions and moments of it, and their cultural tastes, ways of thinking, of 'dispositions'. The habitus … is at one and the same time, a position in the social and a historical trajectory through it: it is the practice of hiring within that position and trajectory, and the social identity, the habits of thoughts, tastes and dispositions that are formed in and by those practices. The position in social space, the practices and the identities … mutually inform each other to the extent that their significance lies in their

---

24 Bud Khleif, 'Ethnic Awakening in the First World: The Case of Wales', in Glyn Williams, ed., *Social and Cultural Change in Contemporary Wales* (London: Routledge, 1978), pp. 114-15.

transgression of the categorical boundaries that produced the words I have to use to explain them and which are therefore perpetuated by my explanation.[25]

The habitus is another over-arching term which may be used to consider the variety of identities which coexist in a given geographical space. The identity formations which have been discussed thus far are largely limited to linguistic concerns, and the restrictions on community affiliation based on any criteria will always have an effect on the identities of other communities in the same habitus.[26] For this reason the overall social space created in Wales – Welsh and English, 'native' and 'immigrant', 'us' and 'them' – should be seen as itself an historical construct, evolving in its ethnic composition apart from any linguistic hierarchy, and 'habitus' is a convenient term with which to explore this idea further. John Fiske offers an informative point of departure:

> The habitus is located within a social space which has both spatial and temporal dimensions; the spacial dimension models the social space as a dynamic relationship among the major determining forces within our social order – economic, class, education, culture – and their materialization in the behavior, tastes, and dispositions of those who, because of their differential positioning within the social space, embody and enact those forces differently. The temporal dimension is where we can trace the trajectories by which social formations or individuals within them, change their geographical positioning through historical movements.[27]

The spatial and temporal dimensions of Wales are two contested constructs. While there are (relatively) clear geographical boundaries separating Wales from England, the temporal definition of Wales as a social entity has been in a natural state of evolution.[28] The relationship between Wales and England since the Act of Union in 1536 has determined in large part the composition of the social order in Wales, including economic, class, education and cultural concerns. If we take 1536 as a temporal moment of articulation, every structure of feeling emerging from that point forward has been informed to some extent by the relationship between Wales and England – the 'us' and 'them' grand narrative within which all sub-communities have evolved. Such communities (Welsh-speaking and Anglophone Welsh among them)

---

25 John Fiske, 'The Culture of Everyday Life', in Grossberg, Nelson, and Treichler, eds., *Cultural Studies*, p. 155.

26 This is not to suggest that multiculturalism is not an important element in the construction of Welshness or Britishness, or that we are purposefully limiting our discussion to white ethnicities. I should clarify here that although the large proportion of musicians in the following cultural history of Welsh popular music are white males, it is an historical symptom of the formation of the Welsh-speaking community that it is not racially diverse. There has been important work conducted on the questions of black Welshness, most notably Charlotte Williams, 'Passports to Wales? Race, Nation and Identity', in Ralph Fevre and Andrew Thompson, eds., *Nation, Identity and Social Theory: Perspectives from Wales* (Cardiff: University of Wales Press, 1999) and her *Sugar and Slate* (Aberystwyth: Planet, 2002).

27 Fiske, 'The Culture of Everyday Life', p. 163.

28 An obvious reference here would be Gwyn Alf Williams, *When Was Wales?*.

operate according to different needs and motivations, their geographical positions have been dictated by the larger social model, and the social movements which created them serve as points of reference in the trajectories which Fiske mentions.

> The theory of the habitus collapses many of our conventional distinctions between the individual and the social, between the interior and the exterior, between the micro and the macro, between practices and structures, between time and place. The habitus is not just a pre-given environment into which we are born, it lives in us just as much as we live in it, we embody it just as it informs us. It admits of no categorical distinctions between the inhabitants, the habitat, and the practices of habitation.[29]

The boundaries between cultures can be real or imagined. This notion of the embodiment of difference is significant, for it suggests that 'belonging' is a process as much as 'culture' is a process, and that geographical placement does not determine social organization. Religions, nationalisms, cultures are fluid; languages may be acquired, boundaries may be crossed. The habitus admits of a multiplicity of social organizations, embodied differently at different points in the temporal dimension. This is of fundamental importance to the construction of Welshness, for it allows for the possibility of cultural border-crossings. In order to map the social history of Welsh popular music and to consider social movements on the micro level, it is important to bear in mind how the embodiment of Welshness has been expressed differently in the last half of the twentieth century, and how cultural border-crossings have impacted on the 'traditional' ideal of Welshness.

> A habitus is not distinguished from others by a categorical boundary; rather, it is a conjunctural process by which we experience and enact the forces that form (and potentially transform) the social space and the locatable practices of habitation within it. It is a process with historical and social specificity, not a generalized category. But because the habitus disallows traditional categorical distinctions does not mean that its conceptual movement is towards a polymorphous homogeneity: far from it. [...] The 'habitus' offers a theoretical framework within which physical difference and social difference can be related contingently, not metaphorically, and within which social processes can be analyzed in terms of concrete practices intersecting with the structuring forces of a particular social order.[30]

Culture is a process shaped by social and political change, initiated by emerging or established communities. The coexistence of different communities within one social space can restrict or magnify the changes enacted in that space; the habitus encompasses the network of changes shaping the overall culture. This is in some ways evocative of the notion of a postmodern condition, which in part celebrates the multiplicity of ways of being in the world. In its referential connection to the past and tradition it is a similar process of embodiment. Of particular importance here is the intersection of social processes with the structure of the social order.

In the example of social movements, an interaction can be seen between community and societal structure, which may have no bearing on other communities

---

29 Fiske, 'The Culture of Everyday Life', p. 163.
30 Ibid.

within the structure, or which may impact their organization as well. In the Welsh context, for example, the actions of *Cymdeithas yr Iaith* may have had little bearing on the everyday lives of Anglophone Welsh; but the ramifications of their actions affected the societal structure of Wales in fundamental ways, notably the visible presence of two languages on road signs, in public places, on government-issued documents, and in all public schools. The elevation in status of the Welsh language became a public issue for non-Welsh speakers whose own organization was impinged upon by the added presence of a 'foreign' language. The shift in governmental representation for the people of Wales has been two-fold: from London to Cardiff, and from monoglot English to bilingual English-Welsh. The impact of the Welsh language on the different communities in Wales is not metaphorical; it is a result of a process of social change.

These experiences of social change are reflected in the art forms of a given period. To understand the impact of social change on a given community one must examine that community's artistic expression. In order for us to map the articulations of Welshness in popular music we must first locate the 'Welsh community' as an historical presence. Only then will we be able to approach the notion of a Welsh cultural identity and explore in greater detail the evolution of that identity through the post-war decades.

Chapter Three

Placing Welsh Pop

The next factor to consider is the cultural organization of Welsh popular music. Is it a community or a scene? Is it a subculture within 'British culture', or is it a culture unto itself? If it is a culture unto itself, is it a national ('high') culture, or a popular culture? Or would it be more appropriate, given its political grassroots and crucial development in the 1960s, to consider Welsh popular music a counterculture? And what, more to the point, is so 'Welsh' about it? Where are its roots? Where is it located? How is it received? How is Welsh popular music received differently by Welsh speakers and by non-Welsh speakers? How are all of these perceptions re-configured in Wales' changing social and political climates? And how can we re-locate Welsh popular music in the changing social and political climates of the Anglo-American culture?

To begin, we should look at production and consumption, at musicians and their audience. In order to locate Welsh popular music, or Welsh popular culture, we must define its terms and imagine its boundaries. We are considering primarily a cultural product which is created and expressed through the medium of the Welsh language. Welsh is a minority language spoken by approximately 500,000 people, the largest percentage of whom, for the sake of this study, reside within the geographical boundaries of the principality of Wales.[1] Having located the intended audience (Welsh-speakers in Wales), it is important to qualify their position within Wales as a whole. When the notion of 'popular music' arose in Wales, when musicians began singing in the popular music idiom, audiences congregated in village halls or chapel vestries; it would have been a 'local' performance for a 'local' audience. People may have traveled from neighboring villages for an evening's entertainment, but there was a small collection of performing venues which dictated, on certain unspoken moral grounds, the nature of the entertainment to be had. When the BBC began broadcasting the first Welsh light entertainment program, *Noson Lawen*, in 1946, the nature of the program remained the same as its regional predecessors, but the audience was now spread geographically throughout Wales. Local entertainment thus became 'national' culture.

Yet even in 1946 there were sections of the population who neither spoke nor understood Welsh, for whom this 'national culture' was, simply put, meaningless.

---

1 While the media have the power to disseminate Welsh music beyond its immediate geographical home (most notably via S4C Digidol, the digital sister-station of the Welsh Channel 4, available throughout Britain on a subscription basis; and Radio Cymru'r Byd, the BBC's website, which transmits Radio Cymru broadcasts throughout the day for the benefit of anyone in the world with the RealPlayer plug-in), the physical, rather than virtual, location is at issue here.

Thus the geographical location of our cultural audience is fractured into smaller pockets, into what are generally termed 'Welsh-speaking *communities*'. The historical shift of these communities, their linguistic transitions from monoglot Welsh to bilingual Welsh/English to predominantly English, has been the subject of many academic studies and the subject of much Welsh popular music, and it is an issue to which we will return; we can only define the consumers of Welsh popular music as a community, though it is a community which is scattered throughout the geographical space known as Wales, a community of (imagined) communities.[2] Furthermore, the various pockets of Welsh-speakers in the North differed socially and linguistically from those in the South; the distinctions between them gradually blurred with the establishment of the Welsh-language media, and the onslaught of Anglo-American culture further homogenized these distinctions.

It is necessary to define as 'imagined' a community of persons who share a common language and a common cultural background (chapel, Eisteddfod), especially when considering the role the media have played in locating and mobilizing their audience.[3] The print media in Wales, with the notable exception of *The Western Mail*, Wales' 'national' newspaper, is generated primarily in England, in English. *Y Cymro* is a weekly newspaper in the Welsh language; the chapel convenes once a week; local Eisteddfodau are staged throughout the summer, and the National Eisteddfod, alternating each year between North and South Wales, is held for the first week in August. These are sporadic outlets for the formation of community. With the advent of radio, an aural cohesion was possible. Thousands of people could be tuned in to the same program at the same time; one could feel part of a larger community simply by staying at home, listening to the radio. Though these programs were limited in frequency, especially in the early days of radio in Wales, as the Welsh content increased so, perhaps, did the Welsh audience's expectations of continued and varied service. By the time Radio Cymru was established as a BBC service in 1979 the Welsh audience had long been mobilized. *Cymdeithas yr Iaith* played no small role in the development of Radio Cymru, and kept a close eye on the amount of Welsh-language content broadcast, for Radio Cymru offered – and continues to offer – the only nationally-broadcast Welsh-language radio service in Wales. Everything else is English. The imagined Welsh community therefore has a home, open to all between the hours of six a.m. and midnight.

The establishment in 1962 of *Cymdeithas yr Iaith* marks the intersection of popular culture and Welsh national politics, and the beginning of the temporal curve encompassing the development of contemporary Welsh popular music. The musicians who emerged in the early moments of this temporal boundary did so from within the 'Welsh community'. Many would have been involved with *Urdd Gobaith Cymru*, the Welsh League of Youth, though they did not necessarily come from Welsh-speaking households. Any allegiances these young people may have developed could have been to the exclusion of their larger linguistic community. But the alliances which formed from such organized youth activities led in no small way to

    2   See Graham Day, 'A Community of Communities? Similarity and Difference in Welsh Rural Community Studies', *The Economic and Social Review* 29/3 (July 1998): 233–57.

    3   Benedict Anderson, *Imagined Communities* (London: Verso, 1991).

the development of Welsh popular music. The popularity of the contemporary 'folk' idiom for the relaying of political messages had entered into Welsh youth culture by the mid-1960s, and as such found its way to both *Urdd* and National Eisteddfod competitions. 'Folk' music, in the international sense of the word (embodied by such figures as Pete Seeger, Bob Dylan et al.), was eventually embraced by the Welsh establishment; popular (and political) youth culture became mainstream. Within the Welsh community, here was a sub-community of Welsh activists with roots in Anglo-American popular culture. This was a group of people who banded together to make music, who formed groups of varying abilities and influences, many of whom remained active for a decade or more. What developed was a cultural organization focused on political resistance.

In most first-hand accounts of the early development of the 'Welsh popular music scene', musicians active at the time will mention a sense of 'community', a sense of 'family'. It appears to have begun as a network of musicians organized around a central cultural aim, which then developed into a more widespread network of musical communities, divided along generational and then linguistic boundaries. But how can this development really be defined? The tendency toward utilization of the term 'scene' is understandable, but it comes from the position of the Anglo-American center, which would see any regional variation as a 'scene' within the greater whole. Is it appropriate to use a regional qualifier to discuss a linguistically unique cultural development which spanned a geographical space of over eight thousand square miles? And when the Welsh 'scene' developed and splintered, what terms could then be used to define the more localized activity, i.e., the Teifi 'scene', the Bethesda 'scene'? Furthermore, what were the individual, local factors which contributed to the emergence of scenes in Cardigan and Bethesda? And is Welsh popular music an organic enough entity to warrant its own cultural labels? That is, is it a culture, a community, or a scene? Furthermore, is it local, or is it national?

Theories of Place

'Place' is a vital keyword in the discussion of Welsh popular music. Because this element of Welsh culture was born out of a need to articulate the experiences of contemporary Wales and to enable a political discourse within her youth population, the notion of 'place' is woven into the very fabric of Welsh popular music. This is evident in the symbolic drawing of boundaries between Wales and England, linguistically and culturally; it is evident in the sympathetic adoption of symbols from other cultural struggles; and it is evident in the integration of Welsh musicians into the Anglo-American dominant culture. What is more difficult to define is the audience's *perception* of the place of Wales. How can a small minority from within a minority culture define such a small place in the face of the dominant culture? And does it really matter to the audience – at least the audience outside of Wales – what or where that place is?

Theories of place generally involve discussions of 'community' and 'scene'. A community signifies a more organic whole; a scene a dynamic process within that whole. In the Welsh situation, most reference to popular music has come under the aegis *Y Sîn Roc Cymraeg*, the Welsh (language) Rock Scene. This implies a movement within the Welsh musical community toward a common cultural utterance, a common sound, or a common sonic referent. This label, 'rock', is therefore applied to all non-traditional, non-classical musical idioms which originate from the same linguistic and geographical source; but the geographical source is disparate, the linguistic value has shifted in the past decades, and the resulting product rarely coheres to a prescribed consensus. So defining Wales as the 'place' of Welsh 'rock' is problematic.[4]

Doreen Massey has argued for a progressive sense of place, of a non-reactionary identification of location beyond the inside-outside boundary drawings.[5] As she notes, 'communities can exist without being in the same place',[6] and we have determined the same by locating Welsh 'communities' throughout Wales, often within larger Anglophone populations. She argues for the consideration of 'place' as 'articulated movements in networks of social relations and understandings',[7] suggesting four ways in which such a concept of place might be developed:

> First of all, it is absolutely not static. If places can be conceptualized in terms of the social interactions which they tie together, then it is also the case that these interactions themselves are not motionless things, frozen in time. They are processes. [...] [P]laces are processes, too.
>
> Second, places do not have to have boundaries in the sense of divisions which frame simple enclosures. [...] Definition in this sense does not have to be through simple counterposition to the outside; it can come, in part, precisely through the particularity of linkage to that 'outside' which is therefore itself part of what constitutes the place. This helps get away from the common association between penetrability and vulnerability. For it is this kind of association which makes invasion by newcomers so threatening.
>
> Third, clearly places do not have single, unique 'identities'; they are full of internal conflicts. [...]
>
> Fourth ... none of this denies place nor the importance of the uniqueness of place. The specificity of place is continually reproduced, but it is not a specificity which results from some long, internalized history. [...][8]

By freeing the place of Welsh pop from rigid borders and considering it in terms of an 'articulated movement in a network of social relations and understandings', we

---

4   The terminology available to describe variations in popular music is itself problematic. 'Rock'n'roll' is generally used to designate the type of popular music exemplified in the 1950s by Elvis, Little Richard and Chuck Berry; 'rock and roll' generally signifies a later style, and 'rock' is a broader category encompassing any variation of hyphenated qualifiers ('hard rock', 'soft rock', 'psychedelic rock', etc.). Hyphenated -rock music will be discussed more specifically in the following chapters. Where the term 'rock' is invoked, it should be understood that it is used generically to indicate any and all popular musical idioms not drawn from traditional or classical sources. In general, the term 'pop' is therefore preferred.

5   Doreen Massey, 'A Global Sense of Place', in Ann Gray and Jim McGuigan, eds., *Studying Culture: An Introductory Reader* (London: Edward Arnold, 1993): 232—40.

6   Ibid., p. 238.

7   Ibid., p. 239.

8   Ibid., pp. 239–40.

may begin to approach the problematics of Welsh pop within the moments of its articulation. Massey's suggestion of boundaries, of 'penetrability and vulnerability', and of internal conflicts, is particularly poignant. Her progressive sense of place is central to the understanding of the development of Welsh popular music as it is deconstructed in the following pages.

In '(Dis)located? Rhetoric, Politics, Meaning and the Locality'[9] John Street examines the assumed connection between sound and location, and summarizes the problematic by drawing from several different discourses, each of which is instructive to our definition and placement of Welsh popular music:

Locality As Industrial Base

> Here locality stands for a specific way of making music, a particular production process [...] denot[ing] a type of sound associated with a particular industrial regime in a particular place – much as British cheeses are associated with places (Cheshire, Red Leicester, Caerphilly).[10]

Defining a Welsh 'sound' is nearly impossible. Given that Welsh popular music was built on borrowed roots and began to develop at a time when English pop had already splintered into many 'scenes' of its own,[11] the notion of a distinctive 'sound' can only enter the discussion in a select few instances (i.e., Geraint Jarman and the 'sound' of Cardiff; Teifi bands and the movement toward ska and 'new wave'), and it must be noted that these were largely *adaptations* of popular Anglo-American or African-American styles, which were themselves based on imported models (reggae, ska). Nonetheless, a certain collection of musicians associated with particular geographical communities were responsible for the majority of such musical product; they tended toward the same modes of production and developed their own fan base. However small the numbers, however brief the period of time in which their music adhered to a particular 'sound', it is possible to associate Fflach Records with a particular music, in the same way that Sun Records, for example, may be seen to embody a Memphis aesthetic. That is to say, the trend established by a label such as Sun toward the recording of a specific style of music (early rock'n'roll) generated a pattern of subsequent recordings of music in a similar vein, and as their output became coterminous with a particular style of music, so did the town of Memphis. This type of trend may be interpreted in innumerable small labels; Sun and Fflach are mentioned together as they occupy similarly peripheral geographical positions with relation to the center of mainstream cultural production.

---

9 Published in *Popular Music - Style and Identity*, International Association for the Study of Popular Music Seventh International Conference on Popular Music Studies, ed. Will Straw, Stacey Johnson, Rebecca Sullivan and Paul Friedlander (Montreal: The Centre for Research on Canadian Cultural Industries and Institutions, 1995): 255—63.

10 Ibid., p. 256.

11 There are certain vocal characteristics unique to the Welsh musical tradition which I explore further in Chapter 10; the point I wish to make here is that there are few *stylistic* qualities which would 'sound' immediately Welsh to the listener.

Locality as Social Experience

> It is this dimension that supports the idea of musical roots, most obviously associated with the blues ... It is a discourse also used by rock stars like Bruce Springsteen, both to authenticate their music and to act as a theme within it, to create the juxtaposition of present and past lives. Place here signifies 'rootedness' as authenticity, as a kind of 'realism'.[12]

In this sense, 'locality' can only signify the social experience of Wales as a whole. It is possible in the United States to place Bruce Springsteen in New Jersey just as it is possible (or even necessary) to place the Beach Boys in California, or REM in Georgia; each state is convinced of its own identity, its own way of life, and its individuality. These artists operate within a unique cultural framework dictated by the history of their different states, of that state's position within the United States, and of the particular social and political issues faced by the residents of that state. Thus Bruce Springsteen can be a spokesman for the common man, the Beach Boys can celebrate an idealized version of life on the West Coast (albeit one in which they did not uniformly participate) and REM can politicize their music from the position of a 'marginalized' area, the Southern United States, as unknown to much of the rest of the country as is Canada. But for Welsh musicians, 'social experience' implies the Welsh language. The language authenticates the music, and its roots are sunk deep into the experience of life on the periphery of mainstream culture. Welsh musicians were afforded much the same cultural status in Britain as African-American blues musicians in the segregated United States, and singing of their experience of marginality is what located them within a community.

Locality as Aesthetic Perspective

> Place, though, can give a perspective on music, without requiring social realism. Place can inspire an escapism, or a music which tries to articulate alienation. [...] Place takes on several guises here – wide open spaces, cramped suburbia – but they all connect a locality to sounds and feelings.[13]

Again, the Welsh language is the articulating factor, not the music as such. With particular reference to escapism, the Welsh language can imbue the music with a particular nostalgia for a time when Wales belonged to the Welsh, before the English moved in, literally and figuratively. This is escapism to an idealized nation, 'wide-open spaces' here signifying the mountainous North and the gentle South, before the land was raped by coal mines and slate quarries, when there was no need to defend the Welsh 'way of life' to those who would seek to stamp it out. Musically, this is a constant in the early days of Welsh pop, from Dafydd Iwan's first recordings to the early part of the 1970s: an acoustic folk-based music reminding the young audience of their own mythology, the inevitable infiltration of the English and the common desire to return to a simpler time. The 'aesthetic perspective' serves to

---

12 Ibid.
13 Ibid.

define temporal and geographical boundaries, and to locate the community within them.

Locality as Political Experience

...[L]ocalities can take on an overt political dimension, becoming the site of struggles that inspire the music. Most dramatically, the existence of threats or danger in the making of music can imbue it with a particular meaning and importance. [...] It is a trait borrowed from folk and often applied to world music. More mundanely, certain kinds of suburban setting (code for 'suffocating' and suppression, as opposed to alienation) allow for artistic rebelliousness – Britain's home counties are the embodiment of this....[14]

Here locating a music within a socio-political substructure – Street uses the examples of rap and soul as well as folk and world musics – suggests a grafting of meaning after-the-fact rather than a contemporary understanding of a music from within its community. How did our understanding of South African music alter or increase, for example, with the release of Paul Simon's *Graceland*? How was Cuban music received in the United States before the release of *The Buena Vista Social Club*? What can we know about the daily lives of these musicians if it does not come to us through their music? What can we know of gang warfare in Compton beyond what we hear in the recordings of NWA? To bring these questions home, how can a Welsh community be formed if no one gives voice to its common grievances? In earlier decades of the twentieth century, the insistence upon voicing those grievances – or, indeed, living a day-to-day existence – through the medium of Welsh would have been a mildly punishable offense. By the 1960s, it was merely subversive; but it was a political act nonetheless, and brought a cohesion to an otherwise fractured society.

Locality as Community

Underlying several of the previous rhetorical uses of locality is an assumption that locality translates into community. Sometimes this may be used negatively, to define the artists as part of an out-group.... More typically, it has positive connotations, with community being the receptacle of the shared values and perspectives that shape the artist.[15]

Here Street quotes George Lewis: 'People look to specific musics as symbolic anchors in regions, as signs of community, belonging, and a shared past.'[16] This is a basic issue in the development of the Welsh pop audience. The geographic difficulties inherent in unifying Welsh-speaking communities have already been mentioned. A metaphor for such a collection of communities could be one of an archipelago, separated by a sea of English, off the coast of the Anglo-American dominant. Traveling between these islands is notoriously difficult; there are no

---

14 Ibid.

15 Ibid.

16 George H. Lewis, 'Who Do You Love? The Dimensions of Musical Taste', in James Lull, ed., *Popular Music and Communication* (London: Sage Publications, 1992): 144.

straight passageways and linguistic flexibility is inevitably required for safe passage from one island to another. Welsh musicians travel from island to island, charting their progress as they go, serving as a kind of social constant in a fluctuating soundscape. We have therefore added to our definition of the Welsh pop music community the suggestion of a nomadic culture. On the institutional level, the Eisteddfod, as the largest movable artistic festival in Europe, can be interpreted as another example of this. In Welsh pop, music serves as the anchoring element, encouraging a sense of community, belonging and a shared past.

Locality as Scene

> Here the locality is conceived as a local network, which establishes a negotiated route through the production and consumption of popular music. It mixes institutions with industry, and with experiences peculiar to that region. [...] When employed by rock writers, many of these ways of linking locality to music impute connections between audiences, musicians, industry and infrastructure. They serve as a critical shorthand which rest upon a set of ideological judgements. These are not just judgements about the sound and its connection to a place; they are also judgements of places and their politics. Places come to stand for certain attitudes, or imply certain judgements. [...] So it is legitimate to ask, first, does locality in fact shape the business of producing and consuming popular music? Second, do these specific local conditions make a difference to what is performed and heard? [...] First, there is the role of place-as-infrastructure .... And then there is the idea of place-as-identity, deriving from a sense of a local scene which links to the discovery of local musical identity. ... [T]he rhetoric of locality in music can be addressed both as an issue of, first, structure and politics, and second, of ideology and meaning.[17]

Here we come to the perception of the Welsh pop music community. The production of Welsh pop, the emergence of an indigenous recording industry in 1969, and the series of massive multi-artist concerts prove the inextricable connection between Welsh pop and *Cymdeithas yr Iaith Gymraeg*; politics and popular culture are tightly bound together. The do-it-yourself aesthetic of the Welsh recording industry is a further testament to the marginalization of Welsh culture. In order to create a recording industry it was necessary to invest time and money to build it from scratch, or turn to the English recording industry – and the English language – for a creative outlet. Welsh popular music was therefore built on an amateur aesthetic for a home audience; the place shaped the business. The business was built by a small collection of amateur musicians whose creative self-confidence was exponentially lower than their English contemporaries; and the modes of production and consumption dictated the musical product; the local environment affected what was performed and heard. In this sense there is a 'local' musical identity, defined first by structure and politics, and secondly by ideology and meaning.

The relationship between Welsh popular music and Anglo-American popular music is important to remember. Though the former adapted the latter's product to suit its own cultural and political needs, the two cultures coexisted peacefully for decades. It was not until Welsh musicians began insinuating themselves into the

---

17 Street, '(Dis)Located?', p. 256.

Anglo-American culture that it became necessary to defend and maintain a sense of 'Welshness', on both sides of the equation. But the Welsh musical community's knowledge of itself was never in question; existing in an organic bubble ensured its survival, in however archival a form. Once the bubble burst from rapid expansion, in the 1980s, the danger became one of protecting the nucleus from outside influence. That is, preventing the English language from destroying what had so lovingly been created in the 1960s, and preventing Welsh musicians within the community from turning their backs on their roots for a chance at outside recognition became paramount. One final quote from Street serves preliminarily to suggest a place for Wales in the Anglo-American culture:

> While the business of being recognised entails becoming linked to the national scene, this does not mean that the local becomes completely submerged. Indeed, it is central to the process that a sense of difference be retained. What is to be recognised is what makes the locality different. Indeed, the local is defined against the national. Or, to put it another way, the national is being cut down to size.[18]

Sara Cohen has written extensively about musical scenes and communities, specifically those in Liverpool.[19] She suggests that 'locality should be depicted as relational and contested: people use music to locate themselves in relation to others, just as they find themselves located.'[20] Wales is located in an undeniably contested place, with the Welsh language occupying the space between English-speaking Wales and England. Welsh-language music places its audience firmly in this space and locates it linguistically, in geographic relation to the Anglophone Welsh but in opposition to the English. It is this determination to define such a difference which establishes the political content of most Welsh-language pop, regardless of genre.

In describing 'musical articulations of locality as webs of significance woven through sound in the classification of spaces, places and peoples',[21] Cohen suggests that the term 'locality' be used with reference to popular music in the following ways:

> The first is to discuss networks of social relationships, practices, and processes extending across particular places. This would depict locality not as a bounded entity with a fixed history and geography, but as shifting concepts and representations or, as Doreen Massey has put it, 'as articulated moments'.[22]

This concept of locality recognizes the importance of temporal realignment, of the *process* of locating culture. Especially with regard to communities situated

---

18 Ibid., p. 260.

19 See Sara Cohen, *Rock Music in Liverpool: Popular Music in the Making* (Oxford: Clarendon Press, 1991) for a thorough study of a particular musical community's infrastructure.

20 Sara Cohen, 'Localizing Sound', in *Popular Music - Style and Identity*, pp. 61–7.

21 Ibid., p. 66.

22 Reference to Doreen Massey, 'Power-Geometry and a Progressive Sense of Place', in Jon Bird et al., eds., *Mapping the Futures: Local Cultures, Global Change* (London: Routledge, 1993).

within shifting social or political climates, the 'articulated moments' of their self-location are those moments of cultural production which are most vital to our outside understanding of them. Almost every surge in Welsh musical production, or articulated musical change, occurred at a point of political contention. Those temporal points are vital to our understanding of the Welsh musical community in its shifting self-representation.

> Second, 'locality' could be used to imply a methodological orientation concerned with the particular rather than the general, the concrete rather than the abstract. It could also emphasize interconnections and interdependencies between, for example, space and time, the contextual and the conceptual, the individual and the collective, self and other.[23]

Again, this takes into consideration the changing conception of 'Welshness'. How Welshness was defined in each decade, for example from the 1950s to the 1990s; how the nostalgic longing for an idealized 'Wales' was juxtaposed against the reality of massive unemployment and encroaching Anglicization; how Welsh communities were unified metaphorically yet remained separated geographically; how the musician's concept of him/herself fit within the musical community and within the wider world; all of these questions are raised in an attempt to define Welshness. But the answer to each question changes in the context of each articulated moment. Although we have defined the community, although we have located the community, we must accept the influence of time in the process of Welsh culture.

Line Grenier's study of musical communities and scenes in Quebecois culture provides another useful model,[24] as she similarly locates a minority community within a larger culture – Francophone Quebec within Anglophone North America. But she has also located Quebecois musical culture both historically in the *chansonnier* movement and within the contemporary musical idiom. This contemporary musical idiom is based, naturally, on North American roots, an adopted cultural product. The French language identifies Quebecois music as 'other', just as the Welsh language identifies Welsh pop as 'other'. This 'other-ness' binds the community and, as Grenier states, 'the language acts ... as the seal of authenticity which defines the community's sense of purpose.'[25] She seems to interchange the terms 'community' and 'scene', using the former as the all-encompassing category, and the latter as the more contemporary variant, but nonetheless, an important element of her discussion relates to the ways in which the Quebecois scene is inclusive, namely in building alliances with other Francophone cultures.

The Quebecois musical community exists with its musical roots in an indigenous culture, the *chansonnier* movement. The Quebecois 'scene' implies production within the pop/rock idiom, based on the 'American' model.[26] In Wales, the musical community exists within its own indigenous folk culture, providing, to varying

---

23 Ibid., p. 66.

24 Line Grenier, 'Quebec Sings "E Uassuian": The Coming of Age of Local Music Industry', in *Popular Music - Style and Identity*, pp. 127–30.

25 Ibid., p. 128.

26 American' is of course used loosely here to refer not only to the popular music of the United States but also to that of Canada.

degrees of authenticity, the tradition out of which musicians can develop a 'scene', a network of musicians drawing upon the 'American' model. A vital difference here is the network of alliances developed in Quebec, which enables a richer musical soundscape for the Quebecois community, not exclusively in the French language, but by all accounts not in English. It does not need to be said that the advantage of the *Francophonie* is the wide existence of the French language in a number of disparate cultures; Welsh is part of the larger Celtic consortium of linguistic and musical communities, but this does not extend to cultures whose musical practices are based on unfamiliar or unrelated histories. Still, building alliances with other cultures has been important to the Welsh musical community, and echoes some of the ideas raised by Lawrence Grossberg.[27]

Grossberg explores 'rock and roll' as an overarching cultural form,[28] and his discussion of cultural politics has a particular resonance here. He begins by establishing a framework for discussion, identifying his key terms, 'rock and roll apparatus' (the apparatus 'through which ... music is inflected ... includ[ing] not only musical genres and practices, but styles of dress, behavior, dance, etc., as well as economic and power relations'[29]) and 'affective alliance' ('an organization of concrete material practices and events, cultural forms, and social experiences into a structure which partly determines (always in a struggle with ideological formations) the historical possibilities of desire'[30]). Though the term 'rock and roll' is loaded with signification for a particular *style* of popular music, a particular moment of youth culture, and a particular aesthetic of post-war America, the notion of an 'apparatus' enables a consideration of the environment within which a particular music is located, and which generates a particular cultural reaction. 'Affective alliance' also carries with it suggestions of community, of a social coherence which fosters musical and cultural growth. Both of these terms assist in placing Welsh popular music within a broader cultural context.

Grossberg states that '[t]he best rock and roll always allows different audiences to locate it within their own affective alliances. The affective power of the music will vary with the context into which it is inscribed, potentially effecting specific reorganizations.'[31] Popular music is a commodity which can be adapted into a variety of social and cultural contexts. Similarities in the process and the end result of adaptation can serve to link communities, building affective alliances between, for example, marginalized societies. Although this idea informs each of the following case studies, there is an inherent problem in the building of affective alliances between minority cultures. As Grossberg writes:

> Although good rock and roll is often produced locally, even out of a local community with a set of shared experiences, its audience is always more inclusive. The notion of

---

27 Lawrence Grossberg, 'The Politics of Youth Culture: Some Observations on Rock and Roll in American Culture', *Social Text* 8 (1983): 104—26.

28 Grossberg uses the term 'rock and roll' specifically to indicate the larger cultural movement.

29 Ibid., p. 104.

30 Ibid.

31 Ibid., pp. 113-14.

community (and hence of 'folk art') is problematic when applied to youth culture for the so-called community of rock and roll cannot be defined geographically. But the notion of community is a spatial one: everyday face-to-face interaction has been assumed to be the dominant determinant of shared experience and the criterion for community. But if temporality has replaced spatiality in defining the rock and roll audience, then the music requires widespread dissemination to be shared among the members of its appropriate audience.[32]

The rock and roll community is not geographically located. Its temporal location adheres to rock and roll's own history, and communities are forged out of its particular stylistic shifts, which assumes an effective mode of dissemination across spatial boundaries. This implies, necessarily, the hegemonic position of a particular musical product in the mainstream culture. For the purposes of this discussion we may assume that the following are true: the Welsh language produces a community. This community represents a small cultural market, but the desire for linguistic survival encourages a wide variety in the musical product available in the Welsh language (i.e., traditional folk, folk-rock, country-rock, rock and roll, punk, new wave, reggae, bubblegum pop, techno, dub, experimental rock, etc.). Therefore, the Welsh pop audience is a linguistic community. The fractured nature of the cultural product implies a generational divide in musical taste. (It would be difficult to imagine, for example, a fan of middle-of-the-road Country & Western singers John ac Alun tuning into Radio Cymru's youth-oriented nighttime programs.) While the audiences for traditional folk and Country & Western are fairly distinct and loyal, the Welsh popular music community is too small to sustain a fracturing into those sub-genres which create subcultures of their own (i.e., rave culture, disco, acid, etc.). In order to affiliate oneself with one of these larger rock communities, one must turn to the English language and mainstream culture. But drawing affective alliances with other *non-Anglophone* cultures – as in Line Grenier's *Francophonie* – is a more powerful means of enriching a 'home' culture. A community becomes affiliated with another community; a dialogue begins between cultures; a new sense of place is in the process of becoming. This returns us to Doreen Massey's 'global sense of place':

> ...it is possible to envisage an alternative interpretation of place. In this interpretation, what gives a place its specificity is not some long internalized history but the fact that it is constructed out of a particular constellation of social relations, meeting and weaving together at a particular locus. If one moves in from the satellite towards the globe, holding all those networks of social relations and movements and communications in one's head, then each 'place' can be seen as a particular, unique, point of their intersection. It is indeed a *meeting* place. Instead then, of thinking of places as areas with boundaries around, they can be imagined as articulated movements in networks of social relations and understandings, but where a large proportion of those relations, experiences and understandings are constructed on a far larger scale than what we happen to define for that moment as the place itself, whether that be a street, or a region or even a continent. And this in turn allows a sense of place which is extroverted, which includes a consciousness

---

32 Ibid., p. 115.

of its links with the wider world, which integrates in a positive way the global and the local.[33]

Adoption and adaptation, affective alliances and families of resemblance, domestication and the politics of style, all follow from this idea; but the idea of 'identity' is the next stage in the exploration of those musical articulations of Welshness.

---

33 Massey, 'A Global Sense of Place', p. 239.

Chapter Four

Identifying Welsh Pop

Wales is impossible. A country called Wales exists only because the Welsh invented it. The Welsh exist only because they invented themselves. They had no choice.[1]

Self-invention is fundamental to the process of Welshness. The willingness to 'become', the adherence to some artefact of a past incarnation of 'self', and the creation of group identity based in similar histories and ideals, have contributed to the development of a number of Welsh identities in the decades following the Second World War. At issue here is the development of a contemporary Welsh identity, and the ways in which that identity is negotiated through popular music. The theoretical examples outlined in the previous two chapters are particularly important, as the emergence of new identities of any kind are bound with notions of 'culture' and 'place'.

Theorizing Identity

There are at least two different ways of thinking about 'cultural identity'. The first position defines cultural identity in terms of the idea of one, shared culture, a sort of collective 'one true self', hiding inside the many other, more superficial or artificially imposed 'selves' which people with a shared culture and ancestry hold in common. Within the terms of this definition, our cultural identities reflect the common historical experiences and shared cultural codes which provide us, as 'one people', with stable, unchanging and continuous frames of reference and meaning, beneath the shifting divisions and vicissitudes of our actual history. [...]

There is, however, a second, related but different view of cultural identity.... Far from being eternally fixed in some essentialized past, [cultural identities] are subject to the continual play of history, culture and power. Far from being grounded in a mere 'recovery' of the past, which is waiting to be found, and which, when found, will secure our sense of ourselves into eternity, identities are the names we give to the different ways we are positioned by, and position ourselves within, the narratives of the past.[2]

Defining Welsh 'culture' is inherently problematic. Linguistic affiliation and the community formations centered around linguistic affiliation are sites of political and social struggle. Though it would be possible to follow Stuart Hall's first model for thinking about cultural identity, and invoke unilaterally Welsh 'common historical experiences and shared cultural codes' in an exploration of twentieth-century

---

1 Gwyn A. Williams, *When Was Wales?*, p. 2.
2 Stuart Hall, 'Cultural Identity and Diaspora', in Jonathan Rutherford, ed., *Identity: Community, Culture, Difference* (London: Lawrence & Wishart, 1998), pp. 223, 225.

Welshness, the frame of reference here must be widened to encompass Anglo-American cultural codes and historical experience. It might then be possible to see the ways in which Welshness is positioned by the different Welsh communities within the 'narratives of the past'. That is to say, Wales has to be positioned first as an agent in Anglo-American culture; the development of popular culture in the post-war years then serves as a common cultural referent, a 'continuous frame of reference' apart from the actual, immediate social history of Wales. The emergence of new Welsh identities within this cultural referent is therefore more than a mere 'positioning'; it is a negotiation of power. As Hall qualifies:

> This second position recognises that, as well as the many points of similarity, there are also critical points of deep and significant *difference* which constitute 'what we really are'; or rather – since history has intervened – 'what we have become'. We cannot speak for very long, with any exactness, about 'one experience, one identity', without acknowledging its other side – the ruptures and discontinuities.... Cultural identity, in this second sense, is a matter of 'becoming' as well as of 'being'. It belongs to the future as much as to the past.[3]

'Difference' is fundamental to the creation of identity; one identity is created in relation to, or contrast with, another. The borders drawn around a linguistic community are delineated by the labeling of 'us' and 'them'. These linguistic borders may be crossed with the acquisition or loss of a language, and are therefore fluctuating markers of community identity, of 'who we were' and 'what we have become'. If 'we' have become more like 'them', the balance of power has shifted. If 'we' have assumed and appropriated 'their' cultural attributes, the balance of power is shifted again. The possibility of such shifts in power creates the promise of unknown permutations of identity to encounter and negotiate in the future, of a further 'becoming'.

The idea of future negotiations brings to mind Raymond Williams' theory of selective cultural traditions. The interpretation of the past and the selection of cultural artefacts – or the importance invested in particular cultural artefacts – reveal a kind of processual negotiation of identity. As popular music can be interpreted as a 'structure of feeling', so might the emergence of each new musical style be seen as a renegotiation of culture. If Wales is to be interpreted within this structure of feeling, the articulations of Welshness – the interpretation and selection of cultural artefacts, of common cultural referents – may be seen in temporal contrast to the articulations of other identities; the shifting 'us' and 'them' opposition punctuates these articulations and shows the fractures and strengths in the process of Welsh identity. These shifting oppositions also recall Doreen Massey's 'progressive sense of place', whereby place refers to 'articulated movements in networks of social relations and understandings'. Social relations within the Welsh community and between the Welsh community and the Anglo-American dominant culture over the last half of the twentieth century have certainly informed a shifting sense of 'Wales'. The process of culture and the process of cultural identity, the emergence of new structures of feelings and new cultural organizations, and the fluctuating boundaries between 'us' and 'them', all provide

---

3   Ibid., p. 225.

ways in which the cultural production of popular music in the Welsh language may be interpreted to represent the progression of one such identity.

As I suggested earlier, popular musical taste can be defined according to generational affiliation. On the most simplistic level, each generation from the Second World War to the present day has defined itself with a particular style of popular music: teenagers in the 1950s with early rock'n'roll, 1960s with psychedelia, 1970s with punk, 1980s with rap, 1990s with grunge.[4] The political and social climate in each of these decades dictated to a large extent the importance of group identity. For example, the 'birth' of the teenager in the 1950s was articulated through rock'n'roll; rock'n'roll provided an escape from the moral strictures established in an earlier structure of feeling. Teenagers were able to express their freedom – financial, physical, sexual – through a music which many persons of earlier generational affiliations found difficult to understand. Rock'n'roll was seen by some as a threat to the established moral order, and as such became the musical code for rebellion.

There are two points to be made regarding rock'n'roll and the code of rebellion, which may be extrapolated for the understanding of subsequent musical codes. First, the label 'teenager' is a fundamental identity formation, definable obviously through chronological age, but also through the consumption of certain cultural products, such as records, fan magazines, posters, and clothing; in the communal enjoyment of music, listening to the radio, in homes, in cars, on jukeboxes, exchanging records and tapes, experiencing live or recorded music at dances, clubs and concerts; in the production of music, whether by playing along to a favorite recording, imitating favorite musicians, playing in groups, in private or in public. These are activities common across the many structures of feeling which have emerged since the 1950s, and which enable persons with similar tastes and proclivities to identify themselves within a larger social formation. An understanding of one's own identity as fan of a particular music is reinforced by affiliation with persons of similar identification in the consumption and/or production of that music.[5] Subjective identities lead to larger identity formations, communities are formed, and cultural histories are enacted.

Second, the emergence of new structures of feeling can provide for often discordant juxtapositions of one musical style and another, especially as these styles are used to define the identities of persons of the same generational category. It would be wrong, for example to assume that all persons of similar age identify with the same music. While much is made of teenager culture and rebellion in the 1950s, one must assume that there were some teenagers in the 1950s who preferred big band music to rock'n'roll, or to maintain loyalty to Frank Sinatra rather than to Elvis. Different generational loyalties may be charted throughout the history of popular music, and the history of popular musical style must consider the uses made by pop audiences of the music with which they choose to identify themselves. Meaning may then be inferred, and identities understood.

---

4   This is not to imply that each of these affiliations is restricted to the 'teenager'; on the contrary, the generation normally associated with 1960s psychedelia was somewhat older.

5   For further developments of these themes, see in particular Simon Frith, 'Music and Identity', in Stuart Hall and Paul du Gay, eds., *Questions of Cultural Identity* (London: Sage Publications, 1997): 108–27, which served as a central resource for the present discussion.

If rock'n'roll is invested with a code of rebellion, that code encompasses the entire structure of feeling, the whole 'way of life'. When juxtaposed against the previous structure of feeling, the meanings invested in the consumption of rock'n'roll – the ways in which the music is consumed, the impact of consumption on the whole way of life – are incommensurable, thus 'rebellious' to the established order. Applying this interpretation to the emergence of other identity differences in the history of popular music, one would see similar acts of rebellion in the emergence of disco, for example, and its association with drug consumption and the gay community; or in the emergence of punk, and its association with a particular societal disaffection. The creation and consumption of popular music using a linguistic code other than English, regardless of musical style or form, is incommensurable with the established order, and therefore rebellious. In the history of Welsh popular music this signifies a negotiation of power, for not only does 'Welsh popular music' indicate a structure of feeling, it has itself become a cultural referent within which different identities are negotiated.

Wales and the Language of Identity

> If language is solely a means of communication, an alphabetical as opposed to a numerical system, then its loss would mean little. Indeed, it could be conceived as an advantage, a view certainly held by a number of people in Wales. Its disappearance would eliminate one of those divisive elements in Wales ... in favour of an international language of great richness. But ... language is much more than a means of communication. Not only does it carry a view of the environment, using that word in its proper inclusive sense, but through its vocabulary and its structure, through the associations generated by its literature, through the symbol which it is and the symbols which it transmits, it creates a distinctive identity which is at once a derivative of tradition and an expression of the present. It is difficult to envisage an ethnic identity ... without an awareness through the language of the myths, memories, values and symbols of Welshness. Indeed, where identity has to be created so does a language....[6]

Popular music was a central component in the modernization and survival of the Welsh language. Welsh popular music arose out of a particular identity formation, for a specific political and social need, and was nurtured in that environment in a protective and autonomous way. While Welsh popular music is not the only tool by which one can identify 'Welshness', the communities which have been organized around its production and consumption, and the contestations surrounding its relationship to Anglophone popular music, deserve to be re-evaluated here as 'ruptures and continuities' in the process of Welsh identity.

Raymond Williams' theory of selective tradition and Stuart Hall's process of 'becoming' are shadowed in the above quote by Aitchison and Carter, where language is at once a 'derivative of tradition and an expression of the present'. It is another means of negotiation, whereby the significance of certain codes – in this case, language – is constant over several generations of a single process. As

---

6   John Aitchison and Harold Carter, *A Geography of the Welsh Language 1961–1991* (Cardiff: University of Wales Press, 1994), p. 6.

each generation chooses the significance of its own ancestors, a selective tradition (the Welsh language) could involve a conscious choice of linguistic affiliation, a linguistic rupture rather than a continuity. In the presence of a new tradition – for example, Anglophone popular music – a linguistic tradition such as Welsh may be deemed irrelevant to the new structure of feeling. When a new structure of feeling – for example, Welsh popular music – emerges in response to another – Anglophone popular music – it is important to consider the generational, geographical and social rifts which led to its emergence.

In addition to being a 'new tradition', Anglophone popular music was also a 'derivative of the past' – drawn from blues and country roots – and an 'expression of the present' – a means by which contemporary musicians situated themselves in the larger society. When popular music became the *de facto* 'language' of youth culture in the Anglo-American world, the community which was unified in the consumption and appreciation of the music was international in scope, transcending linguistic and national borders. The adaptation of popular music as cultural 'code' into local languages was a process undertaken in local time. The incidents of non-Anglophone cultures imitating or translating the music of Anglo-American musicians are innumerable, and the inevitable progression from imitation to integration to indigenization can be mapped in different cultures in different ways, according to different societal and political contexts; each culture adapts this 'expression of the present' in terms of its own past (linguistic) traditions. Cultural identity is then positioned by 'what we were' in linguistic terms with 'what we have become' in international cultural terms.

In Wales, linguistic issues of 'what we were' and 'what we have become' are endlessly problematic and dependent upon which of the 'three Wales model' is under consideration. To the Welsh-speaking community in the post-war years, 'what we were' was a larger percentage of the population of Wales; 'what we have become' was more Anglicized. The 'us' and 'them' boundary again was being contested, but the new international cultural tradition of popular music presented an even larger 'them' than merely the English, and it was an accessible and powerful community to join. The process of indigenizing Anglo-American popular music into the Welsh language was a slow one, and was enacted largely as a result of Welsh-language activism. Though Welsh-language light entertainment and popular songs existed in the years before 1963, the emergence of Welsh-language popular music as structure of feeling was inextricably bound with the emergence of *Cymdeithas yr Iaith*, itself a new structure of feeling. The political motivation for the emergence of *Cymdeithas yr Iaith* was one of cultural definition; in Aitchison and Carter's words, it promoted 'an awareness through the language of the myths, memories, values and symbols of Welshness'. Popular music thus became a doubly-infused agent of meaning for the Welsh-speaking community.

As Aitchison and Carter claim, 'where identity has to be created so does a language'. The crisis of Welsh identity in the 1960s was resolved to a degree by the indigenization of popular music, and the language of popular music modernized the Welsh language. Welsh popular music made the Welsh language more relevant to the cultural needs of the younger generation of Welsh speakers. While it would be ridiculous to assume that all Welsh speakers in the 1960s turned uniformly from

Anglophone popular music to Welsh popular music, it must be stressed that the production and consumption of Welsh popular music, with its political and social ramifications, was central to the positioning of Welsh as a language of youth, and therefore as a cultural artefact to be re-considered in subsequent generations.

Representing Welsh Identity

> Though they seem to invoke an origin in a historical past with which they continue to correspond, actually identities are about questions of using the resources of history, language and culture in the process of becoming rather than being: not 'who we are' or 'where we came from', so much as what we might become, how we have been represented and how that bears on how we might represent ourselves. Identities are therefore constituted within, not outside representation. They relate to the invention of tradition as much as to tradition itself, which they oblige us to read not as an endless reiteration but as 'the changing same': not the so-called return to roots but a coming-to-terms-with our 'routes'.[7]

If a 'new' positioning of Wales in the 1960s determined a politicized movement toward a contemporary youth culture, the assumption must be made that the self-understanding within the Welsh-speaking community was based upon a known historical past; an indigenized Welsh popular musical culture could not have appeared, already formed, purely from a spontaneous desire for self-identification. This known historical past places Wales in relation to England, and it is always through difference that identities are constructed. As Hall states:

> Precisely because identities are constructed within, not outside, discourse, we need to understand them as produced in specific historical and institutional sites within specific discursive formations and practices, by specific enunciative strategies. Moreover, they emerge within the play of specific modalities of power, and thus are more the product of the marking of difference and exclusion, than they are the sign of an identical, naturally-constituted unity – an 'identity' in its traditional meaning.... Above all ... identities are constructed through, not outside, difference. This entails the radically disturbing recognition that it is only through the relation to the Other, the relation to what it is not, to precisely what it lacks, to what has been called its *constitutive outside* that the 'positive' meaning of any term – and thus its 'identity' – can be constructed. ...[I]dentities can function as points of identification and attachment only *because* of their capacity to exclude, to leave out, to render 'outside', abjected. Every identity has at its 'margin', an excess, something more. The unity, the internal homogeneity, which the term identity treats as foundational is not a natural, but a constructed form of closure, every identity naming as its necessary, even if silenced and unspoken other, that which it 'lacks'.... So the 'unities' which identities proclaim are, in fact, constructed within the play of power and exclusion, and are the result, not of a natural and inevitable or primordial totality but of the naturalized, overdetermined process of 'closure'.[8]

---

7   Stuart Hall, 'Introduction: Who Needs "Identity"?', in *Questions of Cultural Identity*, p. 4. Reference to Paul Gilroy, *The Black Atlantic: Modernity and Double Consciousness* (London: Verso, 1994).

8   Ibid., pp. 4–5.

The first point to make here with regard to the construction of Welshness and difference is that the 'other' is invoked from the margins. If England is the dominant presence in the United Kingdom, Wales, on its western perimeters, is located geographically on its margins. If English is the dominant language in the United Kingdom, Welsh, as spoken by roughly half a million people, is a minority language, located geographically on the fringes of the dominant culture. Though the 'minority' or 'marginal' status of the Welsh language may not be recognized as such in its strongholds, from an outside perspective – from the dominant perspective – the Welsh language represents an 'other' language spoken in what would seem a geographically and politically non-threatening position. The incorporation of the dominant cultural product into the Welsh language, however, turns this opposition on its head. Once Welsh becomes the primary language in a new musical 'tradition', English becomes the unspoken 'other'. Welsh-language popular music is constructed out of linguistic difference; it is Welsh because it is not English. Its 'constitutive outside' – the 'something more' at the margins of the Welsh identity – is therefore Anglo-American popular culture.

The formation of a Welsh identity through the production and consumption of popular music is in this sense a 'constructed form of closure'. It is a means of closing linguistic and cultural borders to Anglicization. The successful emergence of a new structure of feeling – Welsh popular music – enabled the creation of new cultural codes and the exclusion of the dominant culture from them.[9] That which this particular Welsh identity 'lacks' is the English language, the 'silent and *unspoken* other'. The closure of linguistic and cultural borders to the English language is an act of self-assertion, and it is the way in which this self-assertion is articulated which punctuates the emergences of new constructions of Welshness.

Cultural identity is, however, a process, and the phases through which Welsh identity have passed in the last half of the twentieth century have resulted from certain contestations emerging both from within the identity formation and from outside it. Most commonly these contestations concern linguistic loyalty, and such concerns underline the delicate nature of a Welshness based on ideals of language. When linguistic fissures appear from within the cultural formation, the sense of commonality is lost, and with it a potential loss in the capacity for self-assertion. Linguistic fissures appear throughout the temporal arc of Welsh popular music, are generally prefaced by an external political or social threat, and are often followed by period of struggle before the emergence of a stronger, more unified assertion of Welshness. If the external political or social threat succeeds in destabilizing a unified sense of Welsh identity, further internal fissures appear and new structures of feeling eventually emerge. These are the moments of articulation to be mapped in the following pages.

---

9   This is not to imply that the dominant Anglo-American culture did not continue to influence Welsh popular music, or that Welsh popular music became an autonomous and wholly unique form of cultural expression; it is merely to suggest that the relationship between Welsh and Anglophone popular musics serves to define a Welsh identity, and that identity has developed in a relational way, from margins to center.

It must be stated first, however, that there is an unspoken alternate history of 'Welsh' popular music – Anglophone Welsh popular music – which was similarly marginalized, and nurtured in live performance in small communities throughout Wales.[10] The claim of this music to represent 'Welshness' is as strong as that of the music organized around linguistic characteristics. The early stages of Anglophone Welsh popular music in the 1960s serve as the symbolic construction of Welshness parallel to that of the early stages of Welsh-language popular music. Whether Anglophone Welsh popular music spoke to local social or political issues is a matter to be discussed elsewhere; what is at issue here is the notion of self-representation. Audiences of Anglophone Welsh popular music were united in the enjoyment of 'their' local music, strengthening a particular community in a particular place. If that particular community felt in any way disenfranchised, or marginalized from the dominant culture, there might have been an unspoken (and possibly unrecognized) kinship with the Welsh-language musical communities at similar stages of their formation. In Massey's terms, Wales was a place which supported a 'network of social relations and understandings': here social relations and understandings of 'place' span linguistic boundaries, and self-representation and group identity are negotiated on similar ground. More importantly, the knowledge of two similarly-rooted musical traditions, divided by language but united in a larger social context, coexisting on the geographical territory – the 'habitus' – of Wales, enables an understanding of the internal conflicts caused by linguistic border-crossings, as well as the more general proprietary use of the adjective 'Welsh'.

Of John Street's theories of place outlined in the previous chapter, the idea of 'locality as political experience' must be reiterated here. The Welsh language movement was the primary political motivation behind the creation and development of Welsh-language popular music. 'Welsh' in the larger sense of the word – Welsh-speaking and Anglophone communities located in the geographical space of Wales, and the temporal process spanning the last half of the twentieth century – presents a more over-arching political experience out of which popular music of either (or any) language can be seen to express an historically problematic self-representation. That is to say, the social history of the people of Wales, though problematic in its construction, is yet another common cultural referent which unifies the popular musics of Wales as expressive cultures. Welsh-language popular music can therefore be interpreted as emerging as a new structure of feeling from within 'Welsh' popular culture, or from within Anglo-American popular culture, or from within the former as it emerged from the latter.

The different popular musics emerging in Wales – Anglophone and Welsh – are representative of similar constructions of place; in Street's words, 'the local is defined against the national'. Welsh identity is created in opposition, or relation, to English identity, regardless of linguistic qualification. In terms of Lawrence Grossberg's 'affective alliances', two identity formations inhabit the same geographical space, organized according to different cultural (linguistic) needs, but set in opposition to a common 'other', the English. While this may be overstating the extent to which

---

10 For a useful summary history of Anglophone Welsh Popular Music see Ruth Shade, 'Direct Activists: The Roots of Welsh Rock', *Planet* 145 (February/March 2001): 25–35.

Anglophone Welsh musicians define themselves in opposition to the English, it is merely to suggest that in an Anglophone Welsh identity formation, the 'us' and 'them', both utilizing the same linguistic codes, are most easily distinguished by geographical boundaries. Because of the political ties linking Wales to England, the ease with which an 'us' and 'them' are distinguished on national terms suggests the formation of an affective alliance within Wales against a common 'other', and based on common political experience.

The construction of 'Britishness' is another opposition to be mentioned in relation to both Anglophone Welsh and Welsh-language cultures. As inclusive a term as it sounds, 'Britishness' is controversial in its exclusivity, and has come to stand for 'Englishness' in a way that marks ethnic and racial immigrant communities in Britain as the larger 'other'. For the peoples of the United Kingdom whose first language is not English – and for those whose cultural history does not stem from the Anglo-Saxons – it is a term which attempts to homogenize the nation and to ignore the importance of diversity in favor of a remembered past. 'Britishness' is yet another construction within which the binary opposition 'us' and 'them' can shift the symbolic power from the center to the periphery.

An Anglophone-Welsh 'affective alliance' hinges on linguistic affiliation and challenges the implications of the descriptor 'Welsh'. The insinuation of the English language into the Welsh cultural formation at different points on the Welsh pop timeline has provoked anger and protest; the inverse motion, of Anglophone musicians embracing the Welsh language, has provoked the opposite reaction. There is a multi-leveled territoriality at issue here: whereas it is acceptable for Anglophone musicians to join the Welsh cultural formation, the weakening of the Welsh cultural formation by the migration of its members to English-language culture is tantamount to a betrayal of cultural roots. Though Wales is predominantly an English-speaking nation, there is amongst the Welsh-speaking community a belief in the territorial entitlement of the Welsh language. For those areas of Wales where Welsh is discernible only in the traces it has left in the inflections of local English speech, such a belief is an insult to the Anglophone Welsh whose heritage provided Wales with a great portion of her cultural and industrial history. Though Anglophone popular culture and Welsh popular culture have coexisted rather peacefully in Wales, the exodus from the minority language to the majority has highlighted those moments when linguistic borders have been less secure.

The relationships between Anglo-Welsh and Welsh, and between Welsh and Anglo-American cultures, provide a shifting background against which the cultural history of Welsh popular music can be mapped. 'Welshness' is a cultural process, and the identities emerging from within that cultural process are as much affected by time as they are by internal negotiations of representation. The dialogues which develop between the Welsh-language cultural formation and its Anglophone 'others' are as significant to the development of self-perception and representation as are the internal dialogues and discontinuities which emerge from within the Welsh-language cultural formation.

Welsh popular music is a symbolic negotiation of cultural identity. Much Welsh popular music of the last half of the twentieth century occupied a middle ground between a remembered past and a potential future, in a self-conscious process of becoming. The acceptance and adoption of Anglo-American popular culture by the Welsh language community was a means of creating a type of stability in an otherwise unstable identity formation. The infrastructure which developed from the creation of popular music – record labels, recording studios, television, radio, print media – and which continues to serve as its support mechanisms, allowed for a certain cultural autonomy. This in turn aided the development of a cultural self-confidence, strengthened and weakened over the decades which followed according to the oppositional relations between the perceived and changing 'us' and 'them'. The forms which these oppositions have taken are illustrated not only in the emergence of new structures of feeling, based on the Anglo-American model as well as on the Welsh, but through written and spoken negotiations, through the enactment of community formations, through social movements, and through silence.

As a cultural code, the Welsh language is pregnant with significance, and the grafting of the Welsh cultural code onto the cultural code of Anglo-American popular music imbues the resulting musical product with numerous potential interpretations. Direct references to 'Welshness', either through lyrics or the incorporation of musical signifiers of Welsh culture, are not in and of themselves proof of an actualized identity; rather, they are an acknowledgment of the contestations involved in the understanding of a cultural process. Nonetheless, lyrical expressions of Welshness serve as documentary evidence of the negotiations – the 'border dialogues'[11] – between Wales and the Anglo-American dominant culture. These dialogues are fundamental to understanding the process of Welsh identity and, in Gwyn A. Williams' words, the 'impossibility' of Wales.

---

11 Iain Chambers, *Border Dialogues: Journeys in Postmodernity* (London: Routledge, 1990). The term 'border dialogues' calls to mind the work of Raymond Williams, his novel *Border Country*, and his own identity as border Welshman positioned in the center of English academia.

PART II

A Cultural History of
Welsh Popular Music

Chapter Five

Wales Before 1963: Creating the Culture

The roots of Welsh popular music lie very close to the surface of Wales' recent cultural history. Wales had no indigenous tradition of music hall, vaudeville or cabaret; what historical model for popular entertainment existed in the Welsh language was based largely in the folk tradition, and what developed into Welsh popular music was borrowed entirely from the Anglo-American model. At the same time, the roles which Welsh language activism and popular music played in the development of Welsh-language media are impossible to separate: it is unclear how a Welsh-language popular music would have developed had it not been for Welsh-language broadcasting. The roots of Welsh popular music are therefore at once political and social, and it is this relationship between language activism, Welsh media, and the production and reproduction of popular music which frames the outline of the development of Welsh popular music, for it has been central to the creation of Welsh popular culture as it exists today.

The Roots of Welsh Pop

In the early decades of the twentieth century, Welsh-language 'popular music' – what would now more commonly be called light entertainment – coexisted with contemporary English-language 'popular music'. From the turn of the twentieth century through the Second World War, light ballads and sentimental songs in Welsh and in English grew in popularity as a result of the sales of sheet music and the immediate accessibility of performances via radio broadcasts and gramophone recordings. Band leaders and singers became the vehicles for the dissemination of new music, and evolved, in the most simplified terms, into 'pop stars'.[1]

There are early examples of Welsh 'pop stars' in the decades before and after the Second World War, those who sang on BBC broadcasts from Bangor or Cardiff, or became known through local performances. Many musicians who began their careers in the 1950s and even the 1960s refer back to musicians such as Bob Roberts Tai'r Felin or the Troubadours as representative of the early days of Welsh 'pop',[2] though the musical relationship between these two generations may not be readily apparent.

---

1   For a history of light entertainment and the early days of the BBC, see Simon Frith, 'The Pleasures of the Hearth: The Making of BBC Light Entertainment' in Formations Editorial Collective, eds., *Formations of Pleasure* (London: Routledge & Kegan Paul, 1983): 101–23.

2   I am deeply indebted to Eurof Williams and Cwmni Huw Brian Williams for allowing me access to the complete, unpublished transcripts of the S4C series, *Y Felin Bop* (Cwmni Huw Brian Williams, 1996), which have informed these pages in no small way. Hefin Wyn's

This 'first generation' consisted of musicians whose repertoire, if not gleaned from the folk tradition, consisted largely of translations of contemporary English-language hits, or sentimental ballads of love and loss; the 'second generation' developed a repertoire based on a very different political ideology.

The clearest example of early Welsh light entertainment is the *Noson Lawen* (Merry Evening): a community event held in a village hall or chapel vestry, an evening of music, comedy and light entertainment, with a host introducing each act, and perhaps telling a joke or two. The *Noson Lawen* could be interpreted as representing an indigenous Welsh version of the British music hall tradition, but the moral framework for this entertainment had a profound effect on its development. In terms of artistic content, and in terms of mode of performance, it is much more closely connected to the Eisteddfodic tradition than to vaudeville. Whatever the root of the entertainment, this was the formula which BBC producer Sam Jones refined for the first *Noson Lawen* broadcast from Bangor just after the Second World War.[3] The pool of talent for a variety show was available locally, at the University of Wales in Bangor:[4] there was a Welsh Society at Bangor, as at most other university campuses in Wales, which would organize its own social evenings – sketches, songs, stories. Sam Jones drafted a small group of these university students into writing and performing for a radio audience. Among them were Meredydd Evans, Cledwyn Jones and Robin Williams, known collectively as Triawd y Coleg (The College Trio).

Given the well-documented difficulties encountered in Britain during the war, and the diminution of Welsh-language broadcasting to but a few minutes a week, the need for entertainment was obvious. Once a month *Noson Lawen* was broadcast from Bangor, creating in effect a Welsh popular culture from the ground up. The writing team responsible for each month's show adapted the available resources to fit the established format of stories, jokes, sketches, and popular songs. Melodies may have come from American folk repertory, minstrel shows, or Stephen Foster songs; rarely would a Welsh folk tune be adapted, though hymn tunes might have been used on occasion. The Welsh lyrics – humorous, sentimental – were rarely direct translations of the original English song, but rather were written especially for the radio broadcasts, and generally bore no relationship to the original theme or mood. This became the standard for early 'popular music', or light entertainment, in the Welsh language, and not until the end of the 1940s did musicians begin writing their own melodies.

Coexisting with this burgeoning Welsh popular culture was the larger, more firmly established, American popular culture, which was transmitted over the airwaves to the further reaches of Wales via Radio Luxembourg. This offered early architects of Welsh popular entertainment an introduction to jazz, to crooners such as Bing Crosby, and to close-harmony groups such as the Mills Brothers and the Ink Spots.

Be Bop-a Lula'r Delyn Aur (Talybont: Y Lolfa, 2003) is a more readily available resource for further information on the early days of Welsh popular music, to 1980.

3   *Noson Lawen* was broadcast first as a pilot over the Christmas period, 1945; the first run of *Noson Lawen* as a series began in April, 1946.

4   For tirelessly sharing his recollections of the early days of Welsh light entertainment and popular music I am deeply indebted to Dr Meredydd Evans, 'The Bangor Bing'.

Along with contemporary groups such as Triawd y Coleg, solo artists (primarily song stylists) began to emerge in the Welsh popular music of this period, Esme Lewis and Sassie Rees, among others. The roots of a more confident Welsh popular culture were starting to take hold, and this type of light entertainment lasted through the middle of the 1950s. With the emergence of rock'n'roll in the United States and skiffle in Britain, the first stylistic shift took place in Welsh pop, represented by the influx of 'Bois' and 'Hogia'.

There is a very close familial relationship between Triawd y Coleg and close-harmony groups such as Bois y Blacbord (The Blackboard Boys), Hogia Bryngwran (Bryngwran Boys) and Criw Sgiffl Llandegai (Llandegai Skiffle Crew). The repertoire of these later bands similarly tended toward the humorous or sentimental, yet they would most likely not have come into being were it not for the skiffle craze in Britain. The skiffle craze highlighted the ease with which a group of like-minded young persons could form a musical group and acquire home-made instruments. In the case of Hogia Bryngwran, which formed circa 1955, the absence of electricity in their village accounted for local home-grown entertainment; the fact that they would meet in one another's homes to rehearse over a paraffin lamp only adds to the mystique of the 'early days of Welsh pop'. But on a musical level, Hogia Bryngwran provided Welsh light entertainment with a particularly international flavor. Their penchant for yodeling was a direct reflection of their fascination with cowboys and American popular culture, and perhaps the influence of country roots musicians such as Jimmie Rodgers. That they were able to integrate yodeling, surprisingly yet seamlessly, into an otherwise Welsh context, is the first of many examples in the history of Welsh popular music of a burgeoning cultural self-confidence, as well as the often difficult relationship between Welsh popular music and its Anglo-American precedents.

In the post-war years the BBC imposed needle-time restrictions and encouraged British alternatives to popular American recordings. This was a clear effort to negotiate a new, British popular culture,[5] the implicit assumption being that American culture was detrimental to the youth of Great Britain. Skiffle had been viewed by some in England as the preferred alternative to the largely vulgar and American youth craze of rock'n'roll, but it must be remembered that this alternative had to be taken one step further in Wales, as an effort to encourage participation in popular culture, not in English, but through the medium of the Welsh language. It is this process of indigenization which is central to the social history of Welsh popular music, and it is important to understand that all such music, in its early years, was thus necessarily twice removed from the 'original' American model.

A number of groups emerged in Wales during the 1950s without the benefit of an established network of concert halls, or regular media support. It cannot be stressed enough that the chapel was a silent presence in the development of Welsh popular culture, and exerted its own social influence on the communities which fostered the desire for light entertainment. There was therefore a kind of innocence to much Welsh

---

5   For more on needle-time restrictions and the development of the BBC, see Stephen Barnard, *On the Radio: Music Radio in Britain* (Milton Keynes: Open University Press, 1989).

popular music of the 1940s and 1950s, and it was not until the Welsh community was mobilized and united in protest that Welsh-language popular music became a vehicle for political action.

Protest, The Media, and Welsh Popular Culture

There were two incidents in contemporary Welsh life which informed the creation of the political community: the 1951 census, and, still resonant in Welsh political music today, the parliamentary motion in 1958 to drown Tryweryn Valley and create a reservoir for the Liverpool water supply. The 1951 census recorded that 28.9 per cent of the population of Wales (714,696 people) were able to speak the Welsh language.[6] The majority of these Welsh-speakers lived in rural areas, and no longer represented one solid, contiguous geographical space. In the years leading up to the 1951 census, Welsh had no official status, was not to be seen on buildings, official notices, or public places, and it was projected that the numbers counted on the census would continue in their downward trend until the Welsh language had become all but extinct. The drowning of Tryweryn thus became a metaphor for the fate of the language: an entire Welsh-speaking village was evacuated and all traces of the living language obliterated. The people were powerless in the face of English control, their way of life was disregarded, and the larger Welsh-speaking community witnessed another exodus from the Welsh-speaking heartland to Anglophone Britain. This was a turning point in Welsh political history. In the years following the 1951 census a number of informal protests were held in an attempt to raise the profile of the Welsh language in local councils and businesses, and a gradual increase in the number of Welsh-medium primary and secondary schools complemented the increase in Welsh primary education. The repercussions of these and other early protests were heard clearly in Welsh popular music of the 1960s.

The Broadcasting Council for Wales was established in 1953, and throughout the following decade there was inevitable tension between Welsh speakers and non-Welsh speakers over the relative amount of time each language received. Welsh and English programs were broadcast on separate wavelengths, leading eventually to the establishment of Radio Wales and Radio Cymru two decades later; but for over a decade after the inception of commercial television broadcasting in Wales in 1958, even the limited proportion of Welsh-language programs – broadcast during off-peak times – were met with hostility by non-Welsh speakers, and the motion toward the establishment of a Welsh-language channel eventually began.[7] The importance of this issue cannot be overstated. If state-sponsored English-language media were to impose themselves upon a community whose culture was rooted in a different language, any hope for a modernized, culturally relevant, youth-oriented

---

6   There are many scholarly works devoted to Welsh language demographics. The information contained here is digested from Janet Davies, 'The Welsh Language', in Herbert and Jones, eds., *Post-War Wales*: 55–77, as well as her full-length study, *The Welsh Language* (Cardiff: University of Wales Press, 1993).

7   For an exhaustive survey of the history of Welsh broadcasting see John Davies, *Broadcasting and the BBC in Wales* (Cardiff: University of Wales Press, 1994).

language revival would be lost. The Welsh language needed not only to retain a presence in the rural communities, but also to insinuate itself into the developing urban centers to be cultivated as a language of youth culture. If the unstated – yet widely acknowledged – *modus operandi* of the BBC in its early days was to stem the rising tide of Americanization, the unspoken agenda of the Welsh-language media was to prevent the continued spread of Anglicization.

Apart from the linguistic significance of the slowly-developing Welsh media, there were considerable social implications. The media commented on the present while providing for the future; it was a new industry, requiring education and training, and an imaginative talent pool to supply the entertainment. This talent pool was cultivated in the chapels, and the Nonconformist tradition was responsible in no small part for the rate at which Welsh popular music was allowed to develop, and for several of its particular characteristics. Because many groups and musicians first performed in chapel vestries, the lyrical content of their songs was restricted; it would have been very rare for a song's subject matter to stray from matters of patriotism and chaste love, and actually approach the physical body. Similarly, a ban on electric instruments in Welsh chapels placed restrictions on possible musical accompaniment, and skiffle, with its certain home-made innocence, and solo voice or close harmony singing with piano or acoustic guitar accompaniment, were standard practice for many years, long after English skiffle had gone electric, given way to beat music, crossed the Atlantic, and changed the course of Anglo-American popular music.

In this way, from the humble beginnings of *Noson Lawen*, designed as entertainment for a post-war audience, grew a Welsh popular culture and Welsh media; from the audience united by sporadic Welsh-language broadcasting developed a community mobilized into political action; and from the generation raised amid these early protests emerged the architects of the popular music which developed for the benefit of the media and out of the need for political consciousness.

Summary

Each phase in the process of Welsh popular music represents a particular trend in style and self-identification. In addition to the 'traditions' which emerge in each of the post-war decades, the musical styles also represent particular patterns of ideology – in Raymond Williams' terms, dominant, residual, and emergent,[8] with a

---

8   Raymond Williams, *Marxism and Literature*. These terms are applied, loosely and most notably to the understanding of Hawaiian music in George H. Lewis, 'Storm Blowing from Paradise: Social Protest and Oppositional Ideology in Popular Hawaiian Music', *Popular Music* 10/1 (1991): 53–67, wherein Lewis states that '[s]uch alternative ideologies, created and supported by their own cultural symbols, may be either residual (formed in the past, but still remembered and, to some extent, still a part of the cultural process), or emergent (the expression of new groups outside the dominant group). They may also be either oppositional (challenging the dominant ideology), or alternative (coexisting with it)'. While concerned with the symbolic use of 'traditional' music in an otherwise borrowed context, Lewis' discussion of identity formations and alternative ideologies is of particular relevance here, especially in

further sub-categorization of 'oppositional' and 'alternative' suggesting a political or cultural subtext. The temporal implications of Welsh popular music, and the expansion and contraction of a 'cultural time lag', reflect the negotiations and self-confidence central to the creation and understanding of a shared cultural identity.[9]

Triawd y Coleg (The College Trio) defined Welsh light entertainment in the post-war years. Their contributions to the BBC radio program, *Noson Lawen*, were instrumental to the creation of a national audience for popular songs in the Welsh language, and some of their songs have since entered the 'folk' repertory as common cultural referents in the Welsh-speaking community.[10] One could consider Triawd y Coleg as the point of inception of contemporary Welsh popular music; with the emergence of skiffle in Great Britain as the 'answer' to 1950s American rock'n'roll, Criw Sgiffl Llandegai represent the other end of this early developmental period in Welsh popular music.

Figure 5.1   Four-part harmony: Hogia Llandegai

considering 'traditional' symbols of Welshness – or newly-created symbols of Welshness such as popular music – as belonging 'to the people'.

9   The 'selection' of representative examples from each developmental period of Welsh popular music is not intended in any way to suggest the canonization of those musicians, or songs, which emerge in the text. Rather, these selections are meant to suggest the emergence of stylistic trends *as discernible in* the music selected from each period.

10   A two-volume collection of their songs, written by Meredydd Evans, with piano accompaniment by Ffrancon Thomas, was published as *Caneuon Noson Lawen: Neuadd y Penrhyn, Bangor* (Llandebie: Llyfrau'r Dryw, 1948).

The primary 'tradition' shared by Triawd y Coleg and Criw Sgiffl (later Hogia) Llandegai is a 'folk' sensibility.[11] Whether utilizing melodies from American, English or Welsh folk traditions, whether translating English lyrics into Welsh or writing entirely new Welsh lyrics, the instant familiarity of some songs performed and recorded by Triawd y Coleg and Hogia Llandegai served to unify the early Welsh pop music audience. In the case of Triawd y Coleg, this audience was (virtually) located throughout Wales, during the broadcast times of *Noson Lawen*; in the case of Criw Sgiffl Llandegai, their audience was (actually) located in chapel vestries, town halls or Eisteddfod fields. These community formations are common to the consumption of Welsh popular music throughout the post-war decades; what is of primary importance here is the establishment of a Welsh cultural tradition in the popular music idiom.

Triawd y Coleg were not the first group of Welsh musicians to perform 'popular music'. Light entertainment had existed in Wales in the years preceding the Second World War, and BBC programs such as *Sut Hwyl* (What Fun) and *Shw Mae Heno* (Hello Tonight) provided the forum for the performance of new songs; but *Noson Lawen* established a tradition of entertainment which still exists today, largely unchanged, in local venues and on S4C. Triawd y Coleg, as primary contributors to the *Noson Lawen* broadcasts of the 1940s, therefore serve as a kind of template to the popular musical groups which emerged in the ensuing years. If traditions are to be traced throughout the history of Welsh popular music, Triawd y Coleg would represent one tradition which is still discernible in the music and presentation of more recent groups. Such continuities can be interpreted as ideological patterns informing the emergence of new structures of feeling. Whereas the type of light entertainment introduced by Triawd y Coleg in *Noson Lawen* may have been based on an earlier (British) model, the incorporation of newly-composed Welsh songs into the established format of sketches, jokes, and music suggests the creation of a new tradition, or structure of feeling, based on a common cultural referent: *residual* elements in a selective tradition. From this basis, the sense of kinship between Triawd y Coleg and successive groups can be interpreted either as a strengthening of the (newly-) established tradition, or as an unwillingness to progress. Criw Sgiffl (Hogia) Llandegai can be seen as representatives of both interpretations.

Criw Sgiffl Llandegai was formed in the mid-1950s by eight members of Côr Talgau. Intended as a sideline to the choir's performances, the octet would perform during breaks in the choir's concerts. The call for Welsh skiffle was eventually great enough to encourage them to develop their own repertoire, and they performed their first concert, independently, in Bethesda in April 1957. The popularity in Great Britain of Lonnie Donegan's recordings encouraged Criw Sgiffl Llandegai to adapt and translate a number of his hits for the Welsh audience; the skiffle 'craze' in Wales – following Criw Sgiffl Llandegai, a number of other Welsh skiffle groups

---

11 'Folk' is a contested term which I explore in greater depth in the first of the following five case studies. For the present purposes, any use of the term 'folk' will carry with it the implication of a shared musical tradition, a music 'of the people', and therefore a common (Welsh) cultural referent.

emerged[12] – was contemporaneous with the peak of skiffle's commercial success.[13] The Welsh skiffle 'tradition' was fostered in an environment which could embrace both Anglophone and Welsh 'folk' musics, and the translation of Anglophone into Welsh had become a natural step in the process toward creating a Welsh 'folk' music culture.

More important than the emergence of a Welsh 'folk' repertory was the further establishment of 'light entertainment' as Welsh 'pop'. As Criw Sgiffl Llandegai grew in popularity, their live performances developed to incorporate sketches and jokes as well as music, following the pattern of the *Noson Lawen*.[14] The music remained light-hearted and easily accessible, and the sense of musical decorum was not threatened by the introduction of electronic instruments or inappropriate lyrical content. Welsh skiffle was therefore an alternative to (mainstream) Lonnie Donegan and his contemporaries, and carried with it residual traces of the ideological pattern established by Triawd y Coleg.

---

12 The Welsh skiffle 'craze' was great enough to incite The Great Eisteddfod Skiffle Controversy. At the National Eisteddfod, Anglesey in 1957, skiffle groups were rejected by the Archdruid from playing on the field under the grounds that skiffle was not music, but 'rubbish'. This episode is recounted by Neville Hughes of Criw Sgiffl (Hogia) Llandegai in *Y Felin Bop*.

13 Mike Dewe, in *The Skiffle Craze* (Aberystwyth: Planet, 1998), cites the period 1955–57 as the peak period of skiffle's commercial success. The BBC played a large role in the perpetuation of the skiffle craze, and Mike Dewe's book should be consulted for a first-hand account of the skiffle years in Wales and elsewhere.

14 Criw Sgiffl Llandegai continued in its original incarnation until 1963. They reformed as a quartet in 1964 and began a second, longer career as Hogia Llandegai, making their first recording in 1966 and continuing until 1973, when they made their first of three farewell tours of Wales. Hogia Llandegai reunited for their 35th anniversary and re-recorded a number of their most popular songs, released as *Goreuon Hogia Llandegai* (Sain SCD 2016, 1992). They remain one of the best-selling acts on the Sain label.

Chapter Six

1963–73: Locating the Audience

It is difficult to separate the development of Welsh-language popular music in the 1960s from the founding in 1963 of *Cymdeithas yr Iaith Gymraeg* (the Welsh Language Society). And as Cymdeithas yr Iaith was spurred by *Tynged yr Iaith* (The Fate of the Language), the radio lecture broadcast by Saunders Lewis on 13 February 1962, it is difficult to consider the language movement without considering the development of Welsh-language media.

The Media and the Youth Market

The popularity of the pirate radio stations, notably Radio Caroline, in mid-1960s Britain prompted the BBC to focus on its youth market. For roughly three years from 1964 the pirate stations offered solid programming of popular music from America and England, a service which the BBC could not provide, due to its restrictions on the broadcasting of recorded music. In agreement with the Musicians' Union, the BBC was restricted to twenty-eight hours of needle time per week,[1] spread over its three services; in 1965 forty-seven hours were added, thirty to the Third Programme, seventeen to the Light Programme. In 1965 a European convention outlawed the pirate radio stations, but the British government was unwilling to take action until the BBC could offer a suitable service to replace the pirates' popular music content. The BBC were authorized in 1966 to offer another radio service, splitting the Light Programme into two channels, a 'pop' service (Radio One) and a 'light entertainment' programme (Radio Two). The implicit need for Welsh-language broadcasting was to replicate, through the medium of Welsh, on one channel, all four mainstream services offered by the BBC.

For popular music on Welsh-language television, the turning point came with the TWW program *Y Dydd* (The Day). Dafydd Iwan, at that time studying architecture at the University of Wales and an active member of *Cymdeithas yr Iaith*, was employed to offer a type of musical commentary on current affairs. This provided him with the opportunity to appear regularly on a national broadcast, encouraged him to compose original songs, and offered him the chance to share his views and those of *Cymdeithas yr Iaith*, in an effective and immediately recognizable musical style. And there was plenty of material for comment. Not only were the efforts of the *Cymdeithas* instigating an unprecedented level of civil disobedience in Wales, there were in the latter half of the decade two distinct moments of political and social change in Wales. In 1966 Gwynfor Evans was the first member of *Plaid Cymru* to

---

1 This information is culled from John Davies, *Broadcasting and the BBC in Wales*.

be elected to the Houses of Parliament, the signifying moment when Welsh politics moved from the regional to the national. And in 1969, despite much protest, Charles was invested as Prince of Wales in a ceremony held at Caernarvon Castle. He had spent a period of months studying the Welsh language at Aberystwyth in preparation for his first address to the Welsh people, but contemporary popular opinion held that an Englishman had no right to the title 'Prince of Wales'. The attempt by the establishment at creating a sense of jubilation in the months preceding the investiture – '*Croeso* 69' (Welcome 69) – was lampooned in the eponymous song by Dafydd Iwan, and his song 'Carlo' still stands as a powerful testament to the strengthening sense of unity in the Welsh community.[2]

If the struggles for peace and human rights were common concerns throughout the world in the 1960s, their strength was discernible through the common musical language of the new 'folk' song, developed in pre-war North America by Woody Guthrie and Pete Seeger, and later typified by Bob Dylan and Joan Baez, among many others. This acoustic folk style aimed at disseminating information through simple melodies and uncluttered harmonies, encouraging audience participation; but more importantly, it was a means of creating a common musical heritage.[3] By appropriating the melodies, and occasionally the style, of American folk singers, Dafydd Iwan created a repertory of contemporary Welsh folk songs. Although – or perhaps because – the majority of his audience may have been unfamiliar with the work of American singers such as Burl Ives or Woody Guthrie, Dafydd Iwan could adapt their music, and bring to the collective Welsh consciousness an idea of nationhood, of a developing culture, of the struggles of Welsh people and their relationship to other struggles around the world. He brought an awareness of the language struggle to the popular attention, and brought to the younger audience a sense of their belonging in, of their commonality with, a wider international community.

While the language movement was building momentum,[4] this new folk music was also a forum for updating the Welsh language, for making it more accessible and relevant to the younger generation. For younger Welsh musicians it became clear that English was not the only musical language, and that translating English-language hits into Welsh was but one musical alternative. This burgeoning self-confidence was due in no small part to the close-knit communities created by *Urdd Gobaith Cymru* (Welsh League of Youth) summer camps at Llangrannog and Glan Llyn, and by the increasing activities of *Cymdeithas yr Iaith*. By the end of the 1960s, with a number of bands forming throughout Wales, and with the increasing visibility of popular music at institutions such as the National Eisteddfod and the *Urdd* Eisteddfod, the introduction of regular, weekly Welsh-language music shows on Welsh Radio, *Helo Sut Dach Chi* (Hello How Are You), and on television, *Disg a*

---

2 'Carlo' is one of the three texts I consider in depth in Chapter 10.

3 The term 'folk' music is inherently problematic, and will be discussed in further detail in Chapter 10.

4 In addition to Dylan Phillips' comprehensive survey of the first thirty years of Cymdeithas yr Iaith, *Trwy Ddulliau Chwyldro...?*, see Gwilym Tudur, *Wyt Ti'n Cofio?* (Talybont: Y Lolfa, 1989) for a systematic yearly review of the first quarter century of the language movement.

Dawn, (Disc and Talent), were logical steps toward institutionalizing popular music as an expression of contemporary Welsh culture.

Helo Sut Dach Chi, broadcast from 1968 to 1977, was the first radio show aimed entirely at the contemporary pop music scene. Hosted by Hywel Gwynfryn, it comprised a full half hour of music, a very difficult feat in the early days of Welsh pop. Where there was not a full half hour of vocal music in the Welsh language, Gwynfryn would fill air time with popular Anglo-American instrumentals. This created a new market and served as an open call for new bands, and eventually Hywel Gwynfryn was receiving demo tapes at the BBC studios from musicians based all over Wales. But a more important element in this show was the creation of a contemporary Welsh 'patter', a pop slang in the Welsh language which appealed to the younger audience and gave the music – often suffering from poor production values and old-fashioned sentiments – a contemporary feel.

Top of the Pops, first broadcast in 1964, created the template for televised pop chart shows in Britain, and in the early days of televised Welsh pop the relationship between *Top of the Pops* and *Disg a Dawn* was very close. *Disg a Dawn* was a weekly televised magazine show aimed at Welsh youth. Ruth Price, the producer of the show, and Meredydd Evans, by then Head of Light Entertainment for the BBC in Cardiff, had been instrumental in creating an earlier 'pop music' show, *Hob y Deri Dando*, similar in many ways to a televised barndance, which focused primarily on music of the folk or traditional idiom. Recognizing the importance of pop music to the 1960s generation, with *Disg a Dawn* they created a forum for the promotion of Welsh pop music, and a stimulus for the formation of new bands. Most importantly, they kept a close watch on the English pop charts, and dictated to some extent the direction that Welsh pop music should take: at the end of every week, Ruth Price would commission Welsh translations of contemporary English hits to be written and performed on *Disg a Dawn*. In some cases, record producers would phone the BBC offices requesting contact numbers for the bands who had appeared on *Disg a Dawn* the previous weekend, thereby spawning the early Welsh pop music recording 'industry'.

Disg a Dawn was broadcast live in Wales on Saturday, and re-transmitted in England on the following Tuesday afternoon. It is difficult to know how large an English audience *Disg a Dawn* would have reached, but with the relative paucity of popular music offerings in the early days of British television, one could assume that the show reached more homes than merely those of the displaced Welsh speakers living on the other side of Offa's Dyke. In an attempt, perhaps, to interest the English viewer, one regular feature of the early series was a review of English records, presented by musician Endaf Emlyn. This showed a seriousness of purpose and a discerning trend in musical tastes in Wales, and led eventually to regular on-air reviews of Welsh records and, in the written press, *10 Ucha'r Cymro* (*Y Cymro*'s Top Ten).

The Welsh Record Industry

The popularity of *Helo Sut Dach Chi* and *Disg a Dawn* belies the state of the Welsh recording industry. Although companies such as Welsh Teldisc, Cambrian and Recordiau'r Dryw (Wren Records) were actively recording and producing singles by musicians such as Dafydd Iwan, Heather Jones and Y Tebot Piws into the 1970s, the state of technology available in Wales was equivalent roughly to the state of technology available in England a decade previously.[5] It was not unusual for a musician or band to be recorded in a chapel vestry or town hall, standing underneath one microphone suspended from the ceiling, or for a group to gather around one standing microphone and be recorded live in one take. Or, if the producer wanted to try a different mix, one or two of the band members might take a step back before re-recording the song. As a result, some of Dafydd Iwan's early recordings on Welsh Teldisc,[6] for example, are reminiscent of the early recordings of Woody Guthrie or the Almanac Singers, if only in their raw sound quality and rough performances. Considering that many of these recordings were made after the release of the Beatles' *Sgt. Pepper's Lonely Hearts Club Band*, the cultural time-lag between England and Wales is striking.

Welsh musicians would certainly have been aware of the standards of recording technology in the mainstream market, and some of Dafydd Iwan's contemporaries in the 1960s were actively recording in England as well as in Wales. One such musician, Meic Stevens, had been living in London and recording English-language songs in the late 1960s, returning to Wales to record either translations of his English songs or original songs in the Welsh language. Although he was offered a recording contract with Warner Brothers, and released one album on their label, he continued to record for independent Welsh labels, which led to an ultimatum by Warner Brothers: choose between recording exclusively in English on their label, or turn entirely to the Welsh recording industry. By opting for the latter he forfeited almost certain international fame, but was instrumental in the early development of the Welsh-language recording industry as it exists today.

Another contemporary of Dafydd Iwan, Huw Jones, was a folk singer and Oxford student, as well as host of *Disg a Dawn*. In 1969, having composed the song 'Dŵr' (Water), he arranged with Meic Stevens to secure studio space in London for the recording of the single.[7] Their intention was for a Welsh-language song to be recorded and produced at the same professional standard as contemporary English-language singles. Huw Jones traveled to London with backing vocalist

---

5   For an in-depth survey of the growth of the Welsh recording industry, see Roger Wallis and Krister Malm, '*Sain Cymru*: The Role of the Welsh Phonographic Industry in the Development of a Welsh Language Pop/Rock/Folk Scene', in Richard Middleton and David Horn, eds., *Popular Music* 3; *Producers and Markets* (Cambridge: Cambridge University Press, 1983): 77–105; and their exhaustive *Big Sounds from Small Peoples: The Music Industry in Small Countries* (New York: Pendragon Press, 1984).

6   Available now on *Y Dafydd Iwan Cynnar* (Sain SCD 2180, 1998).

7   For a complete account of the early days of Sain, and graphic reminiscenes of the recording of 'Dŵr', see Elena Morus, ed., *Camau'r Chwarter Canrif: Hanes Cwmni Sain Recordiau Cyf. 1969–1994* (Llanrwst: Gwasg Carreg Gwalch, 1994).

Heather Jones and musician Geraint Jarman, met Meic Stevens and assorted session musicians at the studio, and recorded 'Dŵr', a completely new direction for Welsh pop. Not only was the song itself a departure from the standard three-minute pop song, clocking in at over four minutes, the multi-layered texture included *tablas*, a novelty for Welsh music. But more important than the song was the industry it spawned.

In order to release the single, Huw Jones and Dafydd Iwan formed their own record label, *Cwmni Sain* (Sound Company), and assumed responsibility for all manner of the single's production, from label design to cover art to distribution. When all copies of 'Dŵr' had sold out, they were able to produce another single and re-invest the profits back into the company. Sain changed forever the face of the Welsh recording industry and established a tradition of professional self-sufficiency which was to recur in various guises throughout the next thirty years.

Figure 6.1   The song that started Sain

Music and Language

Despite the centrality of the language movement to the development of Welsh popular music, the linguistic border-crossings which began at the end of the 1960s were not perceived as a threat to the future of the Welsh language. The first case of a Welsh-to-English career move was undoubtedly Mary Hopkin, who was 'discovered' by Twiggy on *Opportunity Knocks* in 1969, signed to the Beatles' Apple Records label, and enjoyed success with her single 'Those Were the Days' and album *Post Card* (Apple, 1969). Having begun her career singing Welsh translations of such 1960s 'folk' hits as 'Turn! Turn! Turn!' and 'Guantanamera', and recording for the Cambrian record label,[8] her success in the English-language charts was more a cause for celebration than for concern. Perhaps the prevailing attitude of the Welsh pop 'industry' at the time was one of innocent mutual encouragement, more concerned with enjoyment than with the long-term implications of cultural development.

Whatever the contemporary opinion of Mary Hopkin's English recording career, her language shift was of course countered by the frequent linguistic border-crossings of Meic Stevens, and his decision to answer Warner Brothers' ultimatum by focusing permanently on recording Welsh-language music. With monoglot English singers such as Tom Jones and Shirley Bassey leaving Pontypridd and Cardiff for the world stage, the profile that Welsh artists were beginning to gain in the Anglo-American popular culture also brought a recognition of Wales as an entity separate to England. If these Anglo-Welsh musicians raised awareness of Wales as an autonomous entity, their motion out of their home culture could be interpreted more positively as one small step toward the future recognition of a distinctively Welsh culture.

Welsh Popular Music and Live Performance

Of course, not all musicians in Wales in the 1960s were acoustic 'folk' musicians, nor were they language activists. Live performance had been a vital tradition throughout the development of a Welsh pop, and in the 1960s, as that tradition moved from the chapel to the dance hall and to the National Eisteddfod, one band in particular was of central importance: Y Blew.

Begun in 1966 as a college band at Aberystwyth, the driving force behind the formation of Y Blew (Hair) and the *raison d'être* of their short career was the desire to develop a dance music through the medium of Welsh. While many Welsh musicians undoubtedly listened to contemporary English and American pop music, few Welsh bands in the mid-1960s actually attempted musical simulation. Mainstream Anglo-American bands performed regularly at King's Hall in Aberystwyth, and the members of Y Blew wanted to emulate the sound of contemporary British beat groups; that is, to create an electric rock music for the Welsh-speaking audience, to move Welsh music out of its acoustic shell and toward a more contemporary sound. At a time when Welsh nationalist issues were garnering attention throughout Great Britain, when an emerging sense of 'Welshness' was taking root, and when Welsh language activism was central to Welsh pop, it is perhaps surprising that Y Blew did not advertise the fact that one of their members was the son of the recently-elected

---

8   Re-released in 1996 as *Mary Hopkin: Y Caneuon Cynnar/The Early Recordings* (Sain SCD2151E).

Plaid Cymru MP, Gwynfor Evans. Y Blew's Welshness was simply a linguistic fact, not a political statement.

The majority of Y Blew's live set was translations of English hits, but their self-managed publicity campaigns were unlike any Wales had seen so far, and as a result they drew consistently large audiences on the two tours they took through Wales. For their primary advertisement they arranged with Robat Gruffudd of the newly-established Welsh press, *Y Lolfa*, to create billboard-sized posters announcing '*Mae'r Blew yn Dod*' (Y Blew Are Coming), unusual both for their monoglot (and relatively obscure) sentiment and for their sheer size.[9] In the summer of 1967 their popularity reached new heights with an infamous last-minute appearance in the *Pabell Lên* (Literature Tent) at the National Eisteddfod in Bala: following the soft vocal sounds of schoolgirl band Sidan and other relatively harmless acoustic acts, Y Blew appeared with their amplifiers and electric guitars and shocked the audience and unsuspecting passers-by. If contemporary pop music had been marginalized in 'mainstream' Welsh culture up to 1967, the effect Y Blew had on the audience at the Bala National Eisteddfod was tantamount to the effect Elvis Presley had on prime-time American family television audiences in 1956.

When approached in the summer of 1967 by a representative of Qualiton Records to record a single, Y Blew were hesitant, aware of the state of the Welsh recording industry and its unfavorable comparison to the recording industry in England. They agreed to record a demo tape for their own archival purposes, and spent a post-concert morning at a studio in Swansea on their way back to Aberystwyth. The recording session consisted of a run-through of their newly-composed song, 'Maes B' (B Field, an allusion to a utopian 'alternative' youth field at the National Eisteddfod),[10] which most of the band had learned in the car on their way to the studio, and backed with a translation of a Spencer Davis song, 'Beth Sy'n Dod Rhyngom Ni' (What's Come Between Us). Upon returning to Aberystwyth they kept in contact with the Qualiton executive, expecting eventually to receive a copy of the demo tape. What they received was a parcel of 45rpm singles, and news that Qualiton had released their demo tape as a record without any written agreement, contract, or payment. The Qualiton label folded shortly thereafter, and 'Maes B' is now a high-value collector's item.

After a span of nine months, having brought a new professionalism to Welsh music, having updated Welsh pop to the standard of its electric counterparts in England, having set a new standard in marketing and promotion, and having unintentionally released the seminal Welsh rock single, the members of Y Blew simply returned to university. It was not until 1973 that another Welsh band ventured into electric territory, again illustrating the time-lag between Welsh and mainstream Anglo-American culture.

---

9 This could be seen as an ironic reference to the beginning of the 'British Invasion' in the United States and the marketing strategies which announced the arrival of the Beatles.

10 The Monterey Pop Festival, the first 'rock' festival, was held 15–17 June 1967. The overall good vibes it engendered in the pop music community were felt even as far away as Wales; the groovy utopian sentiments of 'Maes B' may be interpreted as representing the sole Welsh-language reference to the 'Summer of Love'.

Figure 6.2   Welsh beat: Y Blew

The 1967 Eisteddfod is seen in retrospect as the 'Welsh Woodstock', due in no small part to the performance of Y Blew and the recognition of the youth movement in Wales and beyond, yet the differences are evident:[11] as American and English youth were looking outward beyond their own cultural boundaries, protesting the Vietnam War, demanding civil rights for African-Americans and the emancipation of women, promoting peace and love, Welsh youth were still struggling to define themselves. There could be no looking outward until they had determined themselves inwardly. While the language movement looked toward other social struggles for inspiration, it was necessary for activists in Wales to move toward defining a Welsh nationhood, a sense of 'Welshness'. Only once that process was in motion could the cultural utterances follow, and it was in the 1970s that Welsh music began to move confidently into its larger cultural surroundings and to assert itself in the world system.

---

11 The most obvious problem here is one of chronology: Woodstock took place in 1969, Eisteddfod y Bala in 1967. Because there was no direct Welsh parallel to the former, the latter stands symbolically as the first articulation of Welsh popular (youth) culture.

Summary

The movement from skiffle to electronic rock music in Wales was somewhat difficult and halting, due in large part to the involvement of the chapel in popular music-making in Wales. Though certain musical and technological advancements were made in the 1960s, Welsh pop still remained rooted in an acoustic 'folk' tradition borrowed from the American model. There were a number of traditions in Welsh pop which continued into the 1960s, and which can be summarized in the recorded output of three bands: Y Tebot Piws, Y Bara Menyn, and Y Dyniadon Ynfyd Hirfelyn Tesog.

The one common feature to these three groups is a sense of humor. Not only are individual songs infused with a sense of the absurd or the ridiculous, their very approach to music-making is both irreverent and innocent. Because Y Tebot Piws (The Puce Teapot), Y Bara Menyn (The Buttered Bread) and Y Dyniadon Ynfyd Hirfelyn Tesog (The Foolish Men of the Long Yellow Sunshine) were active at the end of the 1960s and into the 1970s, their music can serve as a bridge between light entertainment and the more 'serious' rock music of the 1970s, and between amateur music-making and more 'professional' compositional and recording processes. If Welsh pop in the 1960s was defined by a type of innocent, nationalistic, sentimental close-harmony singing,[12] Y Bara Menyn emerged as the antidote. Its three members, Meic Stevens, Geraint Jarman and Heather Jones, were all active musicians whose varied activities and experience indicate a wider musical interest than might have been satisfied by Welsh recordings alone.[13] This is not to imply a lack of creativity on the part of Welsh musicians; only to reiterate that the chapel, the *Urdd*, and the Eisteddfod imposed a particular moral framework on the organization of Welsh music which dictated to a large degree instrumentation, lyrical content, and presentation.

Still, it cannot be assumed that all young Welsh persons in the 1960s preferred to listen to Welsh-language popular music instead of its Anglophone counterparts,[14] but the emergence of Welsh youth culture as a structure of feeling involved a particular adherence to rules and moral guidelines established for the benefit of previous

---

12 While this might seem a sweeping generalization, even a cursory look through back issues of Asbri and the BBC television guide will show an abundance of well-groomed, well-dressed young persons gathered together around a microphone or on a stage, usually with one or two of them playing an acoustic guitar. Though not necessarily an accurate gauge of the type of music performed, the type of music sanctioned amongst young persons in the Welsh communities tended toward the sentimental, though certain exceptions exist, notably Meic Stevens and Y Blew.

13 Meic Stevens produced the seminal Sain single, 'Dŵr'; Geraint Jarman and Heather Jones contributed backing vocals to the track, and had established an active musical and personal partnership earlier in the decade, Jarman composing for Jones, amongst other things, a Welsh translation of Joni Mitchell's 'Woodstock'.

14 One anonymous source informed me of an incident in the 1970s at a chapel youth group meeting, when young people were encouraged to bring in their records for an evening's entertainment. Most of the group brought in Welsh recordings; but my source's selection was Yes' *Tales from Topographic Oceans* (1973). He was subsequently given a beating by the minister for refusing to change the record.

structures of feeling. The ease with which a popular musical culture could be nurtured under such strictures denotes an understanding of the needs of the younger generation; the propagation of established values within the new structure of feeling indicates the grounding of such a new tradition in a previous ideological pattern, a *residual* ideology. Y Bara Menyn emerged in *opposition* to that residual ideology.

The members of Y Bara Menyn intended to satirize the type of sentimental, nationalistic music popular in Wales at the time, yet the irony of their first 'hit' single, 'Caru Cymru' (Loving Wales) was not necessarily understood as such. Though easily identifiable in their disguises,[15] their music was perhaps too similar in style to contemporary taste for its intended effect to be felt immediately. Nonetheless, the introduction of irony into Welsh popular music was important to its very survival; for the relative lack of variety, and the adherence to a musical style which was significantly less sophisticated than its Anglo-American contemporaries, threatened the continued growth of the Welsh pop audience. Irony and self-parody are possible and effective when self- or cultural identity is assured; the motion toward irony and cultural self-parody is a motion toward the insistence of identity. In one way, Y Bara Menyn were challenging certain assumptions about Welsh identity perpetuated by the presentation of contemporary musicians; in another, they were continuing in the comic tradition established by *Noson Lawen*. This comic tradition was then adapted for the 1970s by Y Tebot Piws and Y Dyniadon Ynfyd Hirfelyn Tesog.

If the recordings of the Beatles encapsulate the evolution of popular music in the 1960s, the music of Y Tebot Piws could be interpreted as fulfilling the same function in Welsh popular music, though at a more accelerated pace, and with a delayed onset. Their earliest recordings (1969) with Recordiau'r Dryw (Wren) have a very rough quality, and the standard of musicianship suggests the adherence to a certain DIY aesthetic. What distinguished the early skiffle career of Tebot Piws from that of predecessors such as Criw Sgiffl Llandegai was their repertoire. Like many of their Welsh and Anglophone contemporaries, Y Tebot Piws recorded original compositions; but rather than relying on sentimental themes, their songs were generally absurd or topical, infused with an anarchic sense of humor. They may have continued in the comic tradition established by *Noson Lawen* and Criw Sgiffl Llandegai, but there is a certain proclivity in their lyrics which could only have been influenced by late-1960s British popular culture and a more general psychedelic sensibility.[16] There is thus a sense of contemporaneity in the music of Y Tebot Piws, despite their adherence to the acoustic medium. In their coexistence with the dominant trends of the time, both

---

15 For performances on *Disg a Dawn* Y Bara Menyn adopted an unusual system of camouflage, including a handlebar moustache and toy pistol for Geraint Jarman, a feather boa and floppy hat for Heather Jones, and an array of 'flower power' clothes for Meic Stevens which, given contemporary photos, did little to conceal his true identity. A photograph of Y Bara Menyn may be found in the discography of Meic Stevens' *I Adrodd yr Hanes*, ed. Lyn Ebenezer (Gwasg Carreg Gwalch, 1993). The recordings of Y Bara Menyn have recently been re-released as part of the compilation *Meic Stevens: Disgwyl Rhywbeth Gwell i Ddod* (Sain SCD2345, 2002).

16 The tongue-in-cheek manner with which Y Tebot Piws approached psychedelic music would suggest that theirs was not a first-hand association with the effects of mind-altering substances, but rather a comic bemusement on the 1960s counterculture.

Anglophone and Welsh, they represent the first instance of an *alternative* ideology, coexisting with both the dominant Welsh ideology (sentimental, close-harmony, acoustic) and its Anglophone counterpart.

Figure 6.3   Y Dyniadon Ynfyd Hirfelyn Tesog

The position of Y Dyniadon Ynfyd Hirfelyn Tesog in the history of Welsh pop is much the same as that of Y Tebot Piws, with certain notable musical distinctions. The members of Y Dyniadon were largely classically-trained musicians, and their brief career provided the Welsh audience with a musical eclecticism akin to that of the Bonzo Dog Doo-Dah Band in England. Their sonic explorations – utilizing their assemblage of piano, trumpet, fiddle, viola, cello, guitar, sitar, and banjo – did not evolve from any obvious Welsh predecessor, though their tendency toward self-deprecating wit were of a kind with Y Tebot Piws. Given the size and nature of the Welsh pop music community in the 1960s, Y Dyniadon and Y Tebot Piws were commonly found performing at the same concerts and on the same television broadcasts. Collectively they represented a new phase in the developmental arc of Welsh pop, but individually they embraced two different ideologies. Whereas Y Tebot Piws continued in a comic tradition established earlier in the cultural history of Welsh pop, Y Dyniadon represented the motion into new musical territory – an *emergent* pattern. In Raymond Williams' theory, an emergent pattern would suggest a new formation existing outside of the dominant ideology; in Welsh pop the 'dominant ideology' could be summarized on sonic as well as lyrical terms. Y Dyniadon were decidedly a staple of Welsh pop culture, as is proven by their regular appearances on *Disg a Dawn* and their recordings on the Sain label; their antics, captured in the early videos filmed for television broadcast, suggest a close kinship with Y Tebot Piws, and therefore an embracing of a common cultural 'tradition'. But their musicianship suggests an association with an external – art music – tradition, and their career is thus the first notable example in the history of Welsh pop where 'high' and 'low' become blurred, along with 'amateur' and 'professional'.[17]

There are a number of stylistic patterns identifiable in Welsh pop of the 1960s, which serve as 'ancestral' strains in the music of subsequent decades. Certain strains which emerged in the immediate post-war years were adhered to, or developed, in the music of the 1960s; some were supplanted by more contemporaneous trends. As a result, the development of Welsh pop in the first two decades of its cultural history indicate the presence of the ideological patterns mentioned earlier: residual (Triawd y Coleg, Criw Sgiffl Llandegai) and emergent (Y Dyniadon Ynfyd Hirfelyn Tesog), oppositional (Y Bara Menyn) or alternative (Y Tebot Piws). The lyrical and sonic bases upon which these ideological patterns are founded were soon challenged as the development of Welsh pop expanded beyond the confines of its own geographic and linguistic borders.

---

17 As an illustration of this, Y Dyniadon recorded a Welsh translation of the Beatles' 'Yesterday' ('Dyddiau Fu') and an adaptation of a song by Weil/Brecht ('Dicsi'r Clustiau'), both of which appear on their eponymous EP (Sain 10, 1970).

Chapter Seven

1973–82: Establishing New Traditions

With the seeds of an indigenous popular culture taking root, the 1970s in Wales began with a sense of 'catching up' with the popular music of the Anglo-American mainstream. The Welsh recording industry was still in its formative stages, and popular musicians were still acquiring their creative confidence. The relative prominence of Dafydd Iwan as folk musician, chairman of *Cymdeithas yr Iaith Gymraeg*, and now businessman running a small but youth-oriented Welsh record label, inspired a generation of Welsh-language musicians to begin recording, leading to what many regard as the 'Golden Age' of Welsh popular music. The 1970s saw the 'folk' idealism of the 1960s mature into a different kind of national sensibility, creating a palpable split between 'folk' and 'rock' oriented musics; this expanded sensibility allowed non-Welsh speakers to contribute to a unique commentary on contemporary Welsh life within the capital city. By the end of the decade the punk aesthetic had infiltrated the Welsh pop scene and the motion had begun toward widening the scope of the Welsh audience and the focus of the music.

Rock and Folk in Wales

The road from the relatively innocent light entertainment of *Noson Lawen* in the 1940s, through the close-harmony and skiffle bands of the 1950s, to the protest music of the 1960s, was a relatively straight one: from traditional folk songs to humorous songs in a folk idiom to bare social commentary. While the music of the 1940s and 1950s may have been drawn from a nationally recognized repertoire, updated as musical tastes changed, the original music which emerged in the 1960s served as the basis of a new folk music relevant to the politically-charged climate. The mainstays of this new folk repertory were the songs of Dafydd Iwan, and, despite the brief career of Y Blew, in the late 1960s and early 1970s acoustic music was still the norm for Welsh popular music.

One of the central bands of this transition period was Y Tebot Piws (1970–72), who appear on the cusp between amateur and professional, between Welsh pop music as entertainment and Welsh pop as a serious business; and in the developmental period bridging skiffle and folk, folk and rock. Their songs are generally expressions of their unique humor ('Blaenau Ffestiniog'), if not outright nonsense ('Mae Rhywun Wedi Dwyn Fy Nhrwyn' – Someone Has Stolen My Nose), yet they occasionally drew attention to current issues. For example, when *Disg a Dawn* began to be broadcast in color, the show was based in the BBC's Birmingham studio, as BBC Wales was not equipped with color facilities. This created some discontent in Wales, and a demand that a larger studio be built in Cardiff. Y Tebot Piws contributed to the mood with their song, 'Dyn Ni Ddim yn Mynd i Birmingham' (We're Not Going to Birmingham),[1] though its subtle political content was apocryphally unknown to one member of the group. But more important than any social or political commentary they may have offered to the Welsh pop scene was the impact Y Tebot Piws had on their contemporaries, and the role that the four members played in the development of the culture after the break-up of the band in 1972.

By this time, a number of folk-rock bands had emerged across Wales. This was a period when bands were being formed by like-minded students at Aberystwyth, or at the *Urdd* camp in Glan Llyn, and it is safe to say that most musicians active in the early 1970s knew each other, whether by playing at the same concerts, going to the same college, attending the same *Cymdeithas* rallies, or just by being amongst a minority of Welsh-speaking people in a predominantly Anglophone area. In this way the membership of many bands was cannibalistic, if not incestuous: two members of Y Tebot Piws, Emyr Huws Jones and Alun Huws, contributed to two of the more notable contemporary folk-rock bands, Ac Eraill (And Others) and Mynediad Am Ddim (Admission Free), while a third, Dewi 'Pws' Morris, was instrumental in forming the hugely popular Welsh rock band, Edward H. Dafis.

Although Y Blew planted the seeds of electric Welsh rock in 1967 it was not until Edward H. Dafis was introduced to the *Tafodau Tân* audience in 1973 that those seeds took root. Given the developments in Anglo-American rock at the beginning of the decade, including the emergence of Led Zeppelin and the release of David Bowie's *The Rise and Fall of Ziggy Stardust and the Spiders From Mars*, it is perhaps surprising that heavy metal and glam rock remained at bay from Welsh pop.[2] It would hardly be going too far to say that Welsh pop was still in its youth at the beginning of the 1970s; if a relational time-line were to be drawn between Welsh pop and Anglo-American pop, the period 1970–73 in Wales would represent the rough equivalent to late-1950s America, somewhere developmentally between the folk music of Pete Seeger and the rock'n'roll of Bill Haley. When Edward H. Dafis first appeared, they were a direct throwback to 1950s rock'n'roll. Whether they were intended as a rock'n'roll pastiche or were formed out of a desire to establish the next 'moment' in the history of Welsh pop, their emergence provoked in the Welsh audience a remarkable reaction: the sense of communal release is mentioned in many accounts of their debut performance, and the 1973 concert recording captures a kind of audience excitement more readily associated with Elvis Presley or Beatlemania.[3] Yet contemporary with Edward H. Dafis was Hergest, the Welsh country-rock answer to the Eagles and Crosby, Stills & Nash. Hergest continued in the tradition of close-harmony singing established in the early days of Welsh pop,

---

1   The collected singles of Y Tebot Piws were re-released as *Y Gore a'r Gwaetha o'r Tebot Piws* (The Best and the Worst of Y Tebot Piws) (Sain SCD 2049, 1994).

2   Heavy metal and glam rock involve musical as well as physical expression. The influence of the chapel on the development of Welsh popular music prevented the type of sexual revelry associated with the production (and consumption) of contemporary Anglo-American popular music. The ultimate 'embodiment' of Welsh popular music is the subject of Chapter 12.

3   Recorded for posterity and released on the album *Tafodau Tân!* (Sain H.1007, 1973).

but with a decidedly contemporary edge. In this way, in the same year that Welsh rock'n'roll roots were finally established, there was simultaneously a motion toward catching up with the contemporary Anglo-American acoustic rock idiom, and the audience for both groups was the same.

Figure 7.1   Plugged in: Edward H. Dafis

Wales and the Media

Disg a Dawn continued to provide a regular showcase for Welsh music, expanding in the early 1970s from live performances into early music video. The amateur nature of the early Welsh pop 'scene' should not suggest that the BBC were not serious about *Disg a Dawn*: on the contrary, they maintained a strict audition policy for appearances, and in some cases suggested that a band record a single before appearing on the show. This was occasionally countered by a record label suggesting that a band get live performance experience on a show such as *Disg a Dawn* to justify investment in a single. In such a situation, a performance at the National or *Urdd* Eisteddfod would be sufficient to warrant either a recording or an appearance on a live television broadcast. In this way, the BBC were actually promoting the development of a professionally-minded pop music industry, and encouraging musicians to be serious in their aspirations, although the method to their music could remain 'low-brow'.[4]

---

4   Y Tebot Piws and Y Dyniadon Ynfyd Hirfelyn Tesog were the mainstays of early Welsh pop television. Early videos by Y Dyniadon – short films of the band wreaking havoc

Disg a Dawn was followed in the 1970s by the show *Twndish*, and later the ITV show *Sêr* (Stars). On the radio, *Helo Sut Dach Chi* continued through half the decade, leading to the Saturday morning pop institutions *Sosban* (Saucepan) in 1977, and eventually *Cadw Reiat* (Holding a Riot). In the print media the most fundamental contributions to popular culture were the early fanzines, *Asbri* (Vivacity) (1969–78), *Swn* (Sound) (1972–74) and, most importantly, *Sgrech* (Scream) (1978–85). With these three magazines, Welsh popular music developed into something to take seriously, and to criticize. As the scene matured and acquired a new seriousness, so the media began to recognize it as a cultural exploration, rather than merely an expression of youth or a by-product of the language movement.

The Welsh weekly newspaper, *Y Cymro,* published its weekly Top Ten lists, based on record sales reported by the handful of Welsh-language shops scattered throughout the country. The relative scarcity of Welsh-language shops and bookshops at the time presented certain limitations to the amount of product which could be sold, and *Y Cymro* was sometimes found citing as Number One a record which had sold fewer than forty copies. The monthly current affairs journal, *Barn* (Opinion), began publishing regular record and radio reviews toward the end of the decade, and the pop programs on television provided the stage for new bands to perform; but the biggest factor in the growth of the Welsh audience was still *Cymdeithas yr Iaith Gymraeg*.

Music and the Language Movement

When the *Urdd* recognized the draw that popular music held over the younger generation it became clear that pop music could be an effective fundraising tool. The *Pinaclau Pop* (Pinacles of Pop) concerts held from 1969 in the pavilion at Pontrhydfendigaid, in mid-Wales, attracted over three thousand people, exceeding all expectation. So began a period of large organized concerts at Pontrhydfendigaid, based on the *Noson Lawen* model of music-comedy revues and showcasing popular contemporary Welsh talent. The term 'Welsh popular music' at this point in its development encompassed any and all non-'art' music sung in the Welsh language; it was therefore not uncommon to have Dafydd Iwan singing his brand of protest music on the same bill as the popular 'light entertainment' duo Tony ac Aloma, the folk-inflected Ac Eraill (And Others), or the close-harmony groups Hogia'r Wyddfa (Boys of Snowdon) and Hogia (formerly Criw Sgiffl) Llandegai. The unifying feature of these concerts was the language, and the relatively small number of groups performing popular music of any description in Welsh led to a very tight community of musicians and supporters, united in a common cause.

Pinaclau Pop led in 1973 to *Tafodau Tân* (Tongues of Fire), the concerts organized by *Cymdeithas yr Iaith*. The importance of these concerts cannot be overstated, for they represent the maturation process of the embryonic Welsh popular culture.[5] The thirst for community experience and the momentum generated by the

---

through the streets of Cardiff – highlight the eccentric sensibility and humor of early Welsh pop.

5   One, possibly apocryphal, anecdote recounts a sound-check for an early concert at Pontrhydfendigaid. Two young men were passing by, heard the music, and went inside the

early *Cymdeithas* campaigns contributed to the enormous popularity of the festival concerts and the free and ready acceptance of all musicians performing through the medium of Welsh. The kind of community formed at these concerts was central to the formation of a Welsh cultural identity. As the decades progressed, and the musical expressions of this identity changed, it became clear where the relative strengths and fractures lie. In the 1970s, the emerging sense of (linguistic) Welshness could be gauged largely by the support of *Cymdeithas* and *Urdd* concerts, and the lengths to which audiences would go to seek this community experience.

Around this time language activist and amateur disc jockey Mici Plwm was setting up his traveling Welsh disco in communities all over Wales. Again, the relative paucity of Welsh recordings required that he use either 'international' instrumental hits, instrumental covers of English hits, or Welsh pop records not specifically intended for dancing. By traveling through Wales, Mici Plwm was able to gauge the popular taste of the communities he visited, which provided him with creative suggestions for the producers of *Disg a Dawn*, who had by then installed him on the show as host. By keeping abreast of the trends in England and Wales throughout the week and appearing on television on the weekends he could address the needs of his disco audiences and simultaneously take advantage of the situation and advertise to a national audience the concerts being organized in communities throughout Wales.

Considering the distances people were willing to travel to attend Mici Plwm's disco or the gigs organized in Welsh-speaking Wales, it became clear to at least two people, Huw Ceredig (Dafydd Iwan's brother and host of *Tafodau Tân*) and Hywel Gwynfryn (BBC personality and host of *Helo Sut Dach Chi*), that there might be a market in Cardiff for Welsh-language music. The newly-appointed capital city was not an obvious center of the Welsh language, although the concentration of media and student populations, representing all of Wales, suggested a growing population of Welsh speakers. Huw Ceredig and Hywel Gwynfryn decided in 1971 to hire a city center nightclub one night a week for their Welsh disco, *Noson Barbarella* (Barbarella Night), which eventually attracted Welsh speakers not only from Cardiff, but from *Y Fro Gymraeg* (the general Welsh-speaking heartland) as well. The *Urdd* and *Cymdeithas yr Iaith* had created a community of Welsh youth; the discos and gigs organized throughout Wales served this community and created a social outlet for the development of a common popular culture. That some members of this community might then be inspired to forge a more intimate union may have been an unacknowledged subtext in the movement toward the survival of the Welsh language; but whatever the ulterior motives for creating a forum for young Welsh-speaking people to meet, it was another step along the way toward establishing a

---

pavilion to find out what was happening. They approached the person who seemed to be in charge, said they were also in a band, and asked if they could play that night as well. The man in charge thanked them for the offer, but explained that it was a concert organized for *Cymdeithas yr Iaith*, and that only Welsh-language bands were on the bill. The organizer thus rejected the offer of a free performance for the *Cymdeithas* by Jimmy Page and Robert Plant. The dubious veracity of this anecdote merely suggests that there might have been a general unwillingness in the early years of the Welsh language movement to confess to conversance with the contemporary Anglophone popular culture.

sense of unity on the one hand, and toward turning an amateur entertainment into a professional culture on the other.

Although *Cymdeithas yr Iaith* was the common meeting-ground for a large majority of Welsh youth, in 1971 a splinter group, *Adfer* (Return), formed out of the *Cymdeithas*, with much attendant animosity. Where *Cymdeithas* members continued their protests and campaigns, *Adfer* members were united in the belief that the only way to ensure the survival of the Welsh language was to rebuild the Welsh communities that were being decimated by creeping Anglicization and the mass emigration of Welsh-speaking people to urban areas. This involved, at first, purchasing and renovating homes in traditional Welsh strongholds. There was initially some overlap in the activities of *Adfer* and the *Cymdeithas*, primarily in relocating Welsh businesses – Cwmni Sain among them – to *Y Fro Gymraeg*. Though the Welsh musical community had grown very close in the 1970s a rift eventually developed between musicians who supported *Cymdeithas yr Iaith* and those who supported *Adfer*. The politics of both groups were expounded in numerous recordings of the time, released on the Sain label, despite founder Dafydd Iwan's firm commitment to the *Cymdeithas*. By the late 1970s the growth in the number of people who supported the work of the *Cymdeithas* seemed to indicate that the political division had not permanently damaged the spirit of the language movement. Nonetheless, the *Adfer* – *Cymdeithas* rupture was the first sign of fracture within the Welsh musical community in the post-war years, and the only major rift which was not based on linguistic ideology.

Welsh Pop and the City

With so much of Welsh popular music focused on a particular group experience, trying to establish a common cultural referent, and with so much attention paid to the development of Welsh-speaking communities, one musician attempted to bring Welsh life out of *Y Fro Gymraeg* and into the global context. Geraint Jarman had been active as a musician throughout the early stages of Welsh popular music, as a member of the mock-folk trio, Y Bara Menyn (The Buttered Bread), and as a backing musician and vocalist. His career as composer began in 1967, with a song he wrote for Heather Jones' performance at the *Urdd* Eisteddfod competition, and he continued to write a large percentage of her solo repertoire.[6] As a poet he had published two volumes of his own work,[7] and his poetry was featured regularly in the Welsh monthly *Barn*. The most significant factor in all of his work was the unapologetic city perspective from which he wrote.[8] His Welsh experience was inclusive of Welsh-speakers and non-Welsh speakers, native Cardiffians and immigrants, life on the Docks and out in the Valleys.

---

6   It should be mentioned that Geraint Jarman and Heather Jones maintained a long-term personal relationship as well as a professional one, and that their professional relationship has continued long after their personal one dissolved.

7   *Eira Cariad* (Snow of Love) (Llandybie: Christopher Davies,1970) and *Cerddi Alfred St.* (Alfred Street Poems) (Llandysul: Gwasg Gomer, 1976).

8   This issue is re-visited in greater detail in Chapter 11.

When Jarman had compiled a collection of songs he wished to record himself, he chose to work with professional musicians, valuing talent and experience over linguistic affiliation. This was an unprecedented move for Welsh pop, but one which ultimately saved it from certain implosion. There was no question about Jarman's own choice of language, for his artistic tongue was Welsh. Yet there was a different, more inclusive, Welshness embodied by his band, which had not been recognized in the first fifteen years of the Welsh pop 'scene'. It was a Welshness more pertinent to Jarman's own experience, and it developed into a unique fusion of contemporary Welsh life. The major influence on Jarman's musical sound was undoubtedly reggae. His first albums (*Gobaith Mawr y Ganrif* – The Century's Great Hope, 1976; *Tacsi i'r Tywyllwch* – Taxi to the Darkness, 1977), though still rock-based, show a motion toward reggae, hesitant experimentations with reverb and delay, and full experimental use of the limited technology available to him and Cwmni Sain. The punk influence on Jarman was palpable as well, for the Clash had also begun to explore their 'white reggae' fusion, seeing punk and reggae as expressions of similar struggles of oppressed communities. Whatever the initial impetus, Jarman created an immediate cultural statement, at once contemporaneous with the Anglo-American mainstream music, and unique in its fusion of minority community cultures rooted within a minority community.

If punk and reggae were expressions of a similar cultural struggle, it is not surprising that the punk explosion in Britain in the late-1970s was soon appropriated by Welsh bands, anxious to sharpen an edge on the staid nature of Welsh pop. Y Trwynau Coch (The Red Noses) embraced the punk ideal entirely: 'impossibly fast tempos, primitive drum figures, crashing guitar chords, and wailing, out-of-tune vocals... an invitation issued to all would-be musicians to ignore any worries about instrumental competence and join in'.[9] Quite the antithesis of Geraint Jarman and his polished *Cynganeddwyr*, Y Trwynau Coch nonetheless broke new ground for a new wave of bands, and were perhaps the first Welsh band to be noticed by the influential BBC Radio 1 disc jockey John Peel. Y Trwynau Coch released three EPs in 1978, the most notorious of which, *Merched Dan 15* (Girls Under 15) was refused airplay on radio station Swansea Sound. Although the controversy surrounding the ban is said to have been based on a misunderstanding,[10] the negative publicity was invaluable. The ban prompted an enormous amount of publicity – angry letters to *Y Cymro*, interviews on television – and secured the band's popularity with the younger Welsh audience.

Y Trwynau Coch were never a protest band, but gave voice to a general angst, lashing out against the Welsh system in songs like 'Mynd i'r Capel Mewn Levis' (Going to the Chapel in Levis) and making one of the more uncompromising cultural statements of the period with 'Niggers Cymraeg' (Welsh Niggers). There was another

---

9   David Hatch and Stephen Millward, *From Blues to Rock: An Analytical History of Pop Music* (Manchester: Manchester University Press, 1987), p. 169

10   Aled Glynne Davies, Swansea Sound DJ and later the long-standing Director of Radio Cymru, stated in an interview that he refused to play the song not because of the lyrical content but simply because the standard of musicianship was so low (interview with the author, October 1999).

side to the punk aesthetic which Y Trwynau Coch brought to the Welsh scene. Not since Y Blew had a Welsh band attempted a promotional tour through Wales, and no other band had embraced the idea of merchandising to the same extent. Y Trwynau Coch performed at schools in the afternoons and at club gigs throughout the week; they sold t-shirts, posters, jackets; secured a sponsorship from Levis (in exchange for promoting their jeans in 'Mynd i'r Capel') and Fyffes bananas (for the band's cover version of the Meic Stevens song about Y Bara Menyn, 'Mynd i'r Bala Mewn Cwch Banana' – 'Going to Bala in a Banana Boat'). Contemporaneous with Y Trwynau Coch were Llygod Ffyrnig (The Ferocious Rats), whose 1978 single 'NCB' heralded the beginning of a more gritty Welsh 'punk' music and, together with the 'DIY' mentality espoused by Y Trwynau Coch, inspired some of the more fundamental changes to Welsh pop in the 1980s: the establishment of independent record labels, a movement away from the safety of the Welsh pop 'establishment', and a greater self-confidence among the younger bands. This had a galvanizing effect on the one hand, but on the other, initiated a fracture in the Welsh musical network which deepened in the following decades, especially around issues of linguistic loyalty.

Summary

After Y Tebot Piws disbanded in 1972 their two primary songwriters, Emyr 'Ems' Huws Jones and Dewi 'Pws' Morris, continued to contribute to the canon of Welsh popular song; Emyr Jones to the folk-rock band Mynediad am Ddim (Free Admission), and Dewi 'Pws' to the seminal Welsh rock band, Edward H. Dafis. The general musical transition from the 1960s to the 1970s was one of acoustic to electric, and there were agents common to both points in the transition.

Edward H. Dafis was the first Welsh band after Y Blew to use amplified instruments. As a milestone in the history of Welsh pop, their first performance, at a concert organized by *Cymdeithas yr Iaith*, had the same effect, culturally and psychologically, as Bob Dylan's 'rock' performance at the Newport Jazz Festival in 1965 had on the American 'folk' movement. This is not to suggest that Welsh pop would have remained forever acoustic; merely that the motion in 1973 away from 'folk' and toward 'rock' signaled the emergence of a new structure of feeling.[11] And just as the Anglo-American pop music world fractured in the 1960s and 1970s into 'folk', 'folk-rock', 'country-rock' and 'rock' categories, so did Welsh pop expand in the 1970s to embrace its own versions of those same categories.

The Welsh 'folk' category was well represented in the 1970s, and included, most notably, Ar Log (For Rent), Wales' first 'professional' folk band. That a Welsh band could decide to tour outside of Wales, and earn livable wages doing it, was testament to a burgeoning cultural self-confidence;[12] that the first 'professional' Welsh rock

---

11 It is important to remember that there was a six-year interim between the first Welsh 'rock' band, Y Blew, and the first appearance of Edward H. Dafis in 1973.

12 Though not specifically mentioned in this cultural history of Welsh pop, Ar Log does nonetheless represent an important tradition in Welsh music. Their contributions to the folk repertory, and their collaborations with Dafydd Iwan, have informed Welsh popular music in numerous subtle and palpable ways. For a celebration of their achievements and a

band did not emerge until much later in the temporal arc of Welsh pop, is an indication of the tentative nature of non-folk music in the Welsh language. Yet a number of groups emerged in the 1970s which challenged the preconceptions of Welsh 'pop', and the development of the Welsh record industry enabled the production of more contemporary styles of music.

The Welsh 'rock' category was created and represented in the 1970s by Edward H. Dafis. Because Dewi 'Pws' Morris was a prominent member of the group one might have expected a continuation of the irreverent humor of Y Tebot Piws. While humor was certainly an important element in the songs and stage presentation of Edward H. Dafis, more important was the band's determination to establish the roots of Welsh 'rock'. Such a conscious effort at establishing a tradition may be interpreted as ringing false, as Anglo-American rock music in 1973 had already progressed far beyond its 'roots', having fostered Jimi Hendrix, Cream and Led Zeppelin, and reached the height of its 'progressive' phase. The very wealth of Anglo-American rock music again threatened the survival of Welsh pop, for while the Welsh record industry was strengthening and expanding, the music being recorded was not of the standard of contemporary Anglophone popular music. The assumption must therefore be made that the audience for Welsh pop in the 1970s was united in a political ideology, and although Anglo-American popular music would have been omnipresent in their daily lives, the decision made by members of the Welsh community to support Welsh-language pop was one born out of the need for cultural self-expression.[13]

Edward H. Dafis represented not only a change in trajectory for Welsh pop, but a change in the way in which the Welsh community was meant to consume and enjoy the music. For Welsh pop the 1970s was the decade of pavilion concerts, audiences numbering in their thousands, and a new sense of forward momentum.[14] The symbolic community assembled at these concerts was united in political ideals as well as an *alternative* musical ideology: an alternative to contemporary Anglophone popular music, coexisting with, yet not threatening, the dominant (English) ideology; and an alternative to more 'traditional', folk-based, acoustic popular music in the Welsh language. One could interpret the emergence of Edward H. Dafis as following the trajectory set by Y Blew in 1967, in a type of sympathetic emergent ideology; but the participation of some members of Edward H. Dafis in earlier, established bands,

---

comprehensive account of their history see Lyn Ebenezer, *Ar Log ers 20 Mlynedd* (Llanrwst: Gwasg Carreg Gwalch, 1996).

13 One naturally assumes that young Welsh-speaking people in the 1970s were familiar with Anglo-American rock music as well as Welsh rock; a number of people have insisted that this was not always the case. Some Welsh speakers were actually introduced to Anglo-American rock music as a result of their interest in Welsh rock. Welsh rock was therefore not always a *substitute* for Anglophone rock, but an autonomous, parallel cultural tradition.

14 The first two full-length recordings by Edward H. Dafis reflect this momentum, in a typically ironic fashion: *Hen Ffordd Gymreig o Fyw* (Old Welsh Way of Life) (Sain C510N, 1974) and *Ffordd Newydd Eingl-Americanaidd* Grêt *o Fyw* (*Great* New Anglo-American Way of Life) (Sain 1034M, 1975). The recordings of Edward H. Dafis are considered in Damian Walford Davies, '"Rewriting the Law Books": The Poetry of Welsh Pop Music', *Welsh Music History*, 1 (Cardiff: University of Wales Press, 1996): 206–40.

suggests a continuation of a process rather than a disjunct articulation. In a similar vein, the development of Welsh acoustic rock, typified by the band Hergest, suggests an alternative rather than an emergent or oppositional ideology.

The complicated sub-categories of 1970s Anglo-American rock music cannot easily be applied to parallel developments in Welsh pop. The term 'folk-rock' generally indicates less a musical reliance on 'folk', or traditional, material, and more a progressive acoustic sensibility.[15] The category of early-1970s American country-rock is generally understood to include bands such as the Eagles, and Crosby, Stills, Nash (and Young); Hergest represent the Welsh country-rock 'equivalent', and their songs offer a similar sonic quality. Lyrically, however, Hergest represent the continuation of a particular political tradition in Welsh pop. At a time when *Cymdeithas yr Iaith* and *Adfer* were attempting to rebuild the Welsh-speaking heartlands, a loyalty to one or the other ideology might be inferred from the titles of various songs of the period: 'Y Dref Wen' (The White Town) by Tecwyn Ifan, 'Tua'r Gorllewin' (To the West) by Ac Eraill, among many others, including, perhaps, 'Adferwch y Cymoedd' (Return to the Valleys) by Hergest.[16] Whatever their political affiliations, Hergest did manage to create for the Welsh pop canon a collection of songs about Wales, about areas and towns of Wales, with a kind of longing, or *hiraeth*, inherited from the folk repertory, but in the guise of contemporary popular music. In other words, Hergest were perfectly contemporaneous with American country-rock and British folk-rock in a way that Edward H. Dafis were not contemporary with Anglo-American rock. This near-simultaneity of style may signify a greater ease with which 'folk' or 'country' can be re-assessed and redressed in new guises, or it may simply suggest the natural continuation of an earlier strain of pop music: a *residual* musical ideology, part of the 'folk' process.

Occupying a completely alternative musical space from the popular roster of Welsh pop music acts was Endaf Emlyn. Like Meic Stevens before him, Endaf Emlyn secured a recording contract with a major English label; but unlike Meic

---

15 The term 'folk-rock' is inherently problematic when applied to musics of Great Britain and North America. In the latter instance, 'folk', as a generic term, is used to denote the acoustic-based popular music of North America. 'Folk-rock', as a continuation of that process, may be used, for example, to categorize the music of Bob Dylan and The Byrds. 'Folk', in Great Britain, implies an adherence to a particular tradition. 'Folk-rock', in Great Britain, would therefore be applied to a music which is in some way evocative of that tradition, as in Fairport Convention. 'Country-rock', as it is applied to the music of North America, is a somewhat more loosely-defined term, indicating a primarily acoustic medium, perhaps a tendency toward certain textual subjects, and a closer affinity with Southern 'roots' music than with Northern 'rock'n'roll'. These are terms which are explored in greater detail in Simon Frith, *Sound Effects: Youth, Leisure, and the Politics of Rock'n'Roll* (London: Constable and Company, 1987).

16 'Adferwch y Cymoedd' actually represents a reaction to the philosophy of Adfer, suggesting as it does a need to ensure the survival of 'Welshness' beyond the traditional strongholds of the Welsh language in the far west and northern reaches of the country. Ac Eraill, Tecwyn Ifan and Hergest are mentioned together because of common lyrical suggestions of politics and place, though the influence of Anglo-American country-rock is more clearly present in Hergest than in the others, which tended more toward the Celtic folk-rock.

Stevens he was able to record equally in Welsh and in English, thereby contributing to both Anglophone (English) and Welsh musical cultures. In 1974 he recorded and released the first Welsh 'concept' album, *Salem*, based on the eponymous painting by Curnow Vosper.[17] Each song was based on a different character in the painting, creating a type of enclosed world imaginable by anyone familiar with the picture, and resonant for those whose image of Welshness is based on it. Significantly for the period, rather than using the Sain studios, Endaf Emlyn recorded *Salem* on very simple four-track equipment, lending the recording a certain naiveté which belies its depth. *Salem* emerged during a period of concept albums and 'progressive' rock sensibilities in the Anglo-American world, notably Jethro Tull's *Thick as a Brick* (1972), Yes' *Close to the Edge* (1972), Pink Floyd's *Dark Side of the Moon* (1973) and Genesis' *The Lamb Lies Down on Broadway* (1974). A comparison between *Salem* and any of these recordings would be ridiculous, given the differences in production value alone; but it is important to consider *Salem* in a similar tradition as Anglophone 'progressive' rock, for it served much the same developmental function to the history of Welsh popular music.

In Endaf Emlyn's subsequent recordings, *Syrffio (Mewn Cariad)* (Surfing/Falling in Love)[18] (Sain 1051M, 1976) and *Dawnsionara* (Sain 806N, 1981) the influence of American band Steely Dan is obvious; but the sophistication of Endaf Emlyn's music, the sense of his autonomy from the Welsh pop 'scene', and the lack of any direct reference to the Welsh language movement or any political organization in Wales, suggest an ideological distance between Endaf Emlyn and his Welsh contemporaries. One important point to stress here is that Endaf Emlyn was allying himself with a certain kind of *American* identity. The music of Steely Dan typifies a kind of (adopted) West Coast aesthetic, in much the same way that the Eagles defined a kind of (Southern) California sound. That a group such as Hergest, and a musician like Endaf Emlyn, could transplant West Coast music to Wales, and make it relevant to the Welsh experience, speaks volumes about the relative disinterest in contemporary *English* recordings, and a greater attraction to stereotypically *American* sounds.[19] Though not politically or musically oppositional, Endaf Emlyn's method of production and his involvement with both Anglophone and Welsh musical cultures was decidedly different from the established pattern of Welsh pop. In this sense his music represents the beginning of a new approach to music-making in Wales, an *emergent* ideology.

The 'rock' trajectory in Wales, established by Edward H. Dafis (*dominant/alternative*), paralleled by the 'country-rock' of Hergest (*residual*), and shadowed by Endaf Emlyn (*emergent*) also represent the trajectory from amateur to professional, and the movement from the confines of the Welsh community formed within the

---

17 Endaf Emlyn, *Salem* (Sain 1012M, 1974).

18 'Syrffio', appropriated colloquially from the English 'surfing', is also a play on 'syrthio', to fall.

19 The relationship between Welsh popular music and America have been discussed recently in Robert Rhys, 'Yn Erbyn y Graen', *Barn* 467/468 (Rhagfyr 2001/Ionawr 2002): 57–9 and Simon Brooks, 'Miss America: America a Diwylliant Poblogaidd Cymraeg ei Iaith', in M. Wynn Thomas, ed., *Gweld Sêr* (Cardiff: University of Wales Press, 2001): 211–27.

language movement to the wider, Anglophone and bilingual, culture. The paths these trajectories established for the subsequent two decades highlight relative strengths and weaknesses in the process of a Welsh identity, and the emergence of new structures of feeling based on linguistic as well as ideological grounds.

Chapter Eight

1982–90: Breaking the Mold

The 1980s saw a great concentration of developments in Welsh popular culture. This was the decade of independent labels, the Welsh 'underground' scene, local 'scenes', recognition and support of Welsh bands by John Peel, and the beginning of a creeping bilingualism in Welsh pop. With reggae and punk having already expanded the musical palette in Wales, the 1980s brought a greater fragmentation within the culture as bands began to follow more closely the contemporary Anglo-American models.

One related development which took place in the 1980s was the rise of individual 'scenes' within the Welsh pop world. Whereas in the 1960s and 1970s Welsh popular music grew more or less organically throughout the country, in the 1980s smaller pockets of activity located in the predominantly Welsh-speaking areas of Cardigan (Aberteifi) and Bethesda created scenes unto themselves, with bands being inspired primarily by English-language models, and seeking to provide the Welsh-language audience with a sound more relevant to their own experience.

Wales and the Media

Much the most important development which took place in Welsh media was the arrival of S4C, *Sianel Pedwar Cymru*, the independent Welsh Channel Four. This represented the successful campaign by *Plaid Cymru* MP Gwynfor Evans to secure an independent Welsh television channel, following the public announcement of his decision to fast until death if necessary. The Thatcher government relented in their policy against establishing a Welsh channel, fearing that the martyrdom of the former leader of the nationalist party would instigate the kind of civil unrest they had hoped unsuccessfully to quell in Northern Ireland. S4C broadcast its first transmission on 2 November 1982.[1]

Radio Cymru began to target its younger audience in earnest with its nightly show, *Hwyrach* (Later), showcasing a different disc jockey each night, each with his or her own approach to Welsh pop. By this time there was enough variety of music to suit different demographics, and the shows were planned accordingly. New bands were given the opportunity to record live sessions on the radio, filling the gap left empty by the discontinuation of the BBC's *Disg a Dawn* and HTV's *Sêr*. Having witnessed the success of *Cymdeithas yr Iaith*'s concerts and the popularity of the

---

1   The darker subtexts to Thatcher's terms of office are explored in greater detail in Chapter 12 with reference to the music of Datblygu. For background on the ramifications of the Thatcher years on Welsh political and social life, see John Davies, *A History of Wales* (London: Penguin, 1993).

Sgrech awards ceremonies, Radio Cymru launched a series of concerts to promote its show *Sosban*, bringing audiences to the shows and increasing their radio listenership at the same time. And by the end of the decade Geraint Jarman had entered the media world, producing the influential program *Fideo 9*.

Independent Scenes and Independent Labels

Part of the international punk aesthetic was to scorn the establishment, and by the 1980s in Wales, the 'establishment' was the Sain record label. Sain, situated now in Llandwrog, had grown considerably since its inception in 1969, expanding from an 8-track studio into a 24-track studio in March 1980; by 1989 they had built a second studio with multi-track mixing facilities and launched a sister-label, *Crai* (Raw). But at the beginning of the decade, with a new enthusiasm injected into the scene by the likes of Y Trwynau Coch, the 'DIY' approach to music-making reached new heights in Wales.

Brothers Richard and Wyn Jones had formed the band Ail Symudiad (Second Movement) in 1979. Although Cardigan was a largely Welsh-speaking area, the majority of the bands active there sang in English. When Ail Symudiad began performing locally in Welsh, their audiences were attracted to the concerts largely out of curiosity rather than musical interest. There were no other Welsh-language bands in the area to serve as supporting acts. It may be assumed that their younger audience members would have been more likely to listen to Radio 1 than Radio Cymru, and were therefore less familiar with the developments in Welsh pop than they were with the music of contemporary musicians such as Elvis Costello, Madness or the Specials. Once Ail Symudiad began performing more regularly, however, other Welsh bands started appearing, and the 'Teifi Scene' soon developed.

Contemporary with the Teifi Scene was another, much larger and farther-reaching independent scene, centered in Bethesda, North Wales. A major center for slate quarrying, by the mid-1980s there was very little industry left in the area, and there were a number of bands actively performing locally as a means of doing something productive. Inspired much more by the popular contemporary Celtic fringe guitar-rock – U2, Simple Minds, Big Country, The Alarm – than by the British New Wave which inspired the Teifi bands, the Bethesda scene began in earnest with Maffia Mr Huws. It is important to understand that the members of Maffia Mr Huws were of the generation whose parents would have listened to Dafydd Iwan and other early Welsh pop; they therefore represent a second generation of Welsh pop musicians, in every sense of the word. Whereas *Cymdeithas yr Iaith* was the inspiration for the earlier generation of Welsh pop musicians, this next generation created a scene generated on the same principle of speaking to the needs of their community through their native language, but created out of economic necessity rather than social protest. This is an issue to which I shall return.

Maffia Mr Huws began playing straightforward guitar rock with palpable vestiges of Geraint Jarman's brand of Welsh reggae. It was the collaboration between these two generations of Welsh musicians which is of particular interest. Jarman had been active in Welsh pop since its inception in the late-1960s, yet his music was still relevant to Welsh musicians fifteen years later. The music of many of Jarman's contemporaries in the Welsh pop 'establishment', however, was now considered to be something belonging to the older generation, namely the parents of the new wave of Welsh musicians.

As with the Teifi 'scene', the Bethesda 'scene' spawned in the North Wales slate-quarrying triangle[2] a number of bands of different styles, some of whom became the most popular, biggest-selling Welsh acts of the decade – Sobin a'r Smaeliaid (no direct translation), Tynal Tywyll (Dark Tunnel), Y Jecsyn Ffeif (a homophonic play on The Jackson Five), and Ffa Coffi Pawb (Everyone's Coffee Beans; or, homophonically, Fuck Off Everybody). In addition to engendering a healthy live scene, a number of independently-funded establishments were founded in the wake of the popularity of northern Welsh bands: *Pesda Roc*, the biggest rock festivals in Wales through the middle of the decade; *Ysgol Roc* (Rock School), which encouraged the development of another generation of musicians in Bethesda; *Cyngor Roc* (Rock Council), aimed at raising the level of professionalism in the field by organizing, supporting and marketing rock bands throughout Wales; and *Cytgord* (Harmony), a music information service which produced *Sgrîn Roc* (Rock Screen), the music information teletext service, and which continues to produce the Top 10 list published weekly in *Y Cymro*.

The establishments unifying all this activity were of course Radio Cymru, HTV's program *Sêr* and the record label Sain. Ail Symudiad recorded their first single on Sain, but were refused a second single, inspiring them to start their own record label, Fflach (Flash). As the band were performing regularly and making the occasional television appearances on *Sêr*, Richard and Wyn Jones were able to re-invest all of their earnings into their company, and Fflach was able eventually to release an EP of four bands, Y Ficar (The Vicar), Malcolm Neon, Y Diawled (The Devils) and Eryr Wen (White Eagle). They continued to re-invest their profits, and in 1983 were able to purchase their own equipment for recording in their grandfather's chapel vestry. The label continued to grow, and in 1987 they moved the business into the back room of the family home, eventually turning the garage into a studio and adding an extension. Fflach is the second Welsh label to succeed as a full-time business, and like Sain, was born from the need to expand the professional possibilities for Welsh pop.

Although the punk explosion had quieted significantly since 1977, there was still a palpable sense of youth revolution in Welsh pop, yet the limitations of Radio Cymru – the size of its audience, the all-encompassing nature of its programming – spelled a dead end for any ambitious rock band. British pop was a successful export world-wide, and with the newly-launched MTV relying heavily on videos by the British 'new wave' the possibility of succeeding in a wider market became a draw for younger bands. With the exception of its late-night radio shows, Radio Cymru remained rather conservative in its music programming and largely ignored the underground bands cropping up throughout Wales in the wake of the punk explosion. One such band, Anhrefn (Chaos) led this second revolution and instigated a kind of

---

2   It is not right to suggest that all members of each band named here actually came from Bethesda, but rather that Bethesda acted as a locus for a great deal of musical activity.

long-term relationship between Radio 1 DJ John Peel and underground Welsh bands. Anhrefn bassist Rhys Mwyn aimed to promote the Welsh scene outside of Wales, and to explore the possibilities of success outside of the linguistic borderland which had supported Welsh pop to that point. The sameness of much contemporary Welsh pop music had stultified creativity, and many of the older generations of Welsh pop musicians were bemoaning the passing of the 'good old days' of unflagging camaraderie and interchangeable band members. But for the younger generation, there was perhaps an even greater sense of camaraderie and familial ties, the new scene having been nurtured in particular geographical communities rather than the international community of the 1960s protest movement.

What Rhys Mwyn did was to compile a demo tape of four Welsh bands to peddle around to record labels and radio stations in England. Rather than pushing only one band, Anhrefn, his theory was that by promoting a variety of bands he could encourage a wider interest in Welsh music outside Wales. And rather than send the demo tape to a carefully selected list of record label and media executives, he went personally to corporate offices and studios and handed the tapes over to whomever was the most important person available to see him. In this way he caught the attention of John Peel, who began to play Welsh bands on his show, and who continued his relationship with various Welsh producers, promoters and musicians, willingly playing what was given him, not just for the curiosity value but out of his own interest, until his death in 2004.[3] This four-track demo tape marked the beginning of Recordiau'r Anhrefn (Anhrefn Records), the first distinctly underground record label to garner any kind of interest outside of Wales.

Anhrefn's music may not have been progressive in comparison with contemporary British pop, but their sound was easily marketed to non-Welsh and even non-English audiences, due to the certain obvious stylistic influences which informed their songs. There are cultural signifiers to be inferred from different musical styles – the acoustic singer-songwriter in the 1960s may suggest a political activist just as the punk band in the late-1970s would suggest a larger social decay – and Anhrefn's music could be understood by a non-native audience as reflecting a certain political unrest. In the particular climate in which they recorded, deeply enmeshed in Margaret Thatcher's tenure as Prime Minister, the anger evident in their music illustrated the Welshness they wished to export to the wider world and struck a chord across, and beyond, Britain. Their language was not negotiable; they wanted their audiences to infer their messages from the music, not from the words alone.

Despite – or perhaps because of – their recognition by the English media, Anhrefn never endeared themselves to the Welsh media. The reputation Rhys Mwyn cultivated as outspoken critic of the Welsh pop industry and the bands who established it led to a certain amount of bemused press notice, and the occasional interview on S4C or Radio Cymru, but invitations to perform on television or radio were scarce. In this way they gained notoriety in their home territory without acknowledgement of their

---

3   In fact, the most poignant tribute John Peel paid to Welsh music was entirely unforeseen: on the night that his death was announced, BBC1 ended its newscast with a picture of John Peel taken at the Glastonbury Festival, showing the DJ smiling in his *Mwng* t-shirt.

relative success in England and beyond. A similar situation was endured by the band Datblygu (Developing), the most influential Welsh band never to succeed.

Datblygu formed in 1982 and struggled for several years to find a sympathetic Welsh audience. Their early recordings were rejected by Radio Cymru's show *Cadw Reiat* on the grounds that they sounded as though they had been 'recorded in the bathtub'.[4] Although Radio Cymru were not supportive of Datblygu, S4C's pop show, *Fideo 9*, produced by Geraint Jarman, offered them regular exposure, and John Peel not only featured them on his show, but traveled to Wales to see them perform. For the Peel sessions Datblygu produced new material, and offered English synopses of the often wandering, surreal lyrics.[5] The relative success they enjoyed in England served as a sad reminder of the relatively narrow-minded programming in the Welsh media at the time; but the further-reaching influence Datblygu had on younger Welsh bands was belated vindication of their years of performing on the margins of Welsh musical society. This was made apparent by the re-release of Datblygu's earlier recordings on the Ankst record label, the most significant musical venture of the latter part of the decade.

Ankst Records was founded in 1988 by Gruffydd Jones and Alun Llwyd, two students at the University of Wales, Aberystwyth. In keeping with the tradition of the college, many student bands were forming in the Welsh halls of residence, and the idea behind Ankst was to release cassettes of those bands, and specifically music the founders of the company themselves wanted to hear. They moved from producing cassettes to 7-inch singles and then 12-inch singles, releasing as many as was possible on their minimal budget. Upon graduating from college Ankst secured an Enterprise Allowance from the government and turned their part-time college side-line into a full-time business. 1988 was also the year that the Sain record label began to reach out to its younger audience. Having relied heavily on the popularity of middle-of-the-road pop, male voice choirs and light music singer Trebor Edwards for the financial well-being of the company, Dafydd Iwan and his colleagues at Sain realized that they were losing touch with the younger audience. They developed Crai (Raw), the Sain sister-label, to concentrate on releasing recordings by younger bands, and eventually secured Rhys Mwyn as its permanent freelance director. In a telling example of the cycles in which Welsh popular culture has developed, Alun Llwyd, one of the founders of Ankst, became chairman of *Cymdeithas yr Iaith Gymraeg*, just as Dafydd Iwan, founder of Sain, was in the 1960s. Alun Llwyd was imprisoned for protest activities just as Dafydd Iwan before him, and many artists on Ankst contributed to language movement fundraising, as did Sain musicians in the 1970s.

But unlike Sain, Ankst were able to ride into England in the wake of Datblygu's success on the John Peel show, and cultivated from the start an open-minded attitude toward bilingualism in Welsh pop – something considered unthinkable in the early days of its development. Welsh pop maintained its unity by virtue of its shared language; the acceptance of non-Welsh musicians in successful bands such as

---

4   According to Geraint Davies of BBC Radio Cymru and Dave Edwards, singer for Datblygu, in interviews with Eurof Williams for *Y Felin Bop*.

5   Datblygu's lyrics are explored in greater detail in Chapter 12.

Geraint Jarman a'r Cynganeddwyr was possible only because of their silence.[6] For a Welsh-language record label to promote an exploration of the bilingual nature of Wales seemed a contradiction in terms, and spelled for many the imminent demise of Welsh-language pop and the scene which had spawned it.

Welsh Pop and Bilingualism in the 1980s

There was always a precarious balance between the English and Welsh languages in what I have been referring to as 'Welsh pop'. Modern Welsh popular music was founded on a challenge to Welsh-language musicians to explore their creativity in their mother tongue, and perhaps to create a unified sense of Welshness in the process. The very close ties between popular music, the language and the media had been strengthened throughout the first twenty-five years of the language movement, and it was inconceivable that English-language pop music could give voice to the struggle. The English language was, after all, the backdrop against which the struggle was taking place.

This is not to say that bilingual or Anglophone musicians were not accepted into the Welsh-language scene once they had switched the medium of their music to Welsh. Quite the contrary, even at the end of the 1980s Meic Stevens was considered a central pillar of the Welsh pop movement. And the 1980s saw the emergence of another singer-songwriter whose adoption of the Welsh language has produced an important body of work, both musical and literary. Steve Eaves has brought a singularly poetic sensibility to the Welsh pop scene, adapting the blues aesthetic into his own work, performing regularly with at least one winner of the bardic chair at the National Eisteddfod, and editing the first collection of Welsh lyrics-as-poetry, *Y Trên Olaf Adref* (*The Last Train Home*).[7] Opting out of the mainstream English culture and enriching the burgeoning Welsh culture with an outsider's perspective is one matter; fluctuating between the two cultures is another matter, and therein lies a problem.

One of the first bands to straddle the line between English and Welsh was Jess, key players in the Teifi scene. As I mentioned, a large proportion of pop music originating in Cardigan was English, although the Welsh language is a very strong presence in the daily life of the community. Jess began as an Anglophone group, but were convinced by Wyn Jones of Fflach Records to switch to Welsh, with the suggestion that there was more money immediately available from the Welsh media than from the English. Although Jess recorded in Welsh, they never intended to be bound exclusively to one language or the other. They were never closely associated

---

6   I must also mention Bando, the popular contemporary 'supergroup' featuring Caryl Parry Jones, Myfyr Isaac and Geraint Griffiths alongside non-Welsh-speaking musicians. There was a distinct difference between their critical reception and that of Y Cynganeddwyr, whether for reasons of musical style or professionalism.

7   *Y Trên Olaf Adref: Casgliad o Ganeuon Cyfoes* (Talybont: Y Lolfa, 1984). Steve Eaves is discussed in greater detail below.

with the language movement.[8] Their intention was to reach the widest possible Welsh audience, which meant Anglophone Wales as well as Welsh-speaking Wales, and beyond. Geraint Jarman's production company, Criw Byw (Live Crew), sent Jess on a tour to Czechoslovakia to film a program for S4C. They played in western Europe and at Glastonbury, and succeeded in becoming a professional rock band, earning their living from recordings and live performances. But their eventual decision to record exclusively in English was met with hostility in the Welsh press. Whereas their success could have been heralded as bringing an awareness of Wales and contemporary Welsh culture to an international audience, it was seen instead merely as a convenient springboard to their ultimate betrayal of the Welsh language.

So when Ankst began to promote English- and Welsh-language pop music to the Welsh audience there was some disagreement in the establishment as to how it should be received. By now the earlier fragmentation in the Welsh pop movement had splintered further with a progression into techno music and acid house, and Ankst remained on the cutting edge of contemporary taste. Mainstream English publications like the *NME* were regularly taking notice of Welsh bands, and it became clear that the type of eccentric music being produced by the younger generation of Welsh musicians had the potential for real international success. And so it was that many of Ankst's most popular bands – Y Cyrff, Ffa Coffi Pawb, Gorky's Zygotic Mynci – began to aim for the world stage, spawning a new era in Welsh pop: Y Cyrff re-formed into Catatonia; Ffa Coffi Pawb re-formed into Super Furry Animals, and Gorky's Zygotic Mynci blazed the trail to major label recognition and international acclaim.

Summary

The 'mainstream' Welsh music of the 1980s continued largely on its straightforward rock trajectory (Derec Brown, Maffia Mr Huws) but the advent of smaller labels such as Fflach, Anhrefn, and most notably Ankst, expanded the palette of Welsh pop music to include New Wave (Ail Symudiad, Malcolm Neon) as well as more experimental music (Llwybr Llaethog, Datblygu). These pockets of musical activity were centered around particular geographical regions of Wales (Bethesda, Cardigan), and the new independent labels of the 1980s were generally concerned with providing an 'alternative' to the mainstream (Sain) fare. It may be over-complicating a natural development in the cultural history of Welsh pop to suggest that the establishment of each new independent label represented a new structure of feeling, but it is important to consider the place of each of these labels, the communities which formed around the consumption of their music, and the type of ideals which the music represented. Bands such as Datblygu offer political and social contexts for 'independent' Welsh pop in the 1980s; the ideological issues to be addressed here concern linguistic association, and the trajectories established by the fracturing of a musical and linguistic 'tradition'.

---

8   This is perhaps surprising given that Brychan Llŷr, the lead singer of Jess, is the son of Dic Jones, chaired bard, an honor bestowed by the highest establishment of Welsh culture, the National Eisteddfod.

The precedents for linguistic border-crossing have already been mentioned. Mary Hopkin, Meic Stevens and Endaf Emlyn were all musicians active in both English and Welsh, Mary Hopkin beginning her career singing in Welsh and moving into mainstream Anglo-American culture, Meic Stevens and Endaf Emlyn moving from mainstream Anglo-American culture back into the Welsh pop community. The centrality of the Welsh language to the development and survival of Welsh pop should be obvious; but the developmental arc which Welsh pop had taken through the 1960s and 1970s was the result of the work of a relatively small 'family' of musicians. When Welsh pop fractured into its many sub-categories – new wave, post-punk, techno, etc. – the sense of common purpose which might have existed in the 1960s and 1970s was threatened, if not supplanted, by the desire for contemporary expressions of Welsh life. The motion from 'folk' to 'rock' in the 1970s may have been the first step away from an established order; any subsequent motion back toward 'folk roots' may then be interpreted as a return to political or ideological roots. The motion away from 'folk roots' is a motion toward a type of political and linguistic hybridity unimaginable in the developmental stages of Welsh pop. The two examples of Welsh pop in the 1980s offered here represent both symbolic movements: the return to 'roots' and the motion away from them.

Steve Eaves is one of a very small collection of English people in the cultural history of Welsh pop music who have chosen Welsh as their preferred language of daily life and artistic expression. His commitment to Welsh poetry was mentioned earlier; what is of primary importance here is the mutli-leveled influence Steve Eaves brought to Welsh popular music, poetically, musically and culturally. It would be an exaggeration to say that Steve Eaves' music was groundbreaking, but there are elements discernible in his recordings which were unlike those found in other contemporary Welsh music. His first two recordings, *¡viva la revolución galesa!* (Long Live the Welsh Revolution!) (Recordiau Felin, 1984) and *Cyfalaf a Chyfaddawd* (Capital and Compromise) (Sain C941N, 1985) recall the political roots of Welsh pop in their linguistic commitment; indeed, the fact that this political ideology had been adopted by someone who would otherwise be located outside the borders of the Welsh community, infused it with a greater power. Musically, however, Steve Eaves represents a different sort of 'roots' music.

The roots of contemporary Anglo-American rock music may be traced back to southern United States blues.[9] The sympathetic kinship expressed in the Welsh community for African Americans and the civil rights movement in the 1960s was outlined earlier. The fact that the blues, largely an African-American mode of musical and cultural expression, could be adapted into a Welsh political ideology should therefore not be surprising. But it must be remembered that Welsh 'rock'

---

9   Again, a single set of 'roots' is difficult to establish in Anglo-American rock 'n roll. Richard Middleton's suggestion of multiple roots may be found in *Studying Popular Music*; similarly Charlie Gillett, *The Sound of the City: The Rise of Rock and Roll* (New York: Da Capo Press, 1996) provides a useful historical overview of the way in which different 'roots' musics shaped what we now consider 'rock' music; and Simon Frith, *Sound Effects* provides a brief overview of the fractures created in the rock community and the roots which were revealed as a result.

emerged from a different tradition; that light entertainment provided the original basis for musical expression in the Welsh language, and that subsequent musical styles were largely borrowed, fully formed, from Anglo-American culture. The blues, while revisited and revered by British musicians in the 1960s and 1970s, did not have any obvious contemporary Welsh-language counterparts.[10] Though a musical and harmonic structure was borrowed from the blues and formed the basis of a significant portion of Anglo-American popular music, and is therefore discernible in Welsh-language popular music, Steve Eaves was the first musician in Welsh pop to strip his music back to its 'roots' and to create a Welsh 'blues'.[11] This suggests a multi-layered ideology: a newly-rediscovered musical root politicized in a relatively well-established cultural tradition (*residual*); a linguistic repatriotization from dominant to minority, a strengthening rather than a weakening of the Welsh musical formation (*oppositional*); and a music informed by the continued tradition of the Anglo-American dominant culture, existing on a different temporal plane than its precedents (*alternative*). Of these the most clearly definable is the residual, for it suggests a continuation of one tradition in the expectation of its processual development.

The opposite motion – away from 'roots' – can be inferred in the music and career of Jess. Jess were agents in the 'Teifi Scene', 'stars' of the Fflach label, and one of the first Welsh bands to attempt to break into the wider pop market. While they claim always to have considered themselves a bilingual group, their defection to the English language (and to mainstream institutions such as the Glastonbury festival) was met with some hostility from members of the Welsh-speaking community. Their career began at a time when the Ankst label was in its infancy; while Ankst was host to a number of bands who made the same transition from Welsh to English, Jess took the necessary first steps toward enabling a west-to-east border crossing.[12]

Musically, Jess were clearly more affiliated with Anglo-American popular music than with Welsh pop. Because Cardigan was not home to a great number of Welsh groups before the emergence of Ail Symudiad and the creation of the Fflach label, the influence of Anglophone rock music on local youths was significant.[13] The members

---

10 For an account of the development of contemporary Anglophone Welsh rock music and its chronological pace, see Deke Leonard, *Maybe I Should've Stayed in Bed?* (Bordon: Northdown Publishing, 2000) and its 'sequel', *Rhinos, Winos & Lunatics: The Legend of Man – a Rock'n'Roll Band* (Bordon: Northdown Publishing, 2001).

11 One possible exception was Meic Stevens, who claims that his song 'Gwely Gwag' (Empty Bed) from 1972 was his first attempt at a Welsh-language blues. See his *I Adrodd yr Hanes* for a transcription and background information.

12 It would be ludicrous to draw a direct and uninterrupted line of influence from Mary Hopkin to Jess, but it must be remembered that there had been precedents for the Welsh-to-English language shift; Jess is mentioned primarily as representing the inception of a second wave of border-crossers.

13 The singlemost significant Anglophone band to emerge from Wales in the 1980s was The Alarm. Significantly, their lead singer, Mike Peters, became involved in the work of *Cymdeithas yr Iaith*, re-learned the Welsh language, translated their album *Change* (1989) into *Newid*, and recorded *Tân* (Fire) for the Crai label (1991). He also collaborated with members of Jess in The Poets of Justice. While in no way suggesting that their career is a

of Jess formed their band with the intention of competing in the Anglo-American market, but in order to reach the largest home audience, they were encouraged to sing in both English and Welsh. The one language did not preclude the other, and that is the primary distinction between Jess and the other bilingual artists mentioned earlier. The difficulty they had in gaining acceptance by the Welsh pop establishment was born of a particular territoriality, and it is a territoriality established in the unspoken rule that 'Welsh' pop music must necessarily be sung in the Welsh language.

Jess was one of a number of late-1980s Welsh groups to tour parts of Europe and other minority-language cultures. This kind of ambassadorship was praised and encouraged, but it also suggested a lack of exposure given those bands on their home territory. The type of 'alternative' music being created in Wales at this time – Anhrefn, Datblygu, etc. – did not fit easily into the Radio Cymru format, and 'youth' music was generally relegated to late-night slots. There was a safety in the type of 'rock' being recorded on the Sain label, and their output was symbolic of the type of generation gap now palpable within Welsh popular music. Jess represented an alternative to the mainstream, in that they emerged from a relatively unexpected location, recorded on an 'alternative' label, and alternated between Welsh and English. But they represent an *oppositional* ideology, challenging the notion that dominant Welsh popular culture is monolingual, challenging the notion that Welsh pop is relegated to the geographical boundaries of Wales, and challenging the notion that Welsh popular music cannot compete in the Anglo-American market.

Steve Eaves and Jess are only two examples of an increasingly wide variety of Welsh popular music recorded in the 1980s. While they represent opposing linguistic ideologies – minority language chosen over dominant; minority language given a consideration equal to dominant language – they also represent articulations of new structures of feeling. The increased politicization of Welsh popular music in the 1990s, and the political ramifications of bilingual music, are issues which may be traced back to the roots of Welsh pop, but they found definite moments of articulation in the music of the 1980s.

---

footnote to the history of Welsh pop, I mention The Alarm here as a precursor to the final case study, in which they will figure as contributors to the Anglophone Welsh 'roots' of bilingual bands in the 1990s.

Chapter Nine

1990–2000: Broadening the Scope

The most important developments in Wales during the 1990s were political. Prefaced by significant international events such as the release of Nelson Mandela from prison in South Africa and the fall of the Berlin Wall, the decade began with a world-wide movement toward cultural tolerance. The political shift in Britain, from Thatcher to Major to Blair, mirrored or foreshadowed in America by the shift from Reagan to Bush to Clinton, brought with it the movement toward devolution in Wales, Scotland and Northern Ireland and the impression of a new Britain.

The 1997 referendum for a Welsh National Assembly, won by the narrowest of margins, inspired much press speculation about the idea of a Welsh national character, of a renewed sense of Welshness, of a long-awaited national optimism all but defeated by the failure of the previous devolution referendum in 1979 and the attendant years of struggle during the Thatcher administration. The excitement surrounding the establishment of the first elected governmental body in Wales in seven hundred years was bound to wane eventually, despite the on-going battle for the construction of a permanent home for the Welsh assembly in Cardiff Bay, surrounded by a newly-barraged lake and extensive high-end apartment complexes. But the familiar cultural-political debate has again presented itself, with a renewed relevance. As Wales begins to assert the relative power it has been granted, the place of the Welsh language in a new political sense of 'Welshness' has raised more questions than it has answered.

The assumption of an English cultural hegemony in the 1990s was challenged further by the rise in international profile of the Celtic 'fringe': economic resurgence in the Republic of Ireland, literary and cinematic acclaim for Scotland, and the media-inspired moniker, *Cool Cymru*, denoting the seemingly sudden emergence of Welsh artists – Manic Street Preachers, Stereophonics, Catatonia, and Super Furry Animals – onto the British and American charts.

Wales and the Media

Despite the drive toward the 1997 referendum for devolution, the attendant sense of power and national consciousness, and the popularity in Britain of Welsh and Anglo-Welsh pop groups, the Welsh media did very little to capitalize on the resurgent youth culture, and S4C all but killed a popular music presence on Welsh television. Radio Cymru went through a change in management which introduced a controversial change in format, allowing a greater English-language presence throughout the day, and canceling shows such as Nia Melville's influential *Heno Bydd yr Adar yn Canu* (Tonight the Birds Will Sing), which had championed the Welsh underground scene and provided the Ankst roster with regular media exposure. But of all changes made to Radio Cymru during the 1990s, the new language policy was understandably met with the most vitriolic and long-standing discontent among the listening public.

The discontent over S4C's dismissal of the Geraint Jarman-produced *Fideo 9* was also palpable. Though several short-run series were developed later in the decade, the motion away from a forward-looking popular culture and instead toward a less challenging, middle-of-the-road fare signaled an undeniable aging process amongst those responsible for Welsh-language media programming. The discontent was made all the more bitter by the fact that many of those involved in the Welsh media were former *Cymdeithas yr Iaith* activists, some of whom had fought to establish Radio Cymru and S4C, and former members of seminal Welsh-language rock bands. It was naturally a source of sadness for some that Huw Jones, chairman of S4C until 2005, who began his media career in the 1960s and went on to found the Sain record label with Dafydd Iwan in 1969, would knowingly turn his back on contemporary Welsh music by limiting the amount of prime time programs aimed at the youth audience.[1]

The Welsh print media maintained a level of excitement about Welsh popular music. There were regular contributions to the Welsh monthly *Barn*, occasional articles on popular music in the Anglo-Welsh journal *Planet* and continued Top Ten listings in *Y Cymro*. But the momentum was difficult to regain after the disappearance of popular Welsh pop-oriented magazines such as *Sgrech* and *Sothach* (Trash). Even the weekly magazine *Golwg* (View), which started with a predominantly pop culture-based news format, eventually lost its interest in Welsh pop, by the end of the decade publishing only sporadic feature-length articles on bands and musicians, and relegating music primarily to their monthly color supplement, *Atolwg* (Please!). With so little media support for contemporary Welsh pop, many bands began to turn their attention towards the English-language market.

Sgrîn Roc (The Rock Screen), the teletext service offering an events calendar, a top-ten chart, information on current releases, and general news updates on the Welsh rock scene, was established in 1988 by Cytgord (Harmony), a Bethesda company responsible also for the pop magazine, *Sothach*. By 1990 the service had faced the termination of its contract with S4C, and the tendering of the teletext service into the ownership of a private company. This prompted some musicians to refuse to contribute to the new service, and a movement began toward ensuring the monetary survival of *Y Sîn Roc Gymraeg* (The Welsh Rock Scene). In the short-lived rock bureau formed by Dafydd Bowen Rhys from Cytgord, Rhys Mwyn from Anhrefn, and Alun Llwyd from Ankst, the Welsh rock community had the nearest thing to a governing body as it was likely to have. The first years of the 1990s saw an annual conference, Showbiz Cymru, and the decision in 1992 to establish CRAG – Cyngor Roc a Gwerin (Rock and Folk Council) – was a further step toward institutionalizing what had begun three decades earlier under purely amateur conditions. It was also an attempt to establish an infrastructure to ensure the future of Welsh pop, and to

---

1   As troubling as the cancellation of pop music programs was, it must be pointed out that S4C needed to consider the financial viability of its programming, and the audience numbers for pop-oriented shows were clearly not large enough to sustain them.

work in cooperation with CYD, the society of Welsh learners, to promote and market popular music in the Welsh language. The Welsh rock scene was being kept very close to its cultural roots in many senses, but the necessary financial commitment for CRAG's work soon became less readily attainable, and CRAG did not last through the decade.

The Welsh media's apparent apathy toward popular music had its greatest repercussions in the splintering in 1997 of the Ankst label into two distinct but complementary factions: Ankst Management, responsible for representing early Ankst successes such as Super Furry Animals and Gorky's Zygotic Mynci; and ankst*musik*, which continues to release recordings by contemporary Welsh musicians. Even a renegade label like R-Bennig (a play on the word 'special') diversified, launching an on-line broadcasting service for alternative music. The larger labels such as Sain and Fflach are still able to profit by the sales of their more popular recordings (male voice choirs, established folk artists); but with little media investment in contemporary youth-oriented (otherwise 'independent') music, the decision by musicians and management alike to diversify and find a wider audience seemed a natural one.

Wales and the Postmodern Condition

With a renewed political optimism in Wales as a nation and the cultural confidence inspired by the success of Welsh bands in Britain, the idea of contemporary Welshness emerged in a variety of contexts. The motion toward devolution has been significant culturally for a number of reasons, but primarily for the breakdown of the Anglo-centric notion of the United Kingdom. For this reason, it must be noted that devolution came amid the waning of the musical phenomenon dubbed 'Britpop' by the media.

One of the stylistic traits common to Britpop products such as Blur's *Parklife* (1994) and Oasis' *Definitely Maybe* (1994) was a plundering of earlier musical styles. They share a free association with common cultural referents – the sounds of the Beatles in the case of Oasis, and in the case of Blur, a constantly shifting map of the history of popular music, combined with a particularly ironic sense of humor. To some cultural critics, these are key qualities in the postmodern aesthetic. To some Welsh musicians, the postmodern aesthetic is a useful playground in which to explore the idea of a Welsh cultural identity. In the broader cultural context of the 1990s, the postmodern condition could be seen as finding expression in, amongst other things, U2's *Zoo TV* tour, which blurred the lines separating pop construct, commercialism and real life; the film *Pulp Fiction* (1994), which re-defined the narrative process; and the fascination, continued from the 1980s, with 'World Music' and its challenge to the Anglo-centric pop music construct. In the Welsh cultural context, the postmodern condition could be seen as finding expression in, amongst other things, the playful de-contextualization of musical signifiers and the fluctuation between the Welsh and English languages. In an effort to define Welshness, many musicians have plundered from their own musical pasts, which has resulted in a strengthened folk music scene, and across musical genres there has been a greater musical fragmentation, apparent audibly through any extended exposure to Radio Cymru.

Radio Cymru represents, more than any single musical or cultural product in Wales, a manifestation of the postmodern condition. Because of its very nature – a national radio service which exists to provide for the Welsh-speaking population an equivalent to the four main English-language BBC services[2] – there is no rigid format to any of the individual programs. That is to say, there are intended audiences for any given program, but almost any music recorded in the medium of Welsh could be considered for inclusion. In one program a listener might hear the Welsh equivalent of Country & Western, followed by a popular boy band, followed by a folk song; in the night-time slots, aimed at a younger audience, this middle-of-the-road type of mix might be supplanted by a Welsh hip-hop or techno track and supplemented by the more popular, 'Top 40' Welsh bands. While the juxtaposition of these musical styles might be jarring at first, it shows on the one hand the variety of cultural product in the Welsh market, and on the other the relative freedom available in a market which is not driven by financial reward, but rather by linguistic need.

The Fragmentation of Welsh Pop

One constant feature in Welsh popular music since its inception has been the folk element. The folk scene has maintained a solid audience since the mid-1960s, and built such annual festivals as the Cnapan and Sesiwn Fawr Dolgellau (The Big Session in Dolgellau). Of the two festivals, Cnapan was the more traditionally 'folk' of the two (although it began hosting a related rock weekend), but Sesiwn Fawr Dolgellau is the more forward-thinking festival. It is international in scope, attracting folk musicians and fusion bands from non-Celtic and Celtic nations alike. One of the organizers of the festival, Ywain Myfyr, is a member of the local band, Gwerinos, whose own brand of 'new folk' injected a particular irony and political orientation into the standard repertoire. The idea of holding a free weekend festival in a small town in Snowdonia, opening it to Welsh and Anglophone bands alike, revived in some way the flagging sense of contemporary cultural life in Wales. Radio Cymru sponsors the event, broadcasting live from Dolgellau throughout the weekend, and S4C broadcasts a digested 'highlights' show, hosted by Twm Morys, poet and singer/harpist in the band Bob Delyn.

Bob Delyn (literally, Bob Harp, or Every Harp, but clearly a reference to the American singer-songwriter) have developed their own brand of 'folk' music which succeeds both at defining a Welsh sound and at exploring Wales' place in the wider culture. This Welsh sound is filtered through the setting of traditional Welsh texts to a non-traditional musical accompaniment, writing original lyrics in traditionally-structured, strictly metered Welsh, and employing the prominent textural use of the harp. By incorporating a Breton-language element and the occasional use of non-native instruments in their mid-1990s recordings they extended their musical palette to include elements from other Celtic traditions, and this pan-Celtic fusion serves to

---

2   There are notable exclusions, however. One of the more intriguing programs currently on Radio 3 is 'Late Junction', which offers an eclectic mix of world, experimental, ambient, and pop musics. Indeed Radio 3 itself, as the dedicated 'classical' BBC station, is not replicated on Radio Cymru at all.

connect Welsh folk music with a wider musical network. If rootedness in one's own cultural history is a central feature of the 'folk' tradition, readdressing history from a contemporary perspective is what helps to define a culture's place in the global market. This is a matter to which I will return, as it is especially pertinent to the discussion of Welsh musicians who choose to explore their cultural identity through the rock idiom.

As the 1990s progressed the multi-stylistic nature of Anglo-American pop was mirrored in Wales. Whereas in the 1960s and 1970s Welsh pop seemed to lag stylistically behind the mainstream trends, in the 1990s Welsh musicians were artistically contemporaneous with their Anglo-American counterparts. This may have been a result of the prevalence of British popular music in everyday life; or it may have been a reflection of an overall dependence upon English-language media for musical entertainment, given the Welsh media's ultimate indifference to contemporary Welsh music. Whatever the cultural impetus, there was a tendency toward incorporating British popular culture into the Welsh pop scene, evident in the growing presence of dance music, techno pop, and rap. The dichotomy between techno and rap represents an interesting shift in the concept of Welsh music. Rap is largely text-reliant, often inseparable from its political content, and cultivated in a particular cultural formation; techno music, by contrast, is intended for a particular kind of consumption (dance), largely instrument-based, and less reliant on words. In the Welsh musical context, this indicates an uncertain balance in the linguistic relationship. If a musical form does not presume textual content, and therefore precludes linguistic association, what remains to signify it aurally as belonging to any particular culture?

Welsh Pop and the Welsh Language

The fragmentation of the Welsh pop scene in the 1990s served to strengthen what had begun to develop in the 1980s as three distinct sub-categories: monoglot Welsh, bilingual Welsh/English, and monoglot English. Monoglot Welsh bands are active most notably in the folk idiom, but also across the pop strata, and serve as the foundation for Radio Cymru playlists and *Cymdeithas yr Iaith* concerts; they are the mainstream of Welsh music, despite genre. But this categorization is complicated in the rock idiom by a further fracturing into a (sub-) sub-category, of those bands who move subtly across the linguistic divide.

Some bands have always expressed an innate bilingualism, owing to the bilingual nature of the band membership – Ectogram, Melys, and Rheinallt H. Rowlands (all Ankst artists) being three notable examples. Each of these bands produce consistently innovative music, seemingly content to explore their own terrain through the medium of either language. This free linguistic association illustrates the apparent ease with which linguistic barriers have begun to shift in the spoken Welsh of some areas,[3]

---

3   Though it must be noted that the music emerging from urban and rural areas will reflect different attitudes toward bilingualism.

and for this reason such bilingual bands can be seen to represent more accurately the state of the Welsh language in its contemporary cultural context.

A band's shift from monoglot Welsh to bilingual Welsh/English, however, continues to raise concern among some of the listening public, for it signals, more often than not, an intended emigration to the English-language market. This shift assumes many guises: the inclusion on a recording of the occasional English-language song; an English title given to an otherwise Welsh-language song; or the naming of a band in a linguistically ambiguous or intentionally English-language manner – Ectogram, Topper, Catatonia. Big Leaves, one of the more popular bands of the late 1990s, are another example of this shift. Having begun in 1992 as Beganifs, their name change presumably signals an intention eventually to break into the English-language market. But beyond the purely linguistic concern, this supposition raises another important issue: what can secure a band's popularity once they attempt to break into the English-language market? Popularity in Wales does not predetermine popularity in England or America. Will a band's cultural roots in the Welsh 'scene' have any bearing on their admittance into Anglo-American culture?

Then there are those bands who switched the medium of their music entirely from Welsh to English, and succeeded in the wider market: Gorkys Zygotic Mynci, Catatonia, Super Furry Animals. Their international success earned them continued support by Radio Cymru; their roots in the Welsh 'scene' warrant their inclusion on Welsh radio, and the increased tolerance toward the English language on Radio Cymru enables their continued presence on the air. Similarly, those Anglo-Welsh bands who have topped the British pop charts – Manic Street Preachers, Stereophonics – are included on Radio Cymru's playlist both by virtue of their wide popularity and their roots in South Wales. But do they represent another facet of the Welsh pop 'scene', or do they descend from another tradition altogether? What is the relationship between bands such as Super Furry Animals and Stereophonics? How do these bands represent contemporary Wales?

Summary

It is difficult to isolate any single factor common to the enormous variety of Welsh pop in the 1990s. The bands mentioned here are representative of ideological shifts and structures of feeling in Welsh pop at the close of the century, are examples of the expansion of the musical roots established in the early decades of its temporal arc, and are based in the traditions outlined earlier.

The initial fissure between folk and rock emerged in the 1970s. Common to Anglo-American and Welsh popular cultures, it is a distinction which leads through developmental stages to a multiplicity of tangential categories and styles. In the development of Welsh pop music, the 'folk' movement – as in the adherence to 'traditional' musics – has generally followed a parallel course to musics in a 'popular' idiom. Throughout the post-war years there are examples of the 'folk' and the 'popular' merging, as in the utilization of 'folk' elements – instruments, texts – in an otherwise 'pop' context, but none quite so vividly as in the music of Bob Delyn.

'Folk-rock' may be defined as an acoustic-based pop idiom, but the music of Bob Delyn does not easily fit that category. Though they update Welsh folk material into a more contemporary musical context, it is not the only stylistic trait they display; their recordings provide a combination of traditional, folk, pop, and classical pastiche. Furthermore, their bilingualism – Welsh and Breton – does not adhere strictly to either folk or pop categories.[4] There is certainly a close link between Welsh pop and Breton pop,[5] and the linguistic connections between Breton and Welsh create a natural and understandable fusion; the fact that bilingualism in this case does not include the English language is at once a recognition of alternative – Celtic, not Anglo-Saxon – roots, and an adherence to the political ideology of the Welsh language movement.[6]

The historical precedents for Bob Delyn's brand of folk are primarily literary. Their songs utilize texts from medieval Welsh poetry as well as newly-composed texts in strict Welsh meters. Where they adapt Welsh folk tunes, they do so by maintaining the original melody and harmonic structure, and creating a contemporary accompaniment. This is by no means an unusual approach to folk music-making in the twentieth century; it is merely mentioned in order to place Bob Delyn in an historical path – a remembered tradition, a *residual* ideology – and to emphasize the importance of the text, of language, in their music. This resonates with Line Grenier's study of Quebecois pop and the *chansonnier* movement, for it suggests a deeper root to Welsh pop than is normally revealed. The emphasis on language also serves to separate Bob Delyn from the other two examples chosen here to represent the 1990s, Rheinallt H. Rowlands and Gorky's Zygotic Mynci.

Both Rheinallt H. Rowlands and Gorky's Zygotic Mynci follow the trajectory established in the 1960s with Y Dyniadon Ynfyd Hirfelyn Tesog: the music of Rheinallt H. Rowlands is steeped in a classical, 'high art', soundscape, albeit one created electronically rather than acoustically, and Gorky's Zygotic Mynci continue in the kind of eclecticism anticipated by Y Dyniadon. Both Rheinallt and Gorky's exhibit outside (Anglo-American) influences, whether in their compositional style or through lyrical references to external (non-Welsh) literatures and cultures. Unlike

---

4   The Breton element of Bob Delyn's music was largely contributed by vocalist Nolwenn Korbell. The dissolution of her personal relationship with Bob Delyn's harpist and lead singer, Twm Morys, leaves some degree of uncertainty as to the amount of Breton, if any, which will feature in future Bob Delyn projects.

5   Though not mentioned explicitly here, Alan Stivell is often cited as a direct influence on the creation of Welsh pop. His particular fusion of Breton folk and electronic rock idioms, rooted in a minority language and culture, provided a kind of inspiration for the development of popular music in the Welsh language, which should not be overlooked. For more information on Alan Stivell's role in the development of Breton folk music see Stephen D. Winick, 'Breton Folk Music, Breton Identity, and Alan Stivell's *Again*', *Journal of American Folklore* 108/429 (Summer 1995): 334–54.

6   Twm Morys has not necessarily placed himself in the foreground of Welsh language politics, but has stated on numerous occasions that the desire to sing in the Welsh language comes purely from the desire to express himself in his native tongue. Indeed, his commitment to artistic expression in the Welsh language was finally acknowledged at the National Eisteddfod in Montgomeryshire, 2003, when Twm Morys was awarded the bardic chair.

Y Dyniadon, both Rheinallt and Gorky's are constitutionally bilingual, and unlike Bob Delyn, theirs is a bilingualism in the Jess mold. Rheinallt H. Rowlands and Gorky's Zygotic Mynci also represent a generational shift in Welsh pop, from a standard approach to songwriting to the kind of experimental music nurtured on the Ankst label. They represent, therefore, not only a new structure of feeling (a renewed youth interest in Welsh pop), but an ideological shift (from residual to emergent to oppositional) and a cultural crisis (the tendency of young bands to aspire to the Anglo-American dominant culture).

On a very superficial level, the music of Rheinallt and Gorky's exhibit a new kind of experimentation in Welsh pop, in some ways anti-mainstream, in others ironically self-referential. The idea of Welsh pop here becomes a kind of cultural playground, with a wide array of Anglo-American mainstream influences emerging from the musical textures, and the Welsh language acting as the grounding force to a culture existing on the margins of that mainstream. Rather than creating a new kind of Welsh pop, Rheinallt and Gorky's use a number of musical genres to explore the place of Wales in contemporary culture. Whereas Bob Delyn renewed literary and musical traditions in order to explore an historical Welsh identity and culture, Rheinallt and Gorky's seem less interested in defining or defending Welsh identity and culture as such, and more in understanding their individual place in the world, in whichever language comes to hand. The primary distinction between these two bands is the wider acclaim and mainstream exposure enjoyed by Gorky's, and the relative marginal status celebrated by Rheinallt.

While Rheinallt H. Rowlands may be interpreted as emerging from the pattern established by Y Dyniadon, and while they may have adopted their middle initial from Edward H. Dafis,[7] yet they remain slightly removed from 'mainstream' Welsh pop. Located geographically on the island of Anglesey, they are as removed physically from the 'center' of Welsh media, Cardiff, as is possible to be. As such, their music is informed by their ability to play on the fringes of Welsh culture and Anglo-American culture. Because they fit no easily identifiable classification, they can only be considered as representing an *emergent* ideology: bilingual, geographically isolated, creating a possible and playful balance between Welsh and Anglo-American culture as they conform to neither.[8]

The example of Gorky's Zygotic Mynci is somewhat more difficult to elucidate. They emerged at a time when Welsh pop was rejuvenated by the type of musical experimentation supported by the Ankst label. They were given airplay on the John Peel show, like many other Ankst artists, and they signed a recording contract with Mercury.[9] Even on their mainstream releases there was some element of Welsh to

---

7   Rheinallt H. Rowlands and Edward H. Dafis are both fictitious names.

8   The recording career of Rheinallt H. Rowlands came to a tragic end on 23 December 2005, when singer Owain 'Oz' Wright was hit by a car and killed on his way home from a concert given in Bangor by Euros Childs, lead singer of Gorky's Zygotic Mynci.

9   In addition to befriending English media and record company executives, Gorky's Zygotic Mynci boasted, for a period of time, a mutually admiring relationship with John Cale, surely the most influential individual Welsh musician in the history of Anglo-American popular music. For an account of his transition from Welsh classical violist to founding member of the Velvet Underground, see John Cale and Victor Bockris, *What's Welsh for Zen?*

their music, whether in the occasional bilingual lyric or reference to Welsh culture. Despite, or because of, their relative success in the Anglo-American market, Gorky's encountered some resistance from Welsh-language activists, indicating either a continuation of the linguistic territoriality encountered by Jess, or the fear of cultural implosion. That is to say, the potential success of one band in the Anglo-American market might foreshadow the mass exodus of a number of Welsh bands for an attempt at the reward structure of the mainstream culture. But because the music of Gorky's Zygotic Mynci can be traced to a particular 'tradition', they are here isolated as examples of an *opposition* to the dominant ideology. They are oppositional in their insistence on a natural bilingualism, and they are oppositional in their challenge to the dominant culture's perception of Welsh popular music.

The many strands of Welsh popular music perceptible from the end of the Second World War to the end of the century should provide an indication of the means by which members of the Welsh community have negotiated their cultural identity. That certain styles of music may be traced to both Anglo-American and Welsh roots is a central factor in the development of Welsh pop; that certain musical formations emerge from specifically Welsh examples is central to the creation and continued health of Welsh musical culture. The creation of the Welsh audience and the enunciations of Welshness in the post-war decades are evidence of the shifting and developing cultural self-confidence within the Welsh musical community. An awareness of musical roots, and an adherence to cultural roots, both Anglo-American and Welsh, enable the community's ability to express Welshness at any given time in the temporal arcs of Welsh and Anglo-American popular musics. The relationship between the two musics is not equal, but it is constant. What will be addressed now is the extent to which that relationship is accepted, and to which that relationship is resisted.

The Autobiography of John Cale (London: Bloomsbury Publishing, 1999). For a provocative assessment of recordings by Anglo-Welsh bands, and observations about John Cale's influence on Gorky's Zygotic Mynci, see Dai Griffiths, 'Ffordd Eingl-Gymreig Grêt o Fyw?', *Golwg* 9/33 (1 May, 1997). For an analysis of the effect of Gorky's shift from independent to major label (and back again), see Dai Griffiths and Sarah Hill, 'Postcolonial Music in Contemporary Wales: Hybridities and Weird Geographies', in Jane Aaron and Chris Williams, eds., *Postcolonial Wales* (Cardiff: University of Wales Press, 2005): 215–33.

PART III
Case Studies

Chapter Ten

Dafydd Iwan and the New Welsh 'Folk Culture'

Figure 10.1   Dafydd Iwan

As with Anglo-American popular music, the political roots of Welsh pop were planted firmly in the 1960s. Musically, there was both a continuation of the established popular music trajectory (light entertainment, sentimental ballads, close harmony, skiffle) and a need to join in the spirit of radical international social change. Once the political precedent of Welsh music was set, so was the political focus in other areas of Welsh popular music; soon the overriding feeling was that all popular music sung in the Welsh language was, by its very nature, political. Most importantly, Welsh popular music was contributing to the creation of a new political consciousness and a new cultural self-confidence which had been lacking in earlier generations; Welsh culture was joining, albeit slowly, an international youth movement intent on changing its very world. The primary instigator of this movement in Wales was Dafydd Iwan, whose lyrics provide the first articulations of a contemporary, politicized Welsh identity.

It is always tempting to draw connections between Welsh musicians and their likely Anglo-American precedents. As a result, Dafydd Iwan tends to find his name mentioned in conjunction with American singers such as Woody Guthrie, Pete Seeger and Bob Dylan. The similarities are obvious, and the inspirations undeniable: not only does Dafydd Iwan serve as spokesperson for a generation of Welsh activists, his music is firmly grounded in the kind of first-person observation found in the music of the contemporary American folk movement.[1] The obvious contemporary parallel here is Bob Dylan. Like Bob Dylan, Dafydd Iwan looked to Woody Guthrie for musical inspiration; Dafydd Iwan also adapted one of Guthrie's central works, 'This Land Is Your Land', for one of the foremost expressions of Welshness of

---

1   Political similarities do not necessarily suggest stylistic similarities, however. Dafydd Iwan's vocal style is clearly rooted in the Welsh chapel-singing tradition, and not the contemporary Anglo-American folk tradition.

the last century. Although the resulting song, 'Mae'n Wlad i Mi', is regarded as a central component of 1960s Welsh popular music, one question must be raised: how Welsh can a song be if it is based on a song which is essentially inseparable from its American roots? This could also serve as the central question to the discussion of Welsh popular music in general: how can Welshness be defined if it is expressed through an adopted Anglo-American cultural product?

First, a look at Woody Guthrie's 'This Land Is Your Land', in its manuscript version of 1940:[2]

Chorus: This land is your land, this land is my land
From California to the New York Island
From the Redwood Forest to the Gulf Stream Waters
This land was made for you and me.

As I went walking that ribbon of highway
And saw above me that endless skyway
And saw below me that golden valley, I said:
This land was made for you and me.

I roamed and rambled, and followed my footsteps
To the sparkling sands of her diamond deserts
And all around me, a voice was sounding:
This land was made for you and me.

Was a big high wall there that tried to stop me
A sign was painted said: Private Property
But on the back side it didn't say nothing
This land was made for you and me.

When the sun came shining, then I was strolling
In wheat fields waving, and dust clouds rolling
The voice was chanting as the fog was lifting
This land was made for you and me.

One bright sunny morning in the shadow of the steeple
By the Relief Office I saw my people –
As they stood hungry, I stood there wondering if
This land was made for you and me.

---

2   'This Land Is Your Land', words and music by Woody Guthrie. TRO-© Copyright 1956 (Renewed) 1958 (Renewed) 1970 (Renewed) 1972 (Renewed) Ludlow Music, Inc., New York, NY. Used by permission. 'This Land Is Your Land' was originally entitled 'God Blessed America', written in direct response to the Irving Berlin song mentioned below. The title and the final line of each verse is crossed out in the manuscript version, to be replaced by 'This land was made for you and me'. The final verse included above a later addition. For further information on the song and its passage into American folklore, see Joe Klein, *Woody Guthrie: A Life* (London: Faber and Faber, 1998).

Nobody living can ever stop me
As I go walking my freedom highway
Nobody living can make me turn back
This land was made for you and me.

The importance of this song to the collective American consciousness cannot be overstated. It expresses the American experience on a multitude of levels. The first, most obvious, level, is a message of brotherhood: this land was made for you and me. The second level offers a message of the vastness of the country: from California to New York is quite a distance, with all that land in between. A third, related message relates to the beauty of nature: endless skyway, golden valley, sparkling sands, diamond deserts. These are all messages which had been drummed into the American consciousness in a variety of forms, but most notably in the popular songs 'America the Beautiful', 'My Country 'Tis of Thee', and 'God Bless America'. Each of these songs offers a relentless sentimentality and the invocation of God in reference to the American way of life which was undoubtedly the type of utopianism against which Guthrie was rebelling. Take, for example, the following lyrics:

O beautiful, for spacious skies, for amber waves of grain
For purple mountain majesties above the fruited plain!
America! America! God shed his grace on thee
And crown thy good with brotherhood from sea to shining sea![3]

And:

My country, 'tis of thee, sweet land of liberty,
Of thee I sing;
Land where my fathers died, land of the pilgrims' pride
From ev'ry mountainside, let freedom ring.[4]

And:

God bless America, land that I love
Stand beside her, and guide her thru the night with a light from above.
From the mountains, to the prairies, to the oceans white with foam
God bless America, my home sweet home.[5]

It is clear that Guthrie intended to create an alternative, more realistic, picture of America. He begins 'This Land Is Your Land' by following the above models, painting America as a vast country of natural – not God-made – beauty; but proceeds to uncover the other side of the American dream. Nowhere in the other three songs is any mention made of the inequality of life in America, of unemployment, of the dispossessed. Guthrie's one oblique reference to religion – 'in the shadow of the

---

3   'America the Beautiful', lyrics by Katharine Lee Bates, 1913.
4   'My Country, 'Tis of Thee', lyrics by Samuel F. Smith, c. 1890.
5   'God Bless America', lyrics by Irving Berlin, 1938.

steeple' – leads directly back to tangible reality – 'by the relief office'. Guthrie's America is a land of great beauty, but it is also a land of great trouble, where throngs of people in search of the American dream line up for money and for food; where those with the means to buy land do so to the exclusion of those who have nothing; land is parceled off for those with money, and those without money are forced either to wander in search of work, or to survive on charity. Guthrie sang about the reality of life around him. But much the most important message in 'This Land Is Your Land' is its very title. Guthrie is offering to his listeners the very vastness of America, the limitless opportunities available for those with the courage to seek them out, and the ownership of a dream which is not limited to the boundaries of the oceans surrounding the geographical space we call 'America'. In this sense, Woody Guthrie is stating his truth: he had wandered the countryside looking for life, and found it all around, waiting for him to claim it.

It should be clear that 'This Land Is Your Land' speaks very directly to the American consciousness. The simplicity of the message, and of the messages of the rest of Guthrie's songbook, led to the creation of a folk culture in the United States of which Guthrie, Burl Ives, and Pete Seeger (in his solo career, in collaboration with Guthrie in the Almanac Singers from 1941 to 1943, and as a member of The Weavers from 1949 to 1958) played central roles. The American folk music which became the vehicle for political sentiment in the 1960s followed from this tradition in the guise of Joan Baez, Phil Ochs, and Bob Dylan. While Guthrie may have been seen as the initial inspiration for much of the folk music of the 1960s, the folk singers of the 1960s, most notably Bob Dylan, adopted the Guthrie persona as a means to an end. Although he popularized Guthrie's talking blues style and travel narratives, the folk tradition which developed in the 1960s is generally traced back to Dylan himself as the source of a new folk aesthetic, to the extent that the sound of an acoustic guitar and solo voice became a kind of signifier of political 'folk' music.

Because Dafydd Iwan began his singing career in the mid-1960s, accompanying himself on acoustic guitar, the parallel was invariably made between himself and Bob Dylan. It is important now to turn to Dafydd Iwan's lyrics and compare his message with Woody Guthrie's. First, 'Mae'n Wlad i Mi' (1966):[6]

Dwi'n cofio crwydro hyd lwybrau unig	I remember walking down lonely paths
Ar foelydd meithion yr hen Arenig;	On the bare hills of old Arenig;
A chlywn yr awel yn dweud yn dawel:	And hearing the breeze saying softly:
'Mae'r wlad hon yn eiddo i ti a mi.'	'This land belongs to you and me.'

---

6   'Mae'n Wlad i Mi (This Land Is Your Land), Woody Guthrie, translated by Dafydd Iwan, © Tro Essex Music. Originally recorded by Dafydd Iwan and Edward (Welsh Teldisc, 1966). Lyrics reprinted by permission; translation mine. 'Mae'n Wlad i Mi', as well as the other two songs mentioned here have been re-released on the compilation disc, *Y Dafydd Iwan Cynnar* (Sain SCD 2180, 1998).

Chorus: Mae'n wlad i mi ac mae'n
  land wlad i tithau
O gopa'r Wyddfa i lawr i'w thraethau,

O'r De i'r Gogledd, o Fôn i Fynwy

Mae'r wlad hon yn eiddo i ti a mi.

Mi welais ddyfroedd Dyfrdwy'n
  loetran,
Wrth droed yr Aran ar noson loergan,

A'r tonnau'n sisial ar lan Llyn Tegid,

'Mae'r wlad hon yn eiddo i ti a mi.'

Mae tywod euraid ar draeth
  Llangrannog
A'r môr yn wyrddlas ym mae
  Llanbedrog;
O ddwfn yr eigion mae clychau'n
  canu,
'Mae'r wlad hon yn eiddo i ti a mi.'

Chorus: This land is mine and this
  is yours,
From the top of Snowdon down to
  her beaches,
From the South to the North,
  Anglesey to Monmouthshire,
This land belongs to you and me.

I saw the waters of the Dee
  loitering
By the foot of the Aran one
  moonlit night,
And the waves whispering on the
  banks of Bala Lake,
'This land belongs to you and me.'

There's golden sand on
  Llangrannog beach
And the sea is green in Llanbedrog
  bay;
From the depths of the ocean the
  bells are sounding,
'This land belongs to you and me.'

On the most superficial level, Dafydd Iwan retains Woody Guthrie's travel narrative and at least two of the aforementioned messages: brotherhood, and the beauty of the surroundings. The vastness of Guthrie's America cannot be translated realistically into Dafydd Iwan's Welsh narrative, and any size comparisons between the two geographical regions at issue would be ludicrous. Furthermore what Dafydd Iwan's lyric evokes is a different kind of ownership than that of Guthrie's America, and the difference is evoked through the medium of the Welsh language.

It seems an obvious distinction to make, but Dafydd Iwan's Welsh lyrics bring an entirely different message to the song than is present in Woody Guthrie's original. The Welsh language speaks to a different political need, one more pertinent to Wales in 1966. Political life in Wales in 1966 was at a turning point. The country had just seen the eviction of a predominantly Welsh-language village to allow for it to be drowned and turned into a reservoir for the Liverpool water supply; the village school at Aberfan had just been the site of the worst coal tip disaster in living memory; the Welsh Language Society was in its infancy; and *Plaid Cymru* was about to send its first member to the Houses of Parliament. The 1961 census had shown the number of Welsh speakers in Wales to be roughly twenty-six per cent of the population, with numbers dropping; the influx of English people to areas of North Wales had altered the profile of the Welsh language in its traditional strongholds; and the lack of a visible Welsh-language presence on road signs and in public places was leading to an extended campaign of civil disobedience and unprecedented vandalism on the roads and in the villages of Wales. When Dafydd Iwan was heard singing 'Mae'n

Wlad i Mi', invoking the names of places in Wales – their Welsh place names – he was asserting for Welsh-speaking people the right to claim their country in their native tongue.

The qualification should now be made: Dafydd Iwan was asserting for twenty-six per cent of the population of Wales the right to claim their country in their native tongue. He was drawing a map of the country – the Welsh-speaking part of the country – in a language impenetrable by seventy-four per cent of the population of Wales. He was, in essence, crystallizing in words what a minority of the population believed to be true: that Wales, with these specific borders, these specific sites of natural beauty, these resources, has Welsh place names and belongs to Welsh people. For a popular song, it is protective and exclusionary. It is territorial and subversive. And it is the first significant song in the Welsh language to locate the site of its crisis of identity.

It is difficult to interpret 'This Land Is Your Land' as exclusionary. Guthrie was offering the American dream to all who could claim it; Dafydd Iwan offered the Welsh dream to all who could claim it, with the contingency that they do so through the medium of the Welsh language. While the same could be said of Woody Guthrie's 'exclusionary' use of English, it does prompt one to consider the possible political implications of the song, had Woody Guthrie decided to write and sing it in Spanish, or in Chinese, or in one of the Native American languages. Though migrant laborers were decidedly lower-class citizens in 1920s and 1930s America, lower still were the Chinese laborers employed to build vast expanses of the trans-national railroad, or the Mexican immigrants whose heritage provided California with her very identity, or the Native Americans whose enforced exodus in the nineteenth century to Indian Territories informed much of the history of the state where Woody Guthrie was raised. A statement of solidarity between Woody Guthrie, representing the 'Okie' in search of a living in the dustbowl years, and the unspoken others in immigrant communities throughout the country, would have been an even more powerful indictment of the American social system in the early decades of the twentieth century. In this sense, Dafydd Iwan's use of a minority language, located in a dominant Anglophone culture, fulfills a political agenda unimagined by Woody Guthrie.

But we must return to the central difference between the two versions of the song. Where Woody Guthrie opened the landscape of America to the dispossessed and to the common man, Dafydd Iwan closed the boundaries of Wales to those who were seemingly meant to live there.[7] Although this suggests a darker subtext to the song, it should be stressed that 'Mae'n Wlad i Mi' was instrumental in encouraging Welsh-speaking people to recognize their kinship, to unite into a stronger community and to mobilize into political action. It is unclear how many Welsh people would have been familiar with Woody Guthrie's music, but the originality of Dafydd Iwan's version in the context of Welsh popular music has invested in it a significance akin to the significance of 'This Land Is Your Land' to the American consciousness.

---

7   The fact that the line 'o Fôn i Fynwy' invokes both one of the most fervently Welsh counties of Wales (Anglesey) and the most Anglicized (Monmouth), is significant in this regard.

Dafydd Iwan's early recording career presents many examples of such politically-minded songs. 'Bryniau Bro Afallon' was Dafydd Iwan's Welsh 'version' of 'Big Rock Candy Mountain', another American folk song popularized by its illustrative chorus: [8]

In the Big Rock Candy Mountain it's a land that's fair and bright,
Where the hand-outs grow on bushes and you sleep out every night
Where the box cars all are empty and the sun shines every day
On the birds and the bees in the cigarette trees,
The lemonade springs where the bluebird sings,
In the Big Rock Candy Mountain.

'Big Rock Candy Mountain' paints a picture of life on the railroads, and a hobo's version of utopia. In its evocation of the tough working life faced by many in Depression-era America it is similar in affect to some songs by Woody Guthrie, and serves as part of the American folk repertory. 'Bryniau Bro Afallon' was recorded in the same year as 'Mae'n Wlad i Mi', and shows more direct references to the contemporary political climate in Wales, as well as clear indications of Dafydd Iwan's own political affiliations:[9]

Beth amser yn ôl ar noson fel hon
digwyddais gyfarfod â chrwydryn ddyn.

A long time ago on a night like this
I happened to meet a wandering man

Gofynnais iddo i ble'r oedd e'n mynd;
atebodd yntau beth wedaf atat fy ffrind.

I asked him where he was going;
he answered I'll tell you what, my friend.

Dwi'n mynd i wlad sy'n ddi-ofalon,
draw i fryniau Bro Afallon.

I'm going to a land that's carefree,
over to the hills and dales of Avalon.[10]

Ar fryniau Bro Afallon mae pawb yn byw yn hen,
Does neb yn colli'i dymer
ac mae gwg 'run fath â gwên,

In the hills and dales of Avalon everyone lives to be old,
No one loses their temper and a frown is the same thing as a smile,

Mae'n haf ar hyd y flwyddyn

It's summer all year long

---

8   'The Big Rock Candy Mountain', attributed to Harry 'Haywire Mac' McClintock. There are many versions of this song, with the verses seemingly interchangeable. The version cited above is taken largely from a recording of Harry McClintock, released on *O Brother Where Art Thou* (Mercury 2000).

9   'Bryniau Bro Afallon', words and arrangement Dafydd Iwan © Cyhoeddiadau Sain. The lyrics for 'Bryniau Bro Afallon' appear in the songbook *Canwn!* (Talybont: Y Lolfa, 1990), offering an additional two verses than are recorded on the original record (Welsh Teldisc, 1966). The introductory verse offered above is included in the recording, but not in the songbook. Lyrics reprinted by permission; translation mine.

10   Literally, 'the hills of Avalon Vale', but translated here as 'hills and dales' for reasons of economy and scansion.

a Nadolig bob yn ail ddydd Iau.

and Christmas every other Thursday.

Chorus: O bois rhaid mynd am dro i'r nefolaidd fro
Lle mae'r merched, O! mor hardd

Chorus: O boys we must go to the heavenly vale
Where girls, O! – are beautiful enough

i ddenu calon bardd –
Ar fryniau Bro Afallon.
O mae ieir bach yr ha' a'r blodau yn bla

to tug the heart of a poet –
In the hills and dales of Avalon.
O there's a plague of butterflies and flowers

A chwrw yw dŵr pob afon;
Does 'na neb yn jêl, o mae bywyd yn fêl
Ar fryniau Bro Afallon.

And every river flows with beer;
No one is in jail, life is sweet
In the hills and dales of Avalon.

Ar fryniau Bro Afallon mae pawb yn siarad Cymraeg,
'Llythyrdy' ar ddrws pob Swyddfa Bost,

In the hills and dales of Avalon everyone speaks Welsh
'*Llythyrdy*'[11] on the door of every Post Office,

does dim sôn am *Dafod y Ddraig*.
Mae'r enwade i gyd wedi uno
a'r siope'n gwerthu popeth am ddim.

and no mention of *Tafod y Ddraig*[12]
All the denominations are united
and the shops sell everything for nothing.

Ar fryniau Bro Afallon
mae pawb yn rhoi pleidlais i'r Blaid,
Llafur yn colli *deposits* o hyd
a'r Toriaid yn llyfu'r llaid.
Mae'r Steddfod yn para am fisoedd
a deng noson lawen bob nos.

In the hills and dales of Avalon
everyone votes for *Plaid Cymru*,
Labour loses all its deposits
and the Tories lick the mud.
The Eisteddfod lasts for months
and there are ten Noson Lawens every night

There is a utopianism in Dafydd Iwan's song as well as in the original. Dafydd Iwan is invoking a mythical land rooted in Welsh legend much as McClintock invokes a kind of children's candy land with certain adult concessions. But there is a Welsh reality which creeps into the mythical 'Bryniau Bro Afallon' and again, it is a very particular construction of Welsh reality. The first two verses are somewhat faithful to the original model, but in the chorus Dafydd Iwan makes reference to Welsh cultural history: the girls 'beautiful enough to tug the heart of a poet' possibly a reference to the (notoriously randy) late medieval bard Dafydd ap Gwilym, or a blanket reference to the Welsh poetic tradition. In the fifth line of the chorus, 'no one is in jail' is an overt reference to Welsh language activists, whose campaign of civil disobedience led to the incarceration of a number of members of *Cymdeithas yr Iaith*, Dafydd Iwan

---

11 'Letter house'.
12 'The Dragon's Tongue' – symbol and newsletter of *Cymdeithas yr Iaith*.

included. With the beginning of the third verse, 'everyone speaks Welsh / "llythyrdy" on the door of every post office / no mention of *Tafod y Ddraig*' it becomes clear that the song is a rallying cry for the *Cymdeithas*. We see a monoglot Welsh Wales as part of Dafydd Iwan's utopia; the successful outcome of the *Cymdeithas* campaign for governmental adoption of Welsh as an official language of Wales;[13] and the lessened importance of a newsletter aimed at a membership of people devoted to a radical political cause. With his suggestion that 'all denominations are united', he is referring to the Welsh Nonconformist tradition and the occasionally vitriolic disagreements between neighboring chapels even in the smallest villages;[14] a united Nonconformist force would be a united Welsh-language force, and nowhere is the Anglican tradition mentioned in the song.

The final verse seems to be a celebration of *Plaid Cymru* and its successful campaign to send their leader, Gwynfor Evans, to Westminster. Clearly, if the *Plaid* were to assume all Welsh seats in Parliament, London would have no more control over Welsh affairs, and the Anglo-centric Labour and Conservative parties (and, one would assume, the contemporary incarnation of the Liberal Democrats), would finally be pushed out of Welsh politics. With no imposition of an English 'way of life' on Wales, Welsh 'traditions' such as the Eisteddfod[15] and the *Noson Lawen* would not be relegated to special occasions or specific times of the year. So clearly, Dafydd Iwan's utopia is a Welsh (non-English) utopia. The adult concession carried over from the McClintock version is the beer flowing like rivers; otherwise

---

13 In the summer of 1972 *Cymdeithas yr Iaith* published its manifesto in the Welsh language; it was translated by Harri Webb and printed in *Planet* 26/27 (Winter 1974/75), and includes the following remarks about the Post Office:

> There is hardly any government organisation that could make a more valuable contribution towards raising the social and public status of the language than the Post Office, a public service which all kinds of people make use of so often. Equal status for Welsh here would bring speedy results and could have a direct effect on people's attitude to the language.
>
> Priority should be given to the complete transformation of the linguistic nature of the Post Office, those potent symbols of the constant impact of English on our consciousness. Their past attitude has not been encouraging. ... Only grudgingly do they accept the correct forms of place names as official. True, some nice bilingual signs have now begun to appear, under pressure from *Cymdeithas yr Iaith*, but that is all.
>
> We can be satisfied with nothing less than equal status with English. This means that all Post Office publications in Wales should be bilingual, with Welsh given priority: pension books, postal orders, stamps, etc.... [p. 113]

14 To illustrate: an old joke tells of the Welshman who was stranded on a desert island. When, many years later, he was finally rescued, the landing party were surprised to find that the Welshman had built a little village for himself on the desert island. He showed them around his house and other points of interest. When his rescuers asked him why he had built two chapels, the Welshman said, 'that there is the chapel I go to ... and *that* is the chapel that I *don't* go to.'

15 Though a very strong cultural institution, it should be noted that the Eisteddfod was largely re-invented in the nineteenth century from an ancient model. For an historical overview of the Eisteddfod, see Prys Morgan, 'From a Death to a View: The Hunt for the Welsh Past in the Romantic Period', in Hobsbawm and Ranger, eds., *The Invention of Tradition* (Cambridge: Cambridge University Press, 1983): 43–100.

'Bryniau Bro Afallon' is a domesticated version of an existing folk song, adapted in the tradition of the Almanac Singers in the 1940s: giving voice to a political ideal, in simple, unaffected musical terms.

The aesthetic of folk music is one of simplicity of musical construction and directness of message. While the lyrics of 'Mae'n Wlad i Mi' and 'Bryniau Bro Afallon' may leave room for interpretation, still they provided the foundations for one of Dafydd Iwan's most subversive political texts. 'Carlo' was written in 1969 at a time when a great percentage of the Welsh population was united in protest against the investiture of Charles as the Prince of Wales. The history of the Welsh princes cannot be given adequate mention here,[16] but it should be noted that the symbolism of the Queen of England bestowing upon her son titular duties over the principality of Wales in a ceremony held at the castle in Caernarfon, was not lost on many members of the Welsh public. There were extended protests in the months preceding the investiture ceremony, and the country was effectively divided between those who favored the monarchy and those who opposed it, between British Welsh and Welsh nationalists, Anglophone and Welsh-speaking. In the midst of this internal conflict Dafydd Iwan appeared on the TWW program *Y Dydd* and sang a song he had written especially for the occasion:[17]

Mae gen i ffrind bach yn byw ym Mycingham Palas	I have a little friend who lives in Buckingham Palace
A Charlo Winsor yw ei enw e	And Carlo Windsor is his name
Tro dwetha yr es i	The last time I went
I gnocio ar ddrws ei dŷ,	To knock on the door of his house,
Daeth ei fam i'r drws a medde hi wrtha i:	His mum came to the door and said to me:
Chorus: O Carlo, Carlo, Carlo'n ware polo heddi	*Chorus*: Carlo, Carlo, Carlo's playing polo today;
Carlo, Carlo, Carlo'n ware polo gyda'i dadi	Carlo, Carlo, Carlo's playing polo with his daddy
Ymunwch yn y gân,	Join in the song,
Daeogion mawr a man,	Subjects big and small,
O'r diwedd mae gyda ni brins yng Ngwlad y Gân	We finally have a prince in the Land of Song
Fe gafodd e'i addysg yn Awstralia, do a Sgotland	He was educated in Australia, yes, and Scotland

---

16 For a comprehensive history of the Welsh princes see John Davies, *A History of Wales* and Gwyn A. Williams, *When Was Wales?* For contemporary opinion on the investiture of the Prince of Wales see the monthly periodical *Barn* 77 (Mawrth 1969).

17 'Carlo', music and lyrics Dafydd Iwan, © Cyhoeddiadau Sain. Lyrics reprinted by permission; translation mine. The lyrics are also included in *Oriau Gyda Dafydd Iwan* (Talybont: Y Lolfa, 1969) which calls 'Carlo' 'y record a werthodd fwy nag unrhyw record Gymraeg erioed (do!)' – 'the record which has sold more than any other Welsh record ever (really!)'.

Ac yna lan i Aberystwyth y daeth o,	Then he came up to Aberystwyth,
Colofn y diwylliant Cymraeg,	Pillar of Welsh culture,
Cyfrannwr i *Dafod y Ddraig*,	Contributor to *Tafod y Ddraig*,
Aelod o'r Urdd, gwersyllwr er cyn co!	Member of the *Urdd*, camper since time began!
Mae'n faners e'n berffaith	His manners are perfect
Fe wedith e 'plîs' a 'thenciw',	He says 'please' and 'thank you'
Dyw e byth yn cicio'i dad nac yn rhegi i'w fam,	He never kicks his dad or swears at his mum,
Mae e wastad wedi cribo'i wallt,	His hair is always combed,
Mae'i goleri fe wastad yn lan	His collars are always clean,
Dyw e byth yn pigo'i drwyn nac yn poeri i'r tân!	He never picks his nose or spits into the fire!
Bob wythnos mae'n darllen *Y Cymro* a'r *Faner*,	Every week he reads *Y Cymro* and *Y Faner*,
Mae'n darllen Dafydd ap Gwilym yn ei wely bob nos,	He reads Dafydd ap Gwilym in his bed every night,
Mae dyfodol y wlad a'r iaith	The future of the land and the language
Yn agos at ei galon fach e	Are very close to his little heart
A mae nhw'n dweud ei fod e'n perthyn i'r F.W.A.!	And they say he belongs to the F.W.A.![18]

This song has a playfulness which belies its subversive intent. The Welsh Dafydd Iwan uses in the verses and chorus is much different from that of the two songs discussed earlier; it is somewhat more conversational, employing English words where Welsh words exist ('Sgotland', 'prins', 'plîs', 'thenciw'), and suggesting a dialect evident in some areas of Wales which have been affected by the influx of English media and the English language. The narrator is therefore a Welsh speaker much impressed by the arrival of a prince to Wales, and by the efforts of the prince of Wales to embrace Welsh culture. But the relationship of the prince to Welsh society is indicative of the treatment of Wales by the British crown, and is captured with irony in the chorus: 'Carlo's playing polo today … with his daddy'. When the principality calls on their prince he is elsewhere – in England.

The irony in the mode of address is also clear, and is a means of belittling the strength of the Crown. Prince Charles is seen as a little boy much younger than his age at the time of investiture,[19] the queen is just 'his mum', the Duke of Edinburgh is just 'his dad'; he enjoys all the things Welsh children of his age enjoy such as

18 Roy Clews' *To Dream of Freedom* (Talybont: Y Lolfa., 1980), the written history of the Free Wales Army, begins with an account of the investiture of the Prince of Wales and should be consulted for an insight into the more militant campaigns for Welsh independence.

19 Translating 'Carlo' as 'Charlie' would reinforce this interpretation.

Urdd camps;[20] and his education at Aberystwyth suggests a kinship with politically-informed Welsh youth, as does his attention to *Y Cymro* and *Y Faner*. The reality of the situation was of course much different;[21] but it was by mocking the entire procedure that Dafydd Iwan was able to support the actions launched against the investiture, and to unite the community in protest.

That 'Carlo' was broadcast on live television raises certain intriguing questions as to the type of freedom of speech offered to a young political activist at a time when Welsh-language broadcasting was in its infancy. There was a general dearth of popular songs in the Welsh language at the time, and it was not unusual for a news program to offer a few minutes for social commentary to someone with a view to share. In this way Dafydd Iwan was contracted to come in once a week and sing a song, written especially for the broadcast and based either on American tunes, or original compositions. Because he was a long-standing member of *Plaid Cymru*[22] and deeply involved in *Cymdeithas yr Iaith*, these songs were a means by which Dafydd Iwan could raise awareness of the *Cymdeithas*, and involve his listeners in the Welsh nationalist cause. The lyrical content of much of his music of this time may have fitted the current affairs format of *Y Dydd*, but 'Carlo' – and a later song about Margaret Thatcher – were banned from Radio Cymru for their political sentiments.

To put 'Carlo' back into its contemporary context, at the time of its release, attitudes toward the royal family were somewhat different than they are today, and opportunities for voicing those attitudes were not as readily offered as perhaps they are now. As Dafydd Iwan said:

> Mae'r canu wedi bod yn rhan rhyfeddol o'r profiad i mi, ac yn rhan bwysig o gael pobol i feddwl, hyd yn oed – nid bod cân yn gallu troi rhywun, ond mae'n gallu mynd i mewn i'r ffordd mae pobl yn meddwl. A'r peth mwya amdano fe wrth gwrs yw cael pobl i feddwl am genedlaetholdeb fel peth normal, yn meddwl am genedl fel peth normal … a mae hi wedi bod yn ddifyr iawn i weld pobl yn newid. Wedyn mae rhywbeth fel agwedd tuag at y teulu brenhinol … wedi newid. Dwi ddim yn credu bod o'n bwysig iawn, na dwi ddim yn credu gwela i amser lle bydd Cymru o angenrheidrwydd yn torri cysylltiad â'r teulu brenhinol, ond o leiaf dyn ni 'di mynd drwy gyfnod lle roedd y teulu brenhinol yn term bron dwyfol, ddim yn gallu diodde unrhywun oedd yn beirniadu'r teulu brenhinol. Ac ar un adeg roedd canu 'Carlo' yn her, ac yn beryglus bron. Erbyn hyn, fedra i gael – wel, os bydda i'n gofyn yng Nghaernarfon 'pa gân ydych chi eisiau i mi ganu', mae'n nhw bob amser yn dweud 'Carlo'.

> [Singing has been an amazing part of the experience for me, and an important part of getting people to think, even – not that singing can turn someone, but it can get into the way people think. And the biggest part about it of course is getting people to think about nationalism as a normal thing, to think about a nation as a normal thing … and it's been really interesting to see people change. Then there's something about the attitude toward

---

20 Dafydd Iwan began his singing career at the *Urdd* camp in Glan Llyn. While membership in the *Urdd* is a standard feature of life as a Welsh youth, it is to be doubted that reading Dafydd ap Gwilym in one's bed is a common pursuit.

21 It is doubtful, for instance, that Charles would have been familiar with either *Y Cymro* or *Y Faner*.

22 Dafydd Iwan's paternal grandfather was one of the founding members of the *Plaid*.

the royal family ... which has changed. I don't believe that it's very important, and I don't believe that I'll ever see a time when Wales will necessarily sever ties with the royal family, but at least we've been through a time when the royal family was practically divine, when we couldn't stand anyone being critical of the royal family. And at one time singing 'Carlo' was a challenge, and almost dangerous. By now, I could – well, if I were to ask in Caernarfon 'what song do you want me to sing', they always say 'Carlo'.][23]

It is this 'getting people to think' that is at the center of the folk aesthetic, and which leads us now into an exploration of the label 'folk' and the creation of a contemporary 'folk culture'.

'Folk', Folk Ideology and the Construction of Welshness

Much has been written about the political in popular music[24] and there has been an extended re-assessment of the terms 'folk' and 'popular',[25] especially in view of the integration of otherwise 'world' musics into Anglo-American mainstream culture.[26] For these reasons, an application of the term 'folk' must be qualified, especially when considering the trajectory taken by Welsh popular music in the wake of the early recordings by Dafydd Iwan.

The parallels between Dafydd Iwan, Woody Guthrie and Bob Dylan were mentioned earlier. There seems to be no controversy over the application of the term 'folk' to Woody Guthrie, or in the classification of Bob Dylan's early recordings as 'folk'. But when Bob Dylan plugged in his electric guitar at the Newport Folk Festival in 1965, the terms 'folk', 'rock', and 'folk-rock' were variously applied and rescinded. 'Authenticity' became a much more important term, and a singer's 'folk' credentials might be called to question. It must be stressed, by 1965 Anglo-American popular music (in the broadest sense) had evolved from rock'n'roll to a 'pop' fusion of rock'n'roll and 'folk', due in large part to the mutual influence of the Beatles and Bob Dylan; the blues had been re-visited in the music of the Rolling Stones; and a wider political consciousness was emerging in the lyrics of pop music in general, regardless of genre. It is important to note the trans-Atlantic nature of these developments and the cross-fertilization of an American product with its British counterpart; for as we turn back to Welsh popular music of the 1960s, we

---

23 Interview with Dafydd Iwan, Cardiff, 4 June, 1999; translation mine.

24 See especially Street, *Politics and Popular Culture*, and Eyerman and Jamison, *Music and Social Movements*.

25 See Richard Middleton and John Horn, eds., *Popular Music 1: Folk or Popular? Distinctions, Influences, Continuities* (Cambridge: Cambridge University Press, 1981), Denisoff and Peterson, eds., *The Sounds of Social Change*, and Frith, *Sound Effects*.

26 Space prohibits a thorough exploration of the definitions of 'world' music, but it is a term which is treated in great detail by George Lipsitz in *Dangerous Crossroads: Popular Music, Postmodernism and the Poetics of Place* (London: Verso, 1994), Georgina Born and David Hesmondhalgh, eds., *Western Music and Its Others: Difference, Representation, and Appropriation in Music* (Berkeley: University of California Press, 2000), and in numerous articles published in the journal *Popular Music*, many of which have informed the present study of Welsh popular music.

return to a 'folk' music as yet largely untouched by contemporary trans-Atlantic cross-fertilization.

By the time Dafydd Iwan recorded 'Mae'n Wlad i Mi', Bob Dylan had already recorded *Highway 61 Revisited*.[27] For Welsh popular music the fissure between folk and rock was clearly visible; but the fissure was a cultural one, born of a delayed creation of the indigenous audience. That is to say, Welsh popular music needed to find its 'folk' roots before it could produce its version of 'rock'. So how can we define 'folk' music, if it is not based on an indigenous cultural history? How did American 'folk' become Welsh 'folk'? And how did Welsh 'folk' come to define Welshness in the 1960s?

Folk music is inherently political. In their article, 'Have I the Right?[28] Steve Redhead and John Street examine the 'folk ideology' and claim that it is

> deployed to justify claims that music expresses a political view, legitimates a political cause or describes a political predicament. The musical-political ideology, we suggest, rests on the idea that the music is connected with some notion of 'the people'. The music is understood as deriving from a local culture and, as such, is an expression of the feelings and experiences of an everyday reality. The implications of this are that, firstly, people define themselves in terms of some collectivity, secondly, that this collectivity has an associated culture which in turn is mediated through music. And finally, this process expresses, according to the theory, a political divide.[29]

This notion of music as 'of the people' is problematic here, in the knowledge that 'popular', in the Welsh case, cannot be used to define a music accessible by fewer than half a million people. This is not to imply that any and all Welsh popular music is 'folk' music, but it does validate the grass roots nature of much of the history of Welsh pop. Further, when Redhead and Street suggest that a 'music's politics lie in its representation of a people and a culture'[30] they are reiterating the importance of the local in the musical expression. Because the 'local' in the Welsh case extends over a network of linguistic communities, issues of authenticity now come into play.

> The folk ideology works through a notion of a musician's *right to speak* for a community or people. It is the same sort of concept that underpins many versions of democracy. Musicians function like elected politicians; they represent their audience/constituency. Their authority is dependent on their ability to claim to speak for those who follow. For this, they need to be deemed *legitimate*. In music, this sort of argument can apply to the expression of straightforward protest or the individualism of the singer-songwriter. The validity of the music is measured by whether it strikes a chord with those who hear it: is it *authentic* – is it representative, does it provide an accurate picture of the audience?[31]

---

27 Bob Dylan, *Highway 61 Revisited* (Columbia, 1965) is considered a seminal moment in the history of rock music, and its opening single, 'Like A Rolling Stone' signaled definitively Dylan's break with the folk movement.

28 Steve Redhead and John Street, 'Have I the Right? Legitimacy, Authenticity and Community in Folk's Politics', *Popular Music* 8/2 (1989): 177–84.

29 Ibid., pp. 177–8.

30 Ibid., p. 178.

31 Ibid., pp. 178–9.

There can be no doubt as to Dafydd Iwan's 'right to speak' for the Welsh audience. His credentials in radical Welsh politics and his commitment to the nationalist cause were well established. His desire for change echoed the sentiments of many of his contemporaries, and having been given the opportunity to air his views on television, the means by which he spoke had resonance with a large number of people. This suggests that particular authority mentioned by Redhead and Street. Furthermore, the 'straightforward protest' of the three songs mentioned above prove the legitimacy of the music. The validity of the music – 'whether it strikes a chord with those who hear it' – is dependent upon the message being delivered. Even if some members of Dafydd Iwan's audience had recognized the melodies of 'This Land Is Your Land' and 'Big Rock Candy Mountain', or their residual sentiments, the new messages being delivered through the medium of the Welsh language were more important than the origin of the tunes. And the 'authenticity' of a song like 'Carlo' is proved in its reflection of the sentiments of a large portion of the Welsh audience.[32]

So who are 'the people', and what are 'their' folk songs? In his article on folk ideology and the rock community[33] Simon Frith dispels some of the myths surrounding the American folk revival of the 1940s and 1950s, suggesting that folk's 'rural nostalgia' was set in opposition to urban corruption.

> The post-war New York interest in blues and bluegrass echoed the turn-of-the-century British interest in British rural music. ... In the radicals' version of folk ideology, folk music was not a source of regret ... but a source of inspiration, a way of countering the debilitating effects of the mass media and enthusing the working class with 'folk consciousness'. In the 1930s the American communist party adopted rural music as the most suitable means of expression for the urban workers....
>
> The American folk revival was based on a contradiction. The 'spontaneous folk creations' it celebrated were the result of musical judgments made by outsiders, by urban performers (the British folk 'tradition' was, similarly, constructed in the first place by bourgeois scholars). What was at issue was a definition of 'the people' .... The political problem was how to use music to attract people into an organization, to develop their class consciousness; and if the tactics changed – from developing a new form of workers' music to using an old form – the cultural position did not: 'correct' songs were still correct in as far as they built a sense of class solidarity. The authenticity of music was, despite the folk language, still being judged by its effects rather than its sources. Even Woody Guthrie, in social terms the model performer for 1960s rock-folk, made his music for an urban, educated audience rather than for the rural workers about whom he sang – none of Guthrie's songs was found among the Okies and Arkies who fled the Dustbowl; their lives were already dominated by the commercial sounds of the radio and phonogram.[34]

---

32 Though I have not noted whether the Anglophone residents of Wales would have agreed or disagreed with the sentiments offered in 'Carlo', I should say that there is no obvious example of contemporary Anglo-Welsh popular song which broaches the subject of the investiture of the Prince of Wales.

33 '"The Magic That Can Set You Free": The Ideology of Folk and the Myth of the Rock Community', in *Popular Music* 1: *Folk or Popular?*: 159–68.

34 Ibid., pp. 161–2.

There are many important points to note in this passage. First, the opposition between urban and rural musics; second, the suggestion that 'folk' was a constructed tradition; and third, the encroachment of the mass media on the intended 'folk' audience. All of these points are reflected also in the development of the 1960s Welsh folk consciousness, and many serve as connecting threads between the 1960s and present day Welsh popular music.

First, the opposition between urban and rural musics, the romanticism of the rural and the corruption of the urban. In the Welsh instance, the terms 'urban' and 'rural' acquire additional meanings. Generally speaking, the urban industrial areas of Wales are located in the south, while the larger stretches of rural farmland are located in the west and north. The urban areas of Wales demarcate an encroaching Anglicization, while the rural areas – *y Fro Gymraeg* – demarcate the historically Welsh-speaking communities. Urban (Anglicized) Wales represents a corruption of the Welsh way of life; rural (Welsh) Wales represents a romanticized past. To take this opposition one step further, in the broadest terms, urban – Anglicized – music would denote rock; rural – Welsh – music would denote folk. What happens in the 1960s then is the establishment of a Welsh 'popular music' in the folk idiom, in the Welsh language, representing the political values of a nationalist organization. This 'folk music' was adapted from a model constructed in America and intended to service a radical political agenda. The difference in these two cases rests on the third point mentioned above. Where American folk music was intended to represent a rural population sullied by the mainstream mass media, in the Welsh instance 1960s folk music serviced the need of an indigenous mass media aimed at the very community which demanded it. And it did so, in 'Mae'n Wlad i Mi', by mapping the areas of rural, Welsh-speaking Wales; in 'Bryniau Bro Afallon' by the idealization of linguistic purity; and in 'Carlo' by re-acquiring those parts of Wales most in danger of Anglicization.

There is one further point to mention in Simon Frith's discussion of 'folk' and 'rock'. He describes the folk aesthetic as such:

> The folk emphasis was on lyrics and their plain presentation; the central musical instrument was the voice and it was by reference to vocal conventions that sincerity could be judged. In people's music there were no stars or hits, no distinctions between performers and audiences, and this too was established by musical convention, by the norms of collective performance – the use of repetition and chorus and clichéd melody, the lack of vocal flourish, the restriction of instruments (guitars, piano) to accompaniment. The folk community was the community created by the musical performance itself; folk consciousness was the effect of folk singing.[35]

The presentations of the songs mentioned above were simple; the lyrics were unencumbered by excessive accompaniment, and the sincerity of their delivery could not be doubted. The simplicity of the choruses encouraged audience participation, and this audience participation brought to the collective experience the creation of a folk community. Dafydd Iwan was a member of the community for whom he sang; the fact that his audience was largely comprised of people who knew him in one context or another supports the notion that in folk music – as in Welsh popular music

35 Ibid., p. 162.

in general – there are no 'stars'. Those songs considered 'hits' in the history of Welsh popular music were 'hits' by virtue of their significance to the Welsh consciousness. But there are undercurrents which shape our understanding of Welsh popular music as a cultural process, and it is important to reiterate them here.

The history of Welsh popular music is one of music produced within a particular social formation, by and for persons of that social formation. It is a music created in order to define cultural boundaries, to strengthen ties of kinship, and to assert political and social beliefs. There was an underlying assumption of commonality in the development of Welsh popular music which needed to be re-assessed as political and societal needs changed, for the growth from commonality to community requires more than an assumption of universal beliefs. In the early stages of the development of a popular music, 'folk songs' comment on contemporary issues, raise consciousness and mobilize an embryonic community. There is a particularity to the 'folk' message which is in direct contrast to the universality of the 'rock' message: 'folk' assumes political motivation and 'rock' assumes a more general appeal. This could be taken to mean that 'folk' concerns itself with the cerebral and 'rock' with the visceral, or that 'rock' acknowledges the body while 'folk' does not; either way, it raises one important question not yet addressed, namely, is 'folk' necessarily limited by its own mission?

By 1966, the year in which Dafydd Iwan recorded both 'Mae'n Wlad i Mi' and 'Bryniau Bro Afallon', the folk revival in the United States was already fractured. In Wales in 1966, the Welsh community was being fractured from within; it was being threatened by political and social forces imposing themselves from outside its cultural boundaries. In Anglo-American popular music from 1966 until the end of the decade there was a continued trend toward politically-informed lyrical content, which placed the musician in the wider world and drew attention to personal opinions of a social nature. In Wales the most important issue to bring into the public consciousness was the awareness of the Welsh community itself. Self-definition was the most important first step; global awareness would come later. In purely musical terms, while Dafydd Iwan may seem in retrospect to have been out of sync with the contemporary Anglo-American trends, for Wales he was perfectly timely. He could speak with authority about the issues affecting his own environment, and his songs had resonance for that fraction of the population who shared his sense of place. He had located the Welsh 'folk' community, and this was the first important moment of articulation in the evolution of contemporary Welshness.

The argument is not whether or not Dafydd Iwan was a 'folk' singer; the argument concerns the creation of the Welsh 'folk' audience, and the progress that audience made through the decades that followed. The issue is complicated by the changes in musical taste and musical production, in the establishment of counter-hegemonic ideals and the extent to which those ideals were representative of the wider Welsh public. The attendant question is one of community ideals and unification, of a consciousness articulated through contemporary popular music, and the ways in which those articulations changed. It is important in the following chapters to bear in mind the essential oppositions noted above – English and Welsh, urban and rural, rock and folk – for they are the backdrop against which Welshness continues to be negotiated.

Chapter Eleven

Welsh Reggae: The Sound of the City

Figure 11.1 Geraint Jarman

The establishment of the Welsh 'folk' audience was a necessary first step in the development of popular music in the Welsh language. The early recordings and performances of Dafydd Iwan, the early campaigns by *Cymdeithas yr Iaith Gymraeg*, and the gradual inclusion of popular music at the National Eisteddfod, all contributed to the acceptance of 'Welsh popular music' as an acoustic, rural, folk-based idiom. Much of the textual examples mentioned in the previous case study concerned the construction, historic memory, and utopian ideal of a Welsh-speaking Wales. The imagined location of such a Wales was largely in the Northern strongholds of the Welsh language, and the evocation of community based on geographic and linguistic parameters was at once an essential motion toward unity, and an exclusionary act. The symbolic boundaries distinguishing the Welsh-speaking community from its constitutive outside were drawn figuratively as a protective measure; the music which developed from within those boundaries remained relatively untouched by the larger culture surrounding them.

This type of cultural environment would have threatened to inhibit the natural growth of a Welsh musical network. The opening of boundaries to outside influence and creativity was viewed at first as a danger to the survival of the new sense of 'Welshness', but it was a natural and necessary progression in the process of Welsh identity; for a dialogue between cultures – within the same geographical boundaries, or on opposite sides of them – strengthens the understanding of difference and mutuality which are fundamental to the construction of cultural identity. When Geraint Jarman began his progression from composer to recording artist, his songs paid tribute to the sounds of his surroundings in Cardiff and to the musical expression of the immigrant communities on the margins of the city. In this way Welsh popular culture became 'urbanized', and the musical and cultural boundaries, now opened to West Indian influence, also opened to Anglophone Welsh musicians, in the first successful integration of Welsh and non-Welsh, British and 'other': an inclusive, not an exclusive, cultural product.

The City in Wales, Wales and the City

> The idea of the city as a jungle where bestial, predatory values prevail preceded the large-scale settlement of Britain by blacks in the post-war period. It has contributed significantly to contemporary definitions of 'race', particularly those which highlight the supposed primitivism and violence of black residents in inner-city areas. This is the context in which 'race' and racism come to connote the urban crisis as a whole and that crisis to embody racial problems even where they are not overtly acknowledged or defined.[1]

It could be argued that Cardiff is not a particularly 'Welsh' city. The idea of the 'city' in Wales is relatively problematic, and the acceptance of Cardiff as the representative center of Welsh culture has been a slow and contested one. Cardiff's character was shaped by its centrality to the British coal industry; only with the establishment of the Coal Exchange in 1897 did the municipal character of Cardiff begin to develop. Cardiff earned city status in 1905, and was declared the capital of Wales in 1955. The relative newness of Cardiff provides an interesting dimension to an urban Welshness, for such an identity construction is also informed by the numerous immigrant communities whose experiences and cultures shaped the environment within which Welsh industry developed.

In order to understand the influences on Geraint Jarman's artistic development, it is important to consider the place of the Welsh language in Cardiff. Geraint Jarman's first solo album, *Gobaith Mawr y Ganrif* (The Century's Great Hope)[2] was written in the years immediately following the census of 1971. It is this period which contains the crucial moments at which the Welsh language, Anglophone Welshness, and minority communities in the capital city, found common musical expression. The Welsh-speaking population of Wales at the time of the 1961 census was twenty-six per cent; at the time of the 1971 census, that number had dropped to just under twenty-one per cent. The Welsh Language Act of 1967 was followed by bilingual policies in many county councils; the expansion of Welsh-medium primary

---

1   Paul Gilroy, *'There Ain't No Black in the Union Jack'* (London and New York: Routledge, 2000), pp. 228–9.

2   Geraint Jarman, *Gobaith Mawr y Ganrif* (Sain 1022M, 1976).

and secondary education through the mid-1970s was helped by the establishment of *Mudiad Ysgolion Meithrin* (the Welsh Nursery Schools Movement) in 1971; *Y Dinesydd* (The Citizen), the first *papur bro* (neighborhood paper), was established in Cardiff in 1973, and the campaign to establish a Welsh-language television channel began in the same year.[3] There were therefore numerous attempts at stabilizing and increasing the number of Welsh speakers of all ages in Wales, and the development of an indigenous popular culture was part of this process.

The larger social movements in Wales were reflected in popular music by the symbolic drawing of boundaries between Wales and the Anglophone dominant. This involved reviving the historical memory of a Welsh-speaking Wales, of defining its contemporary location, and strengthening the mutual support Welsh popular music established with the youth-oriented language movements, *Cymdeithas yr Iaith Gymraeg* and *Adfer*. The influx of Welsh-speakers to the capital city in the wake of the growth of bilingual businesses, schools and media, was intended to be offset by the opposite movement *yn ôl i'r Fro*, back to the Welsh-speaking heartland, exemplified by the actions of *Adfer* and, among other things, the relocation of the Sain label from Cardiff to Llandwrog, Gwynedd.

Though the number of Welsh speakers in the Cardiff area at the time of the 1971 census represented a significant percentage of the population of Wales, in terms of percentage per capita it was deceptively large.[4] The Welsh language has a more obvious presence in areas of west and north Wales, and Cardiff, though offering greater employment opportunities than many of the more rural areas of Wales, was therefore a relatively foreign – urban – quantity. The 'urban crisis' mentioned by Paul Gilroy is in this context as much a matter of inner-city violence as it is a statement of concern about the out-migration of Welsh speakers from rural areas of Wales into a predominantly Anglophone capital city. A much more literal example of the 'urban crisis' in Cardiff is Butetown, the docklands area of Cardiff Bay, primary location of the greater proportion of immigrant communities in the larger metropolitan area.

It was estimated at one time that seventeen different languages were spoken in Butetown. The ethnic diversity of the area is still palpable, despite the rapid gentrification due to the Cardiff Bay development project and the virtual obliteration of all vestiges of the social characteristics for which the former Tiger Bay was infamous, or mythologized.[5] To characterize Cardiff as 'Welsh' would be to deny the international scope of its population; to classify it as a bilingual city would be to deny the cultural veracity of its immigrant populations. Cardiff is therefore a problematic space for expressions of Welshness of the type outlined in previous chapters. The

---

3   This is a condensed account of the type of language preservation tactics outlined in Janet Davies' 'The Welsh Language', in Herbert and Jones, eds., *Post-War Wales*: 55–77, and her *The Welsh Language*.

4   For census statistics and analysis see Aitchison and Carter, *A Geography of the Welsh Language 1961–1991*.

5   For a brief commentary on the importance of Tiger Bay to the early career of its most famous export, see Dai Smith, 'Shirley Bassey', in Trevor Herbert and Peter Stead, eds., *Hymns and Arias: Great Welsh Voices* (Cardiff: University of Wales Press, 2001): 195–208.

concessions to 'Welsh' culture in Cardiff, exemplified by *Clwb Ifor Bach*[6] and the Welsh-language media, are border-defining pockets of linguistic isolation within the larger urban society. It is important therefore to see the formation of Geraint Jarman a'r Cynganeddwyr (Geraint Jarman and the Poets) as the first acknowledgment of inter-cultural influence on Welsh popular music.

Welsh and the Language of Reggae

[T]he [Creole] language developed its own vocabulary, syntax and grammar; but it remains essentially a shadow-language fulfilling in a more exaggerated and dramatic way those requirements, which, under normal circumstances, are satisfied by regional working class accents and group *argot*. Form implicitly dictates content, and poles of meaning, fixed immutably in a bitter and irreversible experience, silently reconstruct that experience in everyday exchange. [...] [T]his fact is intuitively grasped by the members of certain West Indian subcultures, and language is used as a particularly effective means of resisting assimilation and preventing infiltration by members of the dominant groups. As a screening device it has proved to be invaluable; and the 'Bongo talk' and patois of the Rude Boy deliberately emphasise its subversive rhythms so that it becomes an aggressive assertion of racial and class identities. As a living index to the extent of the black's alienation from the cultural norms and goals of those who occupy higher positions in the social structure, the creole language is unique.[7]

The comparative status of the Welsh language within a predominantly Anglophone culture has been the central concern of indigenous political organizations, cultural revivals, and education policies in Wales in the second half of the twentieth century. As one of many minority languages spoken in the capital city, the Welsh language went through a process of urbanization in the 1970s, and became the vehicle for a multi-layered commentary on metropolitan Welsh society and popular culture. This is not to suggest that the Welsh language was experienced at the same degree of separation from Cardiff society as were the seventeen other languages in Butetown; merely that the historically problematic relationship between the Welsh and English languages was challenged further by the influx of Welsh into the capital city. As Dick Hebdige continues in his discussion of Creole:

The expulsion of the black from the wider linguistic community meant that a whole culture evolved by a secret and forbidden osmosis. Deprived of any legitimate cultural exchange, the slave developed an excessive individualism and a set of cultural artefacts which together represent the vital symbolic transactions which had to be made between slavery and freedom, between his material condition and his spiritual life, between his experience of Jamaica and his memories of Africa. In a sense, the transition was never satisfactorily accomplished, and the black Jamaican remains suspended uneasily between two worlds, neither of which commands a total commitment. Unable to repair this cultural

---

6   *Clwb Ifor Bach*, the Welsh-language club in the center of Cardiff, was until recently the only small venue for live music in the city.

7   Dick Hebdige, 'Reggae, Rastas & Rudies', in Stuart Hall and Tony Jefferson, eds., *Resistance Through Rituals: Youth Subcultures in Post-War Britain* (London: Routledge, 1998), p. 136.

and psychological breach, he tends to oscillate violently from one world to the other and ultimately he idealises both. Ultimately, indeed, he is exiled from Jamaica, from Africa, from Britain and from Brixton, and sacrifices his place in the real world to occupy an exalted position in some imaginative inner dimension where action dissolves into being, where movement is invalidated and difficult at the best of times, where solutions are religious rather than revolutionary.[8]

The suggestion of language in exile is very powerful. The symbolic constructions of linguistic communities in an area such as Cardiff necessarily involve the adherence to cultural and religious traditions, while attempting in some cases to assimilate into the adopted, or dominant, society. Whereas Hebdige refers to the slaves' collective memory of a cultural and spiritual homeland, the type of utopian ideal of Wales, as illustrated in some songs by Dafydd Iwan, for example, might serve as an alternative interpretation here. That is to say that a Welsh speaker, having removed him or herself from the rural heartland to seek opportunity in industrial South Wales, might feel him or herself as much an exile from an idealized homeland as would the person displaced from a geographical home by circumstances beyond their control. For a person like Geraint Jarman, whose family moved to Cardiff in the 1950s, a sympathetic understanding of the type of displacement experienced by an immigrant community would find expression in the idioms of that community's expressive culture. In this way, language serves as a common link.

As Creole is the reggae vernacular, distancing the Jamaican from the surrounding dominant groups, so is Welsh a distancing factor. Geraint Jarman was, in a manner of speaking, twice removed from his Welsh pop contemporaries: his particular poetic background is one distancing factor,[9] but more significantly, he represents urban Welsh in an otherwise 'folk' context. As Jarman himself said, 'dwi wastad wedi bod yn dipyn o allanwr ... rhwng bod yn Gymro Caerdydd a bod yn Gymro' ['I've always been a bit of an outsider ... between being a Welsh-speaker from Cardiff and being a Welshman'].[10]

> For ... all Rastafarians, language is an arena, a site of political struggle and personal transformation. Since English was associated with the enslavement of African people, its grammar, phonology, and semantics were not considered to be 'heartical', that is, capable of expressing African culture and consciousness.[11]

---

8 Ibid., pp. 136–7.

9 Though many poet/musicians have contributed to the development of Welsh popular music, Jarman is the first example of a composer/performer who classified himself first and foremost as a poet. His poetry, though written in the Welsh language, follows the model established by contemporary Anglo-Welsh and British poetry, rather than the Welsh tradition, and is therefore cited as a distancing factor.

10 'Ethiopia Newydd: Ail-Greu Clasur Cymraeg', *Golwg* 3/15 (13 December 1990); translation mine.

11 John W. Pulis, '"Up-full Sounds": Language, Identity, and the Worldview of Rastafari', in Chris Potash, ed., *Reggae, Rasta, Revolution: Jamaican Music from Ska to Dub* (London: Books With Attitude, 1997): 25–6.

The indigenization of popular music into the Welsh language was a process of realizing the means toward a meaningful expression of Welsh identity. Given that such an identity was threatened by anglicization, the act of appropriating an essentially Anglo-American cultural product and domesticating it was much the same process as the creolization of the English language.

> Jamaica Talk was the 'chosen tongue', the means of communication by which trade unionists and street preachers assaulted British hegemony. It was the tonal semantics of Creole and the worldview of Afro-Christianity that inspired the publications of West Indian poets, historians, and political activists. It was not the printed word that inspired Dread Talk, but the spoken. In addition to verifying local prophesy concerning an African Messiah, the events that unfolded in Ethiopia substantiated a linguistic praxis that subordinated spoken and printed English to the tonal or sound-based semantics of Creole. The acoustic structure of English words and the grammatical structure of printed texts were 'penetrated'; that is, read aloud, broken apart, and reassembled into a discourse that renegotiated traditional constructions of identity. If the words and sounds of this prophecy were first spoken during the 1930s in Kingston, by the 1980s they were heard in Africa, Europe, and North America, as a cohort of Rastafarians matured, a number of formal organizations were established, and an international music industry proliferated.[12]

Though the linguistic structure established in the early years of Welsh pop did not allow for much English infiltration, the use of English in some Welsh songs mentioned earlier was entirely ironic; where these lyrics were printed, the English was spelled through the phonetic structure of the Welsh language.[13] This is suggestive of the type of counter-hegemonic 'penetration' of the English language by the Creole-speaking population of Jamaica. If the Welsh language itself is a site of contention between the Anglo-American and Welsh cultures, the juxtaposition of the Welsh language with a counter-hegemonic idiom such as reggae infuses that music with the potential for deeper political resonance. The effect of this resonance on the negotiation of a Welsh identity is of particular importance here. The means by which Creole was the vehicle for the negotiation of a Jamaican identity, and the association of this identity with Rastafarianism, should be considered as a preface to the discussion of the filtering of reggae through the Welsh language.

Rastafari and Welsh Reggae

The history and tenets of Rastafarianism are central to the discussion of reggae as cultural expression.[14] Dick Hebdige has distilled the Rastafarian belief system thus:

---

12 Ibid., p. 23.

13 The lyrics to Dafydd Iwan's song, 'Carlo' are a good example of this. In its intention to belittle the power of the monarchy and to protest the investiture of Charles as the Prince of Wales, this is a significant and subversive act of linguistic rebellion.

14 The relationship between Rastafarianism and Jamaican music, and the development of Jamaican music, from ska to reggae to dub, have been explored in a number of general and academic articles, many of which have been edited and anthologized in Potash, ed., *Reggae, Rasta, Revolution*.

The Rastafarians believe that the exiled Emperor Haile Selassie of Ethiopia was God and that his accession to the Ethiopian throne fulfils the prophecy made by Marcus Garvey, 'Look to Africa, when a black king shall be crowned, for the day of deliverance is near.' But the religious milieu in which Rastafarianism was evolved demanded a specifically Biblical mythology and this mythology had to be re-appropriated and made to serve a different set of cultural needs.... By a dialectical process of redefinition, the Scriptures, which had constantly absorbed and deflected the revolutionary potential of the Jamaican black, were used to locate that potential, to negate the Judaeo-Christian culture. Or, in the more concise idiom of the Jamaican street-boys, the Bible was taken, read and 'flung back rude'. [...]

The most striking feature is how the Biblical metaphors have been elaborated into a total system – a code of seeing – at once supple and holistic, universal in application, and lateral in direction. The black races are interpreted as the true Israelites and Solomon and Sheba are the black ancestors of Haile Selassie, the black god. Babylon really covers the western world.... The police, the Church, and the Government ... are the agents of imperialism and will share the terrible fate of the white oppressors. Ethiopia is the true name for all Africa. [...] All black men are Ethiopians and the Jamaican Government is not their government. It subordinates itself to Great Britain which still regards Jamaica as a colony. The only true government is the theocracy of the Emperor Haile Selassie....[15]

The infusion of Rastafarianism and music in the 1970s effects the interpretation of reggae as the only essentially religious popular music in the world.[16] The message propounded in reggae of exile, of Ethiopia and Babylon, are understandable from the perspective of a number of marginalized communities. In the Welsh instance, the idea of Babylon is doubly poignant, for the linguistic territory called Wales was colonized by the English language, and Welsh speakers located within that space are effectively linguistic exiles in their own geographical land.

For all the cultural and social parallels between Jamaican and Welsh communities, the religious element of reggae music presents an unusual problem for Welsh popular music. The role of the chapel in the development of Welsh pop has been a constant subtext here. The chapel dictated, to a large degree, the rate at which Welsh pop progressed from acoustic to electric, as well as the lyrical content of the songs sung. Yet for a music which was sponsored by a religious institution, the lyrics of Welsh pop are rarely, if ever, religious. The tendency in Welsh pop toward lyrics expressing a nationalist, political agenda are far more common, and the occasional examples of

---

15 Dick Hebdige, 'Reggae, Rastas and Rudies', pp. 138–9. A similar summary of the tenets of Rastafari may be found in Brian Longhurst, *Popular Music and Society* (Cambridge: Polity Press, 1995), p. 142.

16 This is a suggestion made by Verena Reckord in 'Reggae, Rastafarianism and Cultural Identity', in Potash, ed., *Reggae, Rasta Revolution*, p. 11. The argument could be made that gospel music is essentially 'popular' and 'religious', and that soul music, as a musical expression which evolved from gospel, is likewise infused with religious overtones; but the religious implications of reggae as a diasporic music are somehow more universal than gospel or soul music, which relate to a particular temporal and geographical space in United States history. For more on soul music see Peter Guralnick, *Sweet Soul Music: Rhythm and Blues and the Southern Dream of Freedom* (Boston: Back Bay Books, 1999) and Brian Ward, *Just My Soul Responding: Rhythm and Blues, Black Consciousness, and Race Relations* (Berkeley: University of California Press, 1998).

a 'Christian' message are generally couched in more explicit social commentary.[17] This commentary often refers to a mythologized Wales; and though divine right has not figured in the Welsh pop discussed to this point, the sense of entitlement to linguistic and cultural power – the 'exile' seeking the homeland – is a theme common to both Welsh pop and reggae.

When Geraint Jarman began his explorations of reggae, he attempted also to find a role for Wales in a music otherwise loaded with religious signification. As Stuart Hall suggests:

[I]n particular social formations, where religion has become the *valorized* ideological domain, the domain into which all the different cultural strands are obliged to enter, no political movement in that society can become popular without negotiating the religious terrain. Social movements have to transform it, buy into it, inflect it, develop it, clarify it - but they must engage with it. You can't create a popular political movement in such social formations without getting into the religious question, because it is the arena in which this community has come to a certain kind of consciousness. This consciousness may be limited, it may not have successfully helped them to remake their history. But they have been 'languaged' by the discourse of popular religion. They have, for the first time, used religion to construct some narrative, however impoverished and impure, to connect the past and the present: where they came from with where they are and where they are going to, and why they are here....

In the case of the Rastafarians in Jamaica: Rasta was a funny language, borrowed from a text – the Bible – that did not belong to them; they had to turn the text upside-down, to get a meaning which fit their experience. But in turning the text upside-down they remade themselves; they positioned themselves differently as new political subjects; they reconstructed themselves as blacks in the new world; they *became* what they are. [...] This is a cultural transformation. It is not something totally new. It is not something which has a straight, unbroken line of continuity from the past. It is transformation through a reorganization of the elements of a cultural practice, elements which do not in themselves have any necessary political connotations.[18]

The fundamental differences between Rastafarianism and Welsh Nonconformity are too enormous to itemize and too obvious to mention; but the creation of a modern Welsh cultural identity, nurtured through the chapel and informed by common cultural history and mythologized past, was by its nature engaged with the religious establishment. The chapel, in Hall's sense, connected the past with the present – the past sense of community with the present sense of political consciousness. The chapel, as a focus for the formation of Welsh-language communities, served a central role in the development of Welsh popular culture. The music of that culture may not have 'spread the word' of the chapel in the sense that reggae 'spread the word' of Rastafari; but a similarity in religious doctrine is not essential to the respect for, and appropriation of, the musical expression of another culture. The work of

---

17 Arfon Wyn is one example of a Welsh musician with a Christian message.

18 Lawrence Grossberg, 'On Postmodernism and Articulation: An Interview with Stuart Hall', in David Morley and Kuan-Hsing Chen, eds., *Stuart Hall: Critical Dialogues in Cultural Studies* (London: Routledge, 1996), p. 142.

Geraint Jarman has fluctuated between reggae and Anglo-American 'rock' idioms, but it is clear that his music has been inflected by Rasta culture.

Though not an example of reggae in rhythm or production, Jarman's 'Ethiopia Newydd' (New Ethiopia) serves as the first example of the musical negotiations between Welsh and West Indian cultures:[19]

Rhywbeth newydd ddaeth i'r Fro	Something new came to the heartland
Gweld ein gwlad yn mynd o'i cho'	Seeing our country going crazy
Yr ieuenctid yn codi baneri ac yn rhathu'r craeth	The youth raising banners and rubbing wounds
Mae'r rebel wrthi'n cysgu nawr	The rebel is sleeping now
Yn gorwedd yma ar y llawr	Lying here on the ground
'Sdim golwg o'r ofnau a berodd ei fywyd	There's no sign of the fears that kept his life
dan gwmwl du.	under a black cloud.
Newyddion heddwch ddaeth am ddiwylliant y comando	The news of peace came from the commando's culture
A chlustiau Cymru fach yn clywed reggae ar y radio	And little Wales' ears are hearing reggae on the radio
A gyda hyn ymhlith y miri a'r llawenydd	And with this amid the joy and merriment
Daw ysfa sydyn am ryw Ethiopia Newydd	Will come a sudden craze for some New Ethiopia.
Dal dy dir, Ethiopia Newydd yn dyfod cyn hir.	Hold your ground, a New Ethiopia is coming soon.
O fyd gwyn â'i ffawd yn sur	From the heavens with its sour fate
Dim eira cariad ar y tir	No snow of love on the ground[20]
Mor ddi-werth â deilyn grin ar goeden y genedl	As useless as a dried leaf on the tree of the nation
Mae'r genod a'r hogiau'n gaeth	The girls and boys are captive
Yn crwydro'n hir ar draws y paith	Wandering long across the prairie
Y rocyrs â'r gwalltau cyrliog yw dyfodol Gwalia nawr.	The curly-haired rockers are Wales' future now.[21]
Newyddion heddwch ddaeth o Amsterdam i Moscow	News of peace came from Amsterdam to Moscow

---

19 'Ethiopia Newydd', music and lyrics Geraint Jarman, © Cyhoeddiadau Sain, from *Hen Wlad Fy Nhadau* (Sain, 1978). Lyrics reprinted by permission; translation mine.

20 Reference to *Eira Cariad* (Snow of Love), Jarman's first published collection of poetry.

21 Jarman is famous for, among many other things, his long, curly hair.

A chlustiau Cymru fach yn clywed
    reggae ar y radio
	And little Wales' ears are hearing
	    reggae on the radio

A gyda hyn ymhlith y miri a'r llawenydd	And with this amid the joy and merriment

Daw ysfa sydyn am ryw Ethiopia
    Newydd.
	Will come a sudden craze for some
	    New Ethiopia.

Dal dy dir, Ethiopia Newydd yn dyfod
    cyn hir.
	Hold your ground, a New Ethiopia
	    is coming soon.

The lyrics of 'Ethiopia Newydd' are couched in metaphor, but the message is inherently one of optimism. References to an unnamed struggle can easily be interpreted as the campaign for language rights; the use of the word *bro* – '*i'r fro*' – is suggestive of *y fro Gymraeg*, the Welsh-speaking heartland, the almost mythical construction of Welsh Wales, and the focal point of the *Adfer* movement. While it could just as easily refer to *Bro Morgannwg*, the Vale of Glamorgan, located just outside Cardiff, '*y fro*' is generally a signifier of a geographical area with a high concentration of Welsh speakers. This 'something new' which appeared in the heartland, inciting the youth population to protest, while suggestive of a local struggle,[22] invokes somehow a more general, international, crisis – 'the commando's culture'; 'from Amsterdam to Moscow' – and reggae here serves as the messenger of peace across the world, both literally and figuratively.

The statement that 'the ears of little Wales are hearing reggae on the radio' suggests first that the musical hegemony of British culture, and therefore the power structure, has somehow been overthrown; and second, that Geraint Jarman – 'the long-haired rocker' – is in some way connected to the cultural revolution. Reggae is a powerful metaphor in this instance, for not only is it invoked as the harbinger of peace and brotherhood,[23] but it also signifies the opening of 'the ears of little Wales' to the sounds of contemporary, international society. That Welsh popular music had progressed slowly from the acoustic to electric, and that the idea of a 'professional' rock band was anathema to the construction of 'Welsh popular music', was reflected in the relatively conservative nature of contemporary Welsh pop.[24] By the time of the release of 'Ethiopia Newydd', Bob Marley and the Wailers' seminal recording,

---

22 Significantly, 'Ethiopia Newydd' and the rest of the songs from the album, *Hen Wlad Fy Nhadau*, were re-recorded by various artists and released on Ankst in 1990 in support of *Cymdeithas yr Iaith*'s campaign for Welsh property law. That law, *Deddf Eiddo*, would allow Welsh people control over their own communities, and curb the 'needless tourist and capitalist developments – currently promoted by the Conservative Government – that are destroying community life, the culture and language of Wales'. See liner notes for *Hen Wlad Fy Nhadau* (Ankst 013, 1990).

23 The implications of reggae on a sense of peace and brotherhood can also be interpreted as deriving from the religious significance invested in the use of marijuana.

24 'Professional' and 'amateur' musicians are distinguished by financial considerations alone. An amateur musician may earn money for a night's work, but a professional musician will earn a living solely from musical activity. The structure of the Welsh music 'industry' was not sufficient for a band to earn a healthy living from the gig circuit, and Geraint Jarman a'r

Catch a Fire (Island, 1973), had long since been released. Because Geraint Jarman was exposed to West Indian music in Cardiff, he began to explore the sounds of reggae in his own music; this incorporation of the popular 'other' infused Welsh pop with a new life, and suggested that the only way to nurture an indigenous Welsh popular music was to appropriate outside influences. The 'curly-haired rockers' named as 'Wales' future now' are therefore unlike their predecessors in Welsh pop, geographically, physically, and musically.

There are utopian references in 'Ethiopia Newydd' which should also be mentioned. The appropriation here of the Rastafarian promised land is a suggestion of an idealized Welsh future; but Jarman's references to Wales in each of the verses are redolent of a mythologized past. Jarman first creates for his audience a sense of (comm)unity – 'gweld *ein gwlad* yn mynd o'i cho', 'seeing *our country* going crazy' – which invests the listener with a sense of kinship, but also a sense of responsibility: 'the youth' were the activists, while the others watched. The diminutive, 'Little Wales' – *Cymru fach* – is a term of endearment as well as an acknowledgment of geographical size and political dependence. The second verse contains the most explicit references to an idealized Wales. The first line begins with a reference to *y fyd gwyn* – literally, the pure world, Heaven; and the verse closes with a reference to *Gwalia*, the poetic name for Wales, loaded with arcadian signification. To invoke this term in the same line with reference to 'curly-haired rockers', is to establish the inherent contradiction in Jarman's own music: Welsh-language *rock* music. Welsh pop to this point had been largely acoustic, 'folk', rural; rock music, by contrast, is electric, urban. 'Rock' music is assuming the representative mantle from 'folk' music, and *Gwalia* is being transformed as a result. Welshness is no longer memorialized as a simple, arcadian, acoustic phenomenon, but as an internationally-informed, politically-charged, *attainable* identity.

'The Welsh Trilogy'

'Ethiopia Newydd' was released on the album *Hen Wlad Fy Nhadau* (Land of My Fathers),[25] the first in a trilogy of recordings by Geraint Jarman a'r Cynganeddwyr which explored Jarman's personal sense of Wales.

> [O]edd yna gyfeiriadau tuag at gobaith newydd, ti'n gwybod, yn Ethiopia a chyfeiriadau i gyd at brotest a reggae a naturoliaeth yn dod i mewn i bethau unwaith eto.... [...] [R]oedd *Hen Wlad Fy Nhadau* ... yn bersonol, heb swnio'n rhy *pretentious* ond oeddwn i'n trio chwilio am y Gymru oedd yn berthnasol i fi, ag oedd hyn yn ddiddorol iawn hefyd achos o'n i dal i gydweithio gyda'r bois 'ma o'r cymoedd, oedd yn ddi-Gymraeg eu hiaith ond hefyd oedden nhw erioed wedi bod yn y gogledd, oedden nhw erioed wedi gweld

---

Cynganeddwyr were perhaps the first to succeed at being full-time Welsh musicians in Wales and elsewhere.

25 The title of the album is itself ironic. 'Hen Wlad Fy Nhadau' (Old Land of My Fathers) is the name of the Welsh national anthem; but the musical effect of Jarman's album is a clear departure from its predecessors. 'Hen Wlad' – 'Old Country' – is as much a statement of the chronological age of Wales as it is a suggestion that old traditions are meant – and about – to be broken.

Cymreictod, ti'n gwybod, ac felly oedd y profiad yna a bois y dociau ddoth i mewn i'r grwp yn ddiweddarach, oedd e'n brofiad anhygoel oherwydd trwy eu llygaid nhw hefyd oeddet ti'n darganfod pethau, *you know, you just take for granted otherwise*, ti'n gwbod.

[There were references to a new hope, you know, in Ethiopia, and references to protest and reggae and naturalism were coming into things once again.... *Hen Wlad Fy Nhadau*, personally, not wanting to sound too pretentious, but I was trying to look for the Wales that was relevant to me, and that was also very interesting because I was still working with these guys from the valleys, who couldn't speak Welsh and who also had never been to the north, who had never seen Welshness, you know, and so that experience and the boys from the docks who came into the group later on, it was an amazing experience because through their eyes you could discover things, you know, you just take for granted otherwise, you know.][26]

In the subsequent two recordings of the trilogy, *Gwesty Cymru* (Hotel Wales, 1979) and *Fflamau'r Ddraig* (The Dragon's Flames, 1980), the sound of reggae was integrated with much more confidence than in earlier releases,[27] and the impact of these recordings on contemporary Welsh popular culture was enormous.

Yn awr, gallwn glywed seiniau reggae yn neuaddau cefn gwlad Cymru, ochr yn ochr â siglo a chraig, ac mae'n braf gweld Cymru yn ymateb i gerddoriaeth o'r math yma.

[Now, one can hear the sounds of reggae in the halls of the Welsh countryside, side-by-side with rock and roll, and it's lovely to see Wales responding to this kind of music.][28]

The name of Geraint Jarman's band, Y Cynganeddwyr, added to the impact. The fact that his band – Anglophone musicians from south Wales – were named after the practitioners of strictly metered, alliterative Welsh poetry, *cynghanedd*, is an ironic form of cultural inclusivity.[29] Moreover, it is a means of paying tribute to them, for calling the band 'poets' is as much a statement of respect for their musical ability as it is of their honorary status in Welsh-language expressive culture. *Cynghanedd*,

---

26 Interview with Geraint Jarman for *Y Felin Bop*, unpublished transcripts; translation mine.

27 Jarman's first two recordings, *Gobaith Mawr y Ganrif* (The Century's Great Hope, Sain, 1976) and *Tacsi i'r Tywyllwch* (Taxi to the Darkness, Sain 1977) are early examples of the type of post-production sonic exploration Jarman refined for the more straightforward dub of his later recordings. His first two records were produced in relatively brief periods of time (*Gobaith Mawr y Ganrif* was recorded and mixed in twenty hours; *Tacsi i'r Tywyllwch* was recorded under similar conditions, but the technology available in the studios had improved considerably in the meantime), and for all the haste in their production, the direct approach toward reggae is clearly evident.

28 Emyr Llywelyn, 'Cynghanedd Gytbwys', *Sgrech* 9 (Nadolig 1979), p. 8; translation mine.

29 *Cynghanedd* is a poetic form for which there is no non-Welsh equivalent. The complexity of its rules is perhaps best explained by Mererid Hopwood, first female *prifardd* in the history of the National Eisteddfod, in her *Singing in Chains: Listening to Welsh Verse* (Llandysul: Gomer, 2005). She offers rough English equivalents of the type of dense alliteration typical of *cynghanedd*, such as 'The Night', by Dic Jones (p. 78):

significantly, can also be translated as 'harmony, sounding well', which suggests an historically close connection between the Welsh bardic and musical traditions, as well as Jarman's attempt at contributing to both.

The recorded performance of 'Ethiopia Newydd' is a good indication of the level of professionalism in the band and the equal importance placed on their contributions to the overall musical product. Jarman's voice is not a particularly forceful instrument, and most of the musical interest lies in the background. The keyboards and the lead guitar are prominent throughout 'Ethiopia Newydd', which in itself is unusual in Welsh pop. Instrumental virtuosity was never a primary trait in Welsh popular music, and there were very few instances of improvisational solos in Welsh recordings before the emergence of Y Cynganeddwyr. The significance of the fact that this type of professionalism was a result of outside – Anglophone – influence cannot be overstated. It was certainly mentioned in contemporary accounts of the Welsh pop 'scene':

> Geraint and his Cardiff-based session musicians have given a literacy to Welsh rock. Theirs is the only full-time band on the scene, and, significantly, with the exception of Geraint, they are all non-Welsh speaking. Geraint is a Cardiffian who has published two volumes of poetry, is heavily influenced by reggae music and the Rastafarian lifestyle, and his acceptance by rock fans is of almost cult proportions. Geraint Jarman is regarded as the future of Welsh rock.
>
> Like most other bands, Jarman a'r Cynganeddwyr perform mostly in the North. A paradox, which proves it's rock that rules, is the avid adulation given to the city boy, with his songs about urban paranoia, by rural audiences at such places as Plas Coch, Anglesey. It is a phenomenon which the editorial of the Welsh fanzine *Sgrech*, with its pro-*Adfer* outlook, has only reluctantly accepted.[30]

No less central a figure in Welsh pop than Dafydd Iwan cited Jarman a'r Cynganeddwyr as examples of creative talent which had succeeded in turning foreign influences into something Welsh:

> Er iddo sugno'i faeth a drachtio'n helaeth o'r holl ffynhonnau pop, ac yn arbennig y *Reggae* a'r *Rastaffariaid*, mae wedi llwyddo i roi marc ei athrylith arbennig ei hun ar ei ganu – sy'n hollol Gymreig. Mae llawer wedi synnu fy mod i'n gwrthod canu yn Saesneg, ond mae'n fwy o syndod fyth fod Geraint Jarman yn gwrthod canu yn Saesneg! Fe allai ef fynd fel tân gwyllt dros y byd!

> [Although he's taken his nourishment and drunk deeply from all the pop fountains, especially reggae and the Rastafarians, he's succeeded at making the mark of his own special talent on his singing – which is completely Welsh. Many people have been

---

No hymn of birds, no tremor – save the sounds
   Of the sea's sad tenor,
   The stars ascend in splendour,
   And the dark creeps round the door.

30 Hefin Wyn, 'The Alternative Eisteddfod', *Arcade*, August 7, 1981, p. 9.

surprised that I've refused to sing in English, but it's even more of a surprise to me that Geraint Jarman refuses to sing in English! He could go like wildfire across the world!][31]

While much was made of the bilingual nature of the band during the 1970s, the implications of a Welsh reggae were not explicitly addressed. And although in the wake of Welsh reggae there emerged Welsh versions of punk and ska, the political significance of parallel stylistic hybrids in the Anglo-American mainstream had a different cultural resonance. As Simon Frith suggests:

> The punk vanguard itself was most inspired by reggae musicians because reggae seemed to suggest a quite different way of musical being. It opened up questions of space and time in which musical choice – the very *freedom* of that choice – stood in stark contrast to the thoughtlessness of rock 'n' roll; it implied, too, a homelessness – this was choice as terror. The music itself – its lack of a hierarchy of sounds, its depth of pulse – was the moment of cultural analysis; it didn't express something else, some prior reality, but *was* the structure of experience, for musician and audience alike.[32]

Reggae was integrated into punk as a tool of social realism, and the establishment of affective alliances between British punk and reggae was of particular significance to Geraint Jarman's late-1970s recordings. Jarman's first recordings were not exclusively reggae-based; 'Ethiopia Newydd' is one example of this fact. His music incorporates elements of contemporary rock and punk as well as reggae and dub, and varies to some extent according to the lyrical content. The title track from *Gwesty Cymru* (Hotel Wales), for example, is stylistically reminiscent of contemporary rock; this provides an interesting juxtaposition to its titular reference to the hugely popular, contemporary work of The Eagles, *Hotel California* (1976). Like the Eagles' 'Hotel California', Jarman's 'Gwesty Cymru' depicts a sinister underside to superficial society; yet the lyrics to 'Gwesty Cymru' are not the focal point of the song. The musical affect has a greater impact than the words being sung, and again, it is reminiscent of a certain late-1970s British societal anger typified by the Clash. Y Cynganeddwyr create a stark backdrop to Jarman's vocal – screeching guitar, heavy bass – which was atypical of contemporary Welsh pop, both in its insistence and its production.

Gwesty Cymru also serves as a type of time capsule of Anglo-American popular music of the late-1970s, encompassing as it does reggae and punk; but it also suggests the larger motion from punk to 'new wave' and a greater reliance on synthesized sounds. One example of this is 'Neb yn Deilwng' (No One is Worthy), a reference to the statement made at the National Eisteddfod if the bardic chair or crown is refused to all entrants on the grounds that no submission reached a high enough standard to be endowed with such a literary honor:

Dyw pob dim ddim yn drychinebus	Not everything is disastrous
Dim fel beirniad yn galw am safonau uwch	Not like a critic calling for higher standards

---

31 '*Barn* yn Holi Dafydd Iwan', in *Barn* 222/223 (July/August 1981), p. 300; translation mine.

32 Frith, *Sound Effects*, p. 163.

Dwi'm yn dweud fod diwylliant yn gysegredig	I'm not saying that culture is sacred
Ceisio campwaith fel tarw'n ceisio buwch	Trying for a masterpiece like a bull going after a cow[33]

While the reggae-influenced songs provide the primary trajectory which Jarman pursued in his subsequent recordings, the immediacy of his non-reggae-inflected work is just as significant to the corpus of Welsh popular music. His continued explorations of reggae were given greater weight in the records which followed *Gwesty Cymru*; two tracks from *Fflamau'r Ddraig*[34] provide evidence of the sophistication and obvious politicization of Jarman's reggae at the end of the decade. This politicization is reflected in the shift in focus from optimism – 'a New Ethiopia is coming soon' – to a much more bleak, pessimistic outlook on the future of Welsh society.

'Fflamau'r Ddraig' (The Dragon's Flames) and 'Rheswm i Fyw' (Reason to Live), though separate tracks, are effectively two sides of the same message, and are considered jointly here:

'Fflamau'r Ddraig'	**'The Dragon's Flames'**
Gweud os wyt ti'n ein adnabod	Say if you recognize us
Y mae'n cadw maes yr haf	They're keeping the summer field
A segurdod yn dirywio	And idleness is getting worse
A does dim ots am daith Magi	And it's no matter about Maggie's[35] visit
Wrth iddi sugno gwaed a chwilio	As she sucks blood and searches
Fflamau, fflamau'n codi, yn goleuo'r nos	Flames, flames rising, lighting the night
Fflamau, fflamau'n codi, gweld tafodau'r tân	Flames, flames rising, see the tongues of fire[36]
Fflamau'n codi, talu'r pwyth yn ôl	Flames rising, pay back the price
Ti wedi cyfaddef y cyfan	You've confessed it all
Ac nawr rhaid talu'n brydlon	And now you must pay up
Talu, talu'r pwyth yn ôl	Pay, pay back the price

---

33 'Neb yn Deilwng', music and lyrics Geraint Jarman, © Cyhoeddiadau Sain, from *Gwesty Cymru* (Sain 1158M, 1979). Lyrics reprinted by permission; translation mine.

34 'Fflamau'r Ddraig' and 'Rheswm i Fyw', music and lyrics Geraint Jarman, © Cyhoeddiadau Sain (Sain 1182M, 1980). Lyrics reprinted by permission; translations mine.

35 In the second statement of this line Jarman changes 'Magi' to 'Thatcher'.

36 'Tafodau Tân' (Tongues of Fire) was the name of one of the larger concerts organized by *Cymdeithas yr Iaith*, in 1973, famous for the debut performance of Edward H. Dafis. 'Tafod y Ddraig', the Dragon's Tongue, is the symbol of the *Cymdeithas*, but a connection between *Cymdeithas yr Iaith* and the *Meibion Glyndŵr* arson campaigns is not intentional.

Maen nhw'n cuddio yn y ffos
Lle wyt ti wedi bod trwy'r nos yn
    dy gwrw
Paid â brolio tra bod clustiau'r glas yn
    gwrando.

They're hiding in the ditch
Where you've been all night drinking
    beer
Don't boast while the cops are
    listening.

'Rheswm i Fyw'

Mae lleisiau gwrthwynebwyr yn
    atsain drwy'r tir
Mae popeth yn y fantol, ysgrifen ar y
    mur
Mae gofyn beth ydy'r prydferth a
    charcharwyr wedi ffoi
Moesoldeb dy gyfundrefn yw'r elw
    maen nhw'n creu

'Reason to Live'

The voices of resistance are echoing
    through the land
Everything is in the balance, the writing
    on the wall[37]
Asking what is beauty when the
    prisoners have fled
The morality of your system is the
    profit they create

Os nad oes gen ti reswm i fyw
Paid troi'n dduw ac rheoli'n ffawd

If you don't have a reason to live
Don't play god and rule our fate

Ond mae'r haul yn tywynnu nawr, mor
    felys ar y stryd
Mae traed y gormeswyr yn cicio'n
    wyllt a bloesg
Mae'n gorthrwm yw'r dewis i'r tlodi
    ym mhob oes

But the sun is shining now, so sweetly
    on the street
The oppressors are kicking wildly and
    indiscriminately
Our oppression is the choice of the
    poor of every age

Bum ganwyd mewn caethiwed
Mi wn am ddim byd gwell
'Sdim gorffwys i'r gorllewin,
af am y tiroedd pell.

I was born into slavery
I know of nothing better
There's no resting in the west,
I'll go away to further lands.

The lyrics of 'Fflamau'r Ddraig' allude to the actions of *Meibion Glyndŵr* (The Sons of Glyndower), whose arson campaign on English-owned holiday homes had begun in December, 1979.[38] With the new Conservative Government recently instated, and Margaret Thatcher beginning her tenure as Prime Minister, the effects of the changes in governmental policy had enormous repercussions for Welsh industry and culture.[39] The *Meibion Glyndŵr* campaign, which continued through the 1980s, was only one Welsh reaction to the changes in contemporary British society. Yet despite the extent of the arson campaign, the authorities failed to

---

37 'The writing on the wall' could also refer to the continued campaigns by *Cymdeithas yr Iaith* and the visual markers of their presence – the Dragon's tongue – in the streets of Wales.

38 For a brief summary of the actions of *Meibion Glyndŵr* and of the media's treatment of the events, see Roger Geary, '*Meibion Glyndŵr*: Folk-Devils or Folk-Heroes?', in *Planet* 92 (April/May 1992): 39-44.

39 The effect of Thatcherism on Welsh culture is of particular significance to Datblygu and 1980s Welsh pop in general, which is explored in the next chapter.

apprehend the parties responsible for destroying two hundred homes over the period of a decade. This infuses 'Fflamau'r Ddraig' with a certain retrospective irony. The melody is almost juvenile, a taunting, teasing challenge to the authorities. There is also a complicity in the lyrics which suggests at once an unspoken knowledge of the movements of *Meibion Glyndŵr*, and a unified (community) support of their actions: 'gweud os wyt ti'n *ein* adnabod' – 'say if you recognize *us*'. The us-and-them opposition is very clear, and the 'us' is understood as a larger collective than *Meibion Glyndŵr* alone. But by interpreting the line, 'don't boast while the cops are listening', in a different way, 'y Glas' – literally, 'the Blue' – becomes a reference to the Conservative Party. 'Don't boast while (they're) listening' then becomes more subversive than the more colloquial translation, and is almost prescient of greater political and societal troubles to come.

It is important to note the disembodiment of the voice which is achieved in 'Fflamau'r Ddraig' through heavy reverb in the chorus and throughout the second half of the song. The overall effect is sinister, despite the simplicity and sweetness of the melody, and creates the impression of a spatially dispersed collection of voices surrounding – and challenging – the listener. When the first verse is repeated toward the end of the song it is done so ahead of the beat – the voice returns on its own time, disjointed from the rest of the band and the rest of the song. Given the nature of the message, the 'disembodiment' of the singer's voice is in itself a political statement, and a suggestion that the campaign will continue until the 'body' is caught – until the listener can overtake the singer's voice.

'Rheswm i Fyw', in contrast to 'Fflamau'r Ddraig', is given a very straightforward interpretation. The voice remains largely unaltered throughout the verses and chorus, and it seems much more a statement of individual, rather than group, protest. As the metaphorical consequent phrase to 'Fflamau'r Ddraig's' antecedent phrase, it is a statement of cultural responsibility, where 'Fflamau'r Ddraig' reveled in the anonymity of the subject. The message in 'Rheswm i Fyw' is much more closely allied with the type of metaphorical language of reggae, and it provides the clearest example of Jarman's sympathetic understanding of the cultural importance of the musical style he had adopted almost a decade earlier.

Jarman had employed the Biblical imagery of Rastafari in 'Ethiopia Newydd' with a type of optimism, an expectation of a better world to come 'before long'. In 'Rheswm i Fyw', it seems as though he has resigned himself to the impossibility of utopia. The direct references to oppression and captivity are clearly drawn from the language of reggae. As Hebdige claims:

> This 'war' ['War inna Babylon' (Max Romeo, Island, 1976)] had a double nature: it was fought around ambiguous terms of reference which designated both an actual and an imaginary set of relations (race-class nexus/Babylon; economic exploitation/Biblical suffering), a struggle both real and metaphorical, which described a world of forms enmeshed in ideology where appearance and illusion were synonymous.
>
> Of course, war had its dubious compensations too: a sense of solidarity and purpose, an identity, an enemy more or less clearly defined.[40]

---

40 Dick Hebdige, *Subculture: The Meaning of Style* (London: Routledge, 1998), pp. 37–8.

Jarman defines the actual and the imaginary in 'Rheswm i Fyw': the actual, vocal expressions of resistance to years of Welsh subjugation, and the West/East dichotomy. The significance of the latter is twofold: first, it suggests the captive leaving Babylon for Ethiopia; but it also suggests an opposite motion, away from the Welsh heartland – the West, *y fro* – into the lion's den – the East, England. The first interpretation is a symbolic motion to the homeland; the second is a pessimistic journey away from the home culture. To contrast this with 'Ethiopia Newydd', in which the narrative voice was awaiting the arrival of better days, the narrative voice in 'Rheswm i Fyw' is convinced that they will never come.

The assumption must be made that the accusatory object in 'Rheswm i Fyw' is, again, the newly-elected Conservative government. But more importantly, Wales had already experienced an internal defeat of substantial proportions when the 1979 devolution referendum was rejected by a margin of 956,330 to 243,048. The sense of national resignation to continued political subjugation was palpable. For the political activists who believed that Wales' future depended on self-government, this result was more than a temporary setback; it all but killed any vestige of cultural optimism. The political climate in Wales had altered dramatically, and the changes which were signalled for Wales in the new administration were reason enough for pessimism. 'Rheswm i Fyw' reflects the general despair of the time, in lyrical content and in vocal delivery.

The political implications of the production of 'Fflamau'r Ddraig' and 'Rheswm i Fyw' are worth considering. As Pwyll ap Siôn has suggested:

> There is a particularly oneiric, unreal and detached atmosphere to 'The Dragon's Flames'. [...] The 'dub' quality of the song ... is also a suitable musical figure for the pervading 'absence of identity' in the song. These are voices without bodies: the resistant voices of the arsonists and the quiet voices of those who are in sympathy with them. In his assessment of a questionnaire on the fire-bombing campaign Denis Balsom says that although 'only a tiny proportion ... showed any support for the campaign itself ... a healthy majority claimed to identify with the aims the arsonists espouse.' 'The Dragon's Flames' thus represents the 'voices of resistance' that are not directly involved with the actions of the campaigners (including, of course, Jarman himself). The absence of 'naming' reinforces further the unreal qualities in the song. The only reference to a recognizable image is that of the dragon: it is the dragon's flames that 'pay back the price' in the chorus line. Apart from being the most obvious symbolic representation of 'Welshness' the dragon is also a creature whose true realization is beyond our own experience and comprehension. In this sense, the arsonists become the anthropomorphic manifestations of the dragon: unseen, mysterious, breathing fire, and associated with the discourse of myth and fantasy. [...] The unreal atmosphere of the song is therefore commensurate with the similarly unreal unfolding of the actual historical events.[41]

---

41 Pwyll ap Siôn, 'Voices of Resistance: Geraint Jarman and the Roots of Reggae in Welsh Popular Music', *Welsh Music History* 2 (Cardiff: University of Wales Press, 1997): 263–77. The excerpt, from pages 272–3, refers to Dick Hebdige, *Cut 'n Mix: Culture, Identity and Caribbean Music* (London, 1987), pp. 82–9, and to Denis Balsom, 'The Smoke Behind the Fires', *Planet* 73 (1989): 16–19.

Jarman's physical remove from the arson attacks allowed not only an intellectual distance, but a cultural one as well, and again, it is a difference defined by his personal location in the capital city. While the campaigns against English-owned holiday homes concerned primarily Welsh-speaking communities in the strongholds of the north and west coasts, it should be stressed that the social effects of people from outside Wales purchasing holiday homes in largely rural areas extend beyond linguistic concerns. A demand for real estate in any given area will lead inevitably to a rise in the cost of local homes; local residents will not be able to afford the cost of a mortgage, and the local community will suffer as a result of a proportion of local houses remaining empty for much of the year. This is a particularly rural concern; for Geraint Jarman to address this issue and contextualize it with the sounds of reggae, is to explore again the ideas of 'exile' and displacement.

To follow this logic into 'Rheswm i Fyw' is to understand that Jarman is speaking from a position of national – not rural, not urban – concern. The disembodied voices in 'Fflamau'r Ddraig' could be emerging from anywhere; 'Rheswm i Fyw' suggests that they are 'echoing across the land'. The borders Jarman is defining here are not geographical, but political. Though he is effectively removing the British government from the social space of Wales, he is encompassing the entire population, Welsh and Anglophone, within its boundaries. And more importantly, he is doing so through the musical medium of a marginalized community. This returns us to the basic cultural significance of reggae:

> The transposed religion, the language, the rhythm, and the style of the West Indian immigrant guaranteed his culture against any deep penetration by equivalent white groups. Simultaneously, the apotheosis of alienation into exile enabled him to maintain his position on the fringes of society without feeling any sense of cultural loss, and distanced him sufficiently so that he could undertake a highly critical analysis of the society to which he owed a nominal allegiance. For the rest, the Biblical terms, the fire, the locks, and Haile Selassie et al served to resurrect politics, providing the mythical wrappings in which the bones of the economic structure could be clothed so that exploitation could be revealed and countered in the ways traditionally recommended by the Rastafarian. The metasystem thus created was constructed around precise and yet ambiguous terms of reference and whilst remaining rooted in the material world of suffering, of Babylon and oppression, it could escape, literally at a 'moment's' notice, into an ideal dimension which transcended the time-scale of the dominant ideology. There were practical advantages to be gained by adopting this indirect form of communication, for if a more straightforward language of rebellion had been chosen, it would have been more easily dealt with and assimilated by the dominant classes against which it was directed. Paradoxically, 'dread' only communicates so long as it remains incomprehensible to its intended victims, suggesting the unspeakable rites of an insatiable vengeance.[42]

It is tempting to infer a deeper significance to the above quote, given the current discussion of 'fire', 'mythology' and 'insatiable vengeance'; but the point here is to reiterate the earlier suggestion that Jarman, through his incorporation of reggae, attempted to create a type of sympathetic cultural network of 'exiled' communities in Britain. By adopting the musical style and sonic imagery of the Rastafarian, Jarman

---

42 Hebdige, 'Reggae, Rastas & Rudies', p. 152.

was able to address from his place 'on the fringes of society' the political and social climates in Britain – 'the society to which he owed a nominal allegiance'. In doing so through the medium of Welsh, his message remained impenetrable by the culture against which it was directed; in the case of 'Fflamau'r Ddraig' and 'Rheswm i Fyw', this language of rebellion had already been 'spoken' by unnamed others, and in a more physically threatening manner.

There was a cultural time-lag evident in the early days of Welsh pop; but with the work of Geraint Jarman, notably his 'Welsh trilogy', the political, social and cultural ramifications of life in twentieth-century Wales found expression in a contemporary popular musical idiom. This differs from the music of Dafydd Iwan on a number of stylistic levels; on an ideological level, it suggests a type of folk-realist opposition. The community for which Dafydd Iwan sang, and which was strengthened through his creation of a new 'folk' canon, was essentially inward-looking. Jarman, in incorporating elements from outside the 'established' Welsh pop formation, created a means by which to view Wales within the wider world, and to create a more all-embracing sense of Welshness. As Jarman's style developed into the 1980s and 1990s, he relied more heavily on dub technique, obscuring the lyrics at times, but emphasizing the spatial qualities of his music and, by extension, his subjective location in Wales.

If Geraint Jarman's intention was to explore his own sense of Welshness in the three records released between 1978 and 1980 and referred to, collectively, as his 'Welsh trilogy', what may be inferred from the result is a belief in the capacity for cultural strength. The inherent optimism of 'Ethiopia Newydd' may have been dashed by the time he recorded 'Rheswm i Fyw', but the spirit of resistance and opposition Jarman celebrated in 'Fflamau'r Ddraig' suggests an abiding hope that political and cultural freedom – a new Ethiopia – is still possible.

Chapter Twelve

Datblygu and the Embodiment of Welsh Pop

Figure 12.1   David R. Edwards of Datblygy

In the two decades after Dafydd Iwan first sang 'Mae'n Wlad i Mi', the political and cultural climate of Wales had changed dramatically. The relationship between the Welsh language and popular music was entering a phase of unusual difficulty, and the music itself was expanding to encompass an unprecedented variety of styles. In the 1980s the relationship between the younger generation of language activists and the generation which spawned the movement had become strained, and it was largely in the musical arena that the relationship between these two generations was contested.

If the 1960s were witness to enormous societal changes in Wales and elsewhere, so were the 1980s a decade in which the value systems of the wider Anglo-American world were altered significantly. The status of the Welsh language had improved since the 1960s, due to the continued efforts of *Cymdeithas yr Iaith Gymraeg*, but the more general concern throughout Wales was a social one. The failure of the devolution referendum in 1979 and the overall rightward progression of Anglo-American politics signaled a decisive shift in the sense of Welshness which had been nurtured over the preceding decades. If Geraint Jarman's 'Welsh Trilogy' was a measure of this shift, illustrating as it does a gradual disintegration of the optimism of *Hen Wlad Fy Nhadau*, the music of Datblygu represents the extreme disillusionment of the generation which followed.

Wales and Politics in the 1980s

It is impossible to consider the music of Datblygu (Developing) without contextualizing their lyrics in the political climate of Thatcherite Britain. The first years of the 1980s were witness to remarkable societal changes, all of which had lasting ramifications for the sense of community identity in marginalized areas of the country. For Wales, the decade began with news that half the jobs in the steel industry would be lost,[1] followed by the Conservative government's decision to renege on their offer of a Welsh-language television channel. Despite rising unemployment and general dissatisfaction the Falklands War in 1982 revitalized public support for the Conservative party, and Thatcher was re-elected in 1983 for another term. The number of jobs lost in the privatization of the steel industry during Thatcher's second term in office, and in the closing of over twenty coal pits by the end of the decade, resulted in massive unemployment and the loss of a certain sense of tradition in the South Wales valleys.

The rightward shift was palpable in the United States as well, with the election of Ronald Reagan in 1980, and his re-election in 1984. The entire decade was colored by the fear of nuclear war and the tense relationship between the United States and the USSR; the magnitude of the potential conflict between these two nations was suggested in the smaller conflicts engaged by the United States in Grenada, Libya and Panama.[2] The unprecedented amassing of personal wealth in 1980s American society, typified by emergence of the young urban professionals as an identity formation, belied the fact that there was a growing concern for the less fortunate and the disenfranchised of the world. But the sense of national self-importance which resulted from enhanced military activity began to promote a less inclusive concept of national identity on both sides of the Atlantic. In Britain especially, a particular idealization of national character began to insinuate itself into public discourse. This

---

1   For an itemized account of unemployment figures in Wales in the 1980s see John Davies, *A History of Wales* and Gwyn A. Williams, *When Was Wales?*.

2   For a comprehensive account of the Cold War see Eric Hobsbawm, *Age of Extremes: The Short Twentieth Century 1914–1991* (London: Penguin, 1994).

had enormous implications for the minority communities, ethnic and linguistic, in Britain. As Stuart Hall explained:

We are beginning to think about how to represent a non-coercive and a more diverse conception of 'Englishness' which, under Thatcherism, stabilizes so much of the dominant political and cultual discourses, and which because it is hegemonic, does not represent itself as an ethnicity at all.

This marks a real shift in the point of contestation, since it is no longer only between anti-racism and multi-culturalism but *inside* the notion of ethnicity itself. What is involved is the splitting of the notion of ethnicity between, on the one hand the dominant notion which connects it to nation and 'race' and on the other hand what I think is the beginning of a positive conception of the ethnicity of the margins, of the periphery. That is to say, a recognition that we all speak from a particular place, out of a particular history, out of a particular experience, a particular culture, without being confined by that position as 'ethnic artists' or film-makers. We are all, in that sense, *ethnically* located and our ethnic identities are crucial to our subjective sense of who we are. But this is also a recognition that this is not an ethnicity which is doomed to survive, as Englishness was, only by marginalizing, dispossessing, displacing and forgetting other ethnicities. This precisely is the politics of ethnicity predicated on difference and diversity.[3]

'Englishness' is an Other against which Welshness is often defined; the location of Welshness in the 1980s, on the political and social margins of Thatcher's Englishness, is in Hall's sense an ethnic one. But within the geographical space of Wales there were at least three formations negotiating their subjective identities in the face of internal and external conflict: the industrial South Wales non-Welsh-speaking Welsh communities (*y Cymry di-Gymraeg*, the non-Welsh-speaking Welsh) struggling to preserve a way of life and the means to earn a living; *Meibion Glyndŵr*, continuing their arson campaign in an attempt to protect the North Wales Welsh-speaking communities from English in-migration; and the geographically dispersed Welsh-language musicians attempting to revive a stagnating Welsh pop scene, to instill in it a sense of professionalism, and thereby to change the nature of the Welsh music industry. This final point is central to the understanding of Welsh popular music of the 1980s and 1990s, and the contested relationship between the Welsh (minority) popular culture and its Anglo-American other. It also reflects a larger generational dissatisfaction, for in the 1980s the notion of 'youth' became important again, as the generations to which Ronald Reagan and Margaret Thatcher belonged seemed increasingly not to understand the needs and dangers of modern life.

Though ethnicity continues to be, in many places, a surprisingly resilient and powerfully reactionary force, the *new* forms of ethnicity are articulated, politically, in a different direction. By 'ethnicity' we mean the astonishing return to the political agenda of all those points of attachment which give the individual some sense of 'place' and position in the world, whether these be in relation to particular communities, localities, territories, languages, religions or cultures. These days, black writers and filmmakers refuse to be restricted to only addressing black subjects. But they insist that others recognize that what

---

3 Stuart Hall, 'New Ethnicities', from Morley and Chen, eds., *Stuart Hall: Critical Dialogues in Cultural Studie*, p. 447.

they have to say comes out of particular histories and cultures and that everyone speaks from positions within the global distribution of power. Because these positions change and alter, there is always an engagement with politics as a 'war of position'.

This insistence on 'positioning' provides people with co-ordinates, which are specially important in face of the enormous globalization and transnational character of many of the processes which now shape their lives. The New Times seem to have gone 'global' and 'local' at the same moment. And the question of ethnicity reminds us that everybody comes from some place – even if it is only an 'imagined community' – and needs some sense of identification and belonging. A politics which neglects that moment of identity and identification – without, of course, thinking of it as something permanent, fixed or essential – is not likely to be able to command the New Times.[4]

Thatcher and Reagan represented a generation whose identities were shaped by the experience of living through the Second World War and its aftermath. The mythologizing of a particular kind of national strength, of patriotism, was predicated on the notion that the American or British dream was shared by all persons occupying the respective geographical spaces. A subtext to this belief is that such persons share common ethnic, religious, and sexual identities. These rather simplified constructions of national identity were challenged in the 1960s by the succeeding generation; and in the 1980s, the generation born to that second generation, whose futures were dictated by the political and social mores established by Thatcher and Reagan, began to question the generational 'distribution of power'. The 'imagined community' of younger people coming of age in the 1980s could then position themselves in opposition to the political structures which denied them power, and assume control of their own political agenda, disseminated through 'alternative' mass media and popular music.

The popularity of MTV, first broadcast in the United States in the summer of 1981, enabled a liberal political agenda to be directed specifically at a youth audience.[5] The reluctance of the United States mass media to assume responsibility for AIDS education, for example, inspired MTV to create a forum to do so; popular music once again became engaged in raising consciousness. Band Aid, organized by Bob Geldof in 1984 to raise money for African famine relief, was another example of popular musicians – and by proxy, the 'younger generation' – deploying messages of social change to challenge the dominant ideology of self-interest. Student demonstrations in the United States to demand corporate and governmental divestment from South Africa, echoed the sentiments of Artists United Against Apartheid, and increased awareness of a political issue which might not have been addressed directly by the government or the mainstream mass media.

---

4   Stuart Hall, 'The Meaning of New Times', from Morley and Chen, eds., *Stuart Hall: Critical Dialogues in Cultural Studies*, pp. 236–7.

5   For further background on the history of MTV and investigations into the impact of music television on popular music and culture, see Simon Frith, Andrew Goodwin and Lawrence Grossberg, eds., *Sound and Vision: The Music Video Reader* (London and New York: Routledge, 1993) and Ann Kaplan, *Rocking Around the Clock* (London and New York: Routledge, 1987). Recent studies on music video and the negotiations of 'alternative' identities include Stan Hawkins, *Settling the Pop Score: Pop Texts and Identity Politics* (Aldershot and Burlington: Ashgate, 2002).

The political messages relayed in some Anglo-American popular music spoke directly to the construction of national identity. The irony of a song such as Bruce Springsteen's 'Born in the USA' (Columbia, 1984) was lost on Ronald Reagan, who chose to divorce Springsteen's symbolic use of the American flag from the song's narrative of the Vietnam veteran losing his faith in the country to which he returns; while an album such as U2's *War* (Island, 1983) introduced a wider public, in no small way, to the complications of Irish politics and Irish identity. A return to 1960s 'folk' ideology, typified by the debut release of Tracy Chapman (Elektra, 1988), spoke to a different kind of domestic politics, uncovering characters on the fringes of American society lost amid the larger drive to amass personal wealth at the expense of less privileged. There seemed therefore to have been a liberal backlash to the extreme conservatism of Anglo-American culture, and the popular music emerging from that culture is testament to it. The situation in Wales, however, was slightly different. For just as it happened in the 1960s at the beginning of the modern Welsh 'folk' movement, the need in Wales in the 1980s to negotiate a new sense of cultural 'self' was greater than the desire to address wider societal and political questions.

Welsh Pop and the 1980s Musical 'Establishment'

The 1980s were the decade of the independent label in Wales. The desire to establish an 'alternative scene' to the mainstream Welsh pop fare recorded on the Sain label, gave rise to the creation of independent labels such as Recordiau Fflach, Recordiau Anhrefn, Recordiau Ofn, and Ankst. This type of musical dissociation began in the 1970s with Geraint Jarman,[6] and in the 1980s came to reflect a further fragmentation, inspired as much by stylistic trends in Anglo-American popular music, as by political and societal shifts within Wales. The anger palpable in much Welsh pop of the mid-1980s is evidence of the younger generation of musicians trying to understand the future being created for them, while attempting at some level to change their present. This 1980s Welsh pop could be summarized as an inward-looking music, addressing the shifting fortunes of Wales, exploring a sense of subjective self in terms of a larger sense of Welshness; again, this type of identity negotiation is redolent of 1960s Welsh pop, but with a stronger emphasis on contemporary personal experience.

The type of subjective experience explored in some 1980s Anglo-American popular music – Joy Division, The Cure, The Smiths – was similarly an alternative to contemporary mainstream pop – Duran Duran, Wham!, Michael Jackson – and the sonic distinctions of the different musics were reflected visually in the accoutrements of the respective audiences. That is to say, the sonic and the visual were married in the 1980s in a way similar to that of the relationship between 1970s punk music and visual style, and the 1960s psychedelia and the 'flower power' aesthetic. This relationship was further solidified in the 1980s with the emergence of hip hop; the connection between the visual and the sonic became codified in the 1980s as a result of ideology as much as of MTV. And the parallel, contemporary, residual and

---

6   Although Jarman recorded on Sain, it should be clear that his musical ideology was somewhat different to that of his label-mates.

alternative forms of cultural expression in Welsh popular music were to be found on the Sain and Ankst labels, respectively.

The 'new wave' of Welsh popular music captured a contemporaneity which had not hitherto been a consistent feature of Welsh pop. With notable exceptions such as Geraint Jarman and Endaf Emlyn, Welsh pop in the 1960s and 1970s followed a rather conservative trajectory. Though still married to the Welsh language movement, and in a mutually supportive relationship with *Cymdeithas yr Iaith*, Welsh pop seemed in the 1980s to have reached a creative standstill. The shift in British politics and the concerns for the future of Welsh society and the Welsh language were generally not addressed in the context of 'mainstream' Welsh popular music; the Anglo-American 'new wave' aesthetic was therefore a much more suitable relationship to nurture.

> You see the difference from the earlier form of identity ...: embattled Britain, in its corsetted form, rigidly tied to the Protestant Ethic. In England, for a very long time, certainly under Thatcherism, even now, you can only harness people to your project if you promise them a bad time. You can't promise them a good time. You promise them a good time later on. Good times will come. But you first of all have to go through a thousand hard winters for six months of pleasure. Indeed, the whole rhetoric of Thatcherism has been one which has constructed the past in exactly that way. That is what was wrong about the sixties and seventies. All that swinging, all that consumption, all that pleasurable stuff. You know, it always ends in a bad way. You always have to pay for it in the end.[7]

The sense of 'bad times' in Wales in the 1980s was embodied in the music of Datblygu.[8] As much a reaction to 'good time' Welsh pop of the 1960s and 1970s as a reaction to contemporary British politics, the lyrics of David R. Edwards were central to the establishment of a Welsh 'underground' aesthetic and the revival of an indigenous popular culture in the process of self-mummification. Their very name, Datblygu, is itself a signifier of change. Welsh bands had uniformly been named after people, real or fictional (Geraint Jarman a'r Cynganeddwyr, Edward H. Dafis); nouns, with or without the definite article (Y Tebot Piws, Eliffant); in reference to places (Hogia'r Wyddfa, Hergest); or as a kind of visual, linguistic joke (Ac Eraill, Mynediad am Ddim). Datblygu, as a verb (to develop) or as a gerund (developing), denotes a distancing, or separation, from that which came before – in this case, thirty years of Welsh popular music.

As lyricist and frontman for Datblygu, Dave Edwards exposed – and represented – a particular kind of Welsh counterculture, which in itself was decidedly contrary to the type of shared identification assumed among the Welsh pop audience, and reflected

---

7   Stuart Hall, 'The Local and the Global', in Anthony D. King, ed., *Culture, Globalization and the World-System* (Basingstoke: Macmillan Education, 1991), p. 31.

8   In the liner notes for the re-release of *Wyau* and *Pyst* (Ankst CD060,1995), Dave Edwards wrote, 'at the time i was employed as a low-paid slave within various u.k. government institutions. like auschwitz etc., if you do an excess of hard labour you end up being cremated before your time, luckily by 1991 i had escaped the stress-inducing situations which inspired these songs. as a child, adults used to elaborate on the good old days. this c.d. documents the bad old days. i dislike my memories but stand by the songs. at best this collection is a time capsule, at worst the songs are the product of a mind incensed by circumstances. i make no apologies for either.'

in the music. He traversed the seamy underbelly of Welsh culture and criticized openly the type of utopian ideology to which early Welsh pop had subscribed:

...Achos putain fawr yw Prydain Fawr	...Because Great Britain is a great whore
Yn marw'n araf ar y llawr	Dying slowly on the ground
Ac mi gewn ni'r sylw rydym yn haeddu	And we'll get the attention we deserve
Gan ein bod ni'n byw mewn Cymru crymi [crymu]	Since we live in a crummy [stooping] Wales[9]
Rwy'n gweld merch â nodwydd yn ei braich	I see a girl with a needle in her arm
Heroin yn cusanu ei gwaed	Heroin kissing her blood
Mae hi wedi cael digon o fywyd creulon	She's had enough of cruel life
Lle nad oes gobaith yn un blaid	Where there's no hope in any party
Ac mae pobl fel moch mewn lladd-dŷ cas	And people are like pigs in a cruel slaughterhouse
Darnau o gnawd yng ngen gwleidyddiaeth ...	Pieces of meat in the jaws of politics ...[10]

Though there had been previous instances in Welsh pop of lyrical explorations of the dangers of modern life, they had been masked as cautionary tales – 'Lisa Pant Ddu' by Edward H. Dafis, for example – or were connected naturally to the 'otherness' of urban life, as in the songs of Geraint Jarman. Dave Edwards wrote from his position as a native of Cardigan, in west Wales, and exposed rural life not as the rustic idyll idealized in some Welsh pop of the 1960s and 1970s, but as a gritty existence, bereft of hope, marginalized from the rest of Wales and ignored by the British political system.

Previous constructions of Welsh identity, based on a sense of community, traditional values and heroic past, were shattered in the music of Datblygu, and the quest for a modern, rural Welsh identity, in all its inherent contradictions and complications, was a common theme:

Oes mwy yn Aberhonddu nag amaethyddiaeth a chymdeithasau adeiladu?	Is there more in Brecon than agriculture and building societies?

---

9 The alternative spellings and translations, Cymru crymi / Cymru crymu, both signify a kind of decay, Cymru crymi (crummy) suggesting an outward physical and social decay, and Cymru crymu (stooping) suggesting a decay in political values and blind obeisance to the British state. The homophonic ambivalence is left to the listener's interpretation.

10 Datblygu, 'Nefoedd Putain Prydain' (The Whore Britain's Heaven), re-released on *Datblygu 1985–1995* (ankst*musik* CD086, 1999). Lyrics reprinted by permission; translation mine.

Oes mwy yn Aberteifi na fod yn ddi-waith a gorfod gwylio'r teledu?	Is there more in Cardigan than being unemployed and having to watch television?[11]

The idea of the Welsh heartland, the Welsh-speaking areas of rural west and north Wales, was a contested location of Welsh identity in the 1970s, and the cause of the rupture between *Adfer* and *Cymdeithas yr Iaith*. The desire to rebuild *y fro Gymraeg*, to ensure a future for the Welsh language in its traditional strongholds, was expounded notably in Tecwyn Ifan's song 'Y Dref Wen' (The White Town, 1977) and Ac Eraill's 'Tua'r Gorllewin' (To the West, 1974). The contemporary political and social contexts, and the optimism which inspired the belief that an indigenous industry could be developed and supported by a relatively small linguistic community based in the further reaches of rural Wales, had changed, if not died, by the time Datblygu recorded 'Dros y Pasg Eto'. And the younger generation of Welsh speakers living in rural Wales during Thatcher's second term were concerned less with seeking linguistic freedom than with ensuring steady employment.

Reit. Gan fy mod wedi gorfod ysgrifennu lot o gachu er mwyn cael cyfweliadau ar gyfer swyddi cachu – clerc, gwerthu petrol, gyrru tacsi, athro – dyma'r unig *curriculum vitae* sy'n cyfri. Hei, ga i fod Siôn Corn?	Right. Since I've had to write a lot of shit just to get interviews for shitty jobs – clerk, selling petrol, driving a taxi, teacher – here's the only *curriculum vitae* that counts. Hey, can I be Santa Claus?
Roedd y BBC yn chwilio am gynhyrchydd *Helo Pobl* beth amser yn ôl. Anfonais ffurflen gais gonest. Dwedon nhw, 'na'. Dwedon nhw, 'na, ti ddim yn ddigon da. Ti'n rhy dda.' Hei, ga i fod Siôn Corn? …	The BBC were looking for a producer for *Helo Pobl* a while back. I sent an honest application form. They said, 'no'. They said, 'no, you're not good enough. You're too good.' Hey, can I be Santa Claus? …[12]

Dave Edwards represents a generation of Welsh speakers born during the first decade of modern Welsh language activism; as local industry jobs were lost and young people began moving to the capital city and beyond, the 'traditional' sites of Welsh cultural practices – the *Urdd*, the Eisteddfod – became less relevant, and cynicism replaced the optimism upon which these institutions were based. The reality of life as lived in the 1980s through the medium of the Welsh language was

---

11 'Dros y Pasg Eto' (Over Easter Again), *BBC Peel Sessions* (Ankst 027, 1992). Lyrics reprinted by permission; translation mine.

12 Datblygu, 'Ga I Fod Siôn Corn?', from *Datblygu 1985–1995* (ankst*musik* CD086, 1999). Lyrics reprinted by permission; translation mine.

far more bleak. The song 'Gwlad ar Fy Nghefn' (Land On My Back)[13] illustrates this point graphically:

Maes Eisteddfod anhysbys	An unknown Eisteddfod field
VD ar werth yn y maes pebyll	VD for sale on the camping field
Ond byddwch slebog cyn bod yn briod	But be a slut before getting married
A cymrwch asid cyn bod yn athro	And take acid before becoming a teacher
Ac rwy'n teimlo fel Cymdeithas yr Iaith	And I feel like *Cymdeithas yr Iaith*
Neu ddyn dall yn chwilio am waith	Or a blind man looking for work
Ac mae pob *cliché*'n ffaith	And every cliché is a fact
Ac mae cerdded un cam gormod fel taith	And taking one step is too much like a journey
Ac mae byw yng Nghymru	And living in Wales
'R un peth â syllu ar y paent yn sychu,	Is the same as watching the paint dry
Ar y gwair yn tyfu lan.	And the grass grow.
Dydd Sul blin ym Mhen Llŷn	A weary Sunday in the Llŷn Peninsula
Ac mae pync yn cuddio ar gornel	A punk is hiding at the corner
Crap apêl y capel	The chapel's crap appeal
Ond mae'i seidar yn surach na'r Beibl	But his cider is more sour than the Bible
Cadwch Talwrn y Beirdd	Keep *Talwrn y Beirdd*
Y maciau plastig, y teiau llydan	The plastic macs, the wide ties
Dyn nhw byth yn gwrthod brechdan	They never refuse a sandwich
Ac mae nhw'n chwerthin pan mae pawb arall yn	And they laugh when everyone else does
Byw yng Nghymru	Living in Wales
'R un peth â syllu ar y paent yn sychu	Is the same as watching the paint dry
Ar y gwair yn tyfu lan.	And the grass grow
Yr un hen Noson Lawen	The same old *Noson Lawen*
Gormodaeth o deisennau menyn	An excess of butter cake
Ehangiad o'r Orsedd a'r Urdd	An extension of the *Gorsedd* and the *Urdd*
Pob dinesig gwledig yn sugno ei laswellt	Every rural citizen sucking on his grass

---

13 'Gwlad' translates not as the verbal 'to land', but as the noun 'land, country'. It is a subtle reference to the Welsh national anthem, and intended as an antidote to it.

Byw yng Nghymru

'R un peth â syllu ar y paent yn sychu,

Ar y gwair yn tyfu lan

Tyfwch lan.

Living in Wales

Is the same as watching the paint dry

And the grass grow

Grow up.[14]

'Gwlad ar Fy Nghefn' is a distillation of criticisms about traditional Welsh culture and, by extension, the loss of hope in modern Wales. The opening verse catalogues a number of stereotypes about the National Eisteddfod: first, that it is never situated in a central location; second, that the community of young people who stay at the nearby site reserved for tents and camper vans might potentially find themselves engaged in casual sexual contact with each other; and third, that the two career paths offered to dedicated *Eisteddfodwyr* – marriage and teaching – would be better served by alternative physical and psychological experimentation. One contemporary campaign slogan introduced by *Cymdeithas yr Iaith*, 'gwnewch *bopeth* yn y Gymraeg' – do *everything* in Welsh – could be interpreted in a similar way: socialize, educate, marry, raise children; but also socialize, drink, take drugs, have sex; *modernize* the language, make it relevant to the contemporary Welsh experience.[15] Dave Edwards recognizes here that certain types of socializing take place in the back fields of the Eisteddfod, and seems to be commenting on the more general social inability in the late-1980s to address the ramifications of casual sex. The alternative to physical and psychological freedom, however – marrying and perpetuating the Welsh language through having children or simply teaching them – is hardly more desirable.

Equating the continuing campaign of *Cymdeithas yr Iaith* with the fortunes of a blind man seeking employment is one of the more pessimistic forecasts of the fate of the language expressed in Welsh pop. The relative status of Welsh speakers in Britain had been compared with the status of African Americans in the United States on other occasions – 'Niggers Cymraeg' by Y Trwynau Coch (1980) and 'Nigger-Boi John-Boi Cymru' by Steve Eaves (1989)[16] – but in a manner intended to inspire unity and strength within the Welsh-speaking community. This comparison between the struggle for the Welsh language and the struggle simply to move through life

---

14 Lyrics drawn from David R. Edwards, *Al, Mae'n Urdd Camp* [literally, 'Al, it's an *Urdd* Camp', but homophonically 'German *Urdd* Camp', a reference to the historical rumor that the *Urdd* was formed on the contemporary model of the Hitler Youth] (Talybont: Y Lolfa, 1992), with slight alterations made to coincide with the version recorded on *Wyau/ Pyst* (Ankst 060). Lyrics reprinted by permission; translation mine. 'Gwlad ar Fy Nghefn' was also recorded for the John Peel Show in 1988 and released on *BBC Peel Sessions* (Ankst 027, 1992). Dave Edwards' explanatory notes for the *Peel Sessions* recording state that it is 'a national anthem in reverse about wales [*sic*] in 1988 where people actually believe in sexually transmitted diseases...'

15 It should be mentioned that sexual terminology in the Welsh language is primarily agricultural in origin, and slang is largely borrowed from the English language.

16 This sympathetic relationship, or 'family of resemblance', between Welsh speakers and marginalized others is an idea which is of central importance to the following case study.

expresses not only a loss of hope, but also a more general loss of self- and cultural direction.

In the third verse Edwards continues his criticism of 'traditional' Welsh culture, notably the chapel and its centrality to the Welsh-speaking community. Edwards here paints an image of a 'lost soul' on the Llŷn Peninsula, a predominantly Welsh-speaking area, attending chapel on a Sunday morning, not for spiritual enlightenment, but for a warm place to drink. *Talwrn y Beirdd* (The Bards' Spot) is a popular and long-running series on Radio Cymru wherein two panels of poets compete in the composition of brief alliterative verses, *englynion*, on a given subject. It is based on a similar 'light, but sophisticated, entertainment' held annually at the National Eisteddfod, known as *Ymryson y Beirdd*, The Bards' Competition. That the people in plastic macs and wide ties 'laugh when everyone else does' is testament to the density of poetic Welsh, which often renders immediate aural comprehension difficult. It is also a suggestion that the literary and cultural in-jokes alluded to in some of the *englynion* are understood primarily by the regular listening audience, and by those with some background in the Welsh literary tradition – in other words, the dedicatees of Welsh culture, not the casual listener. It can only be assumed that the metric structure of Dave Edwards' lyrics were written purposefully and in direct opposition to the rules established by Welsh poetic tradition.

It is in the last verse that the consequences of a rural Welsh ideology are suggested. The legacy of the *Gorsedd*, the bardic institution at the center of the National Eisteddfod, and *Urdd Gobaith Cymru*, the Welsh League of Youth, is a generation of drifters in the Welsh countryside, chewing on a stalk of grass, waiting for better days. The image of the hick, the icon of a particular 'country' way of life in the United States, is suggestive not only of a simpleton, but of the product of extreme poverty in the southern US, or of the migrant workers moving west toward California looking for work during the Dust Bowl years. Superimposing that image to rural Wales in the 1980s, one conjures the image of unemployed youth, passing the time watching 'the paint dry and the grass grow'. The structure of contemporary life in rural Wales seems to allow for no alternative.

'Gwlad ar Fy Nghefn' signals a decisive shift in the established pattern of Welsh cultural commentary. Rather than seeking to strengthen a sense of unity, Edwards is highlighting the fissures developing in a community which had previously been created in adherence to a particular, historically mythologized, ideal of a Welsh-speaking Wales. He represents a solitary, dissident voice in a fracturing identity formation, and is therefore essential to the ultimate strength of the culture. As Raymond Williams states:

> No community, no culture, can ever be fully conscious of itself, ever fully know itself. The growth of consciousness is usually uneven, individual and tentative in nature. An emphasis of solidarity which, by intention or by accident, stifles or weakens such growth may, evidently, bring a deep common harm. It is necessary to make room for, not only variation, but even dissidence, within the common loyalty. [...]
>
> A culture, while it is being lived, is always in part unknown, in part unrealized. The making of a community is always an exploration, for consciousness cannot precede creation, and there is no formula for unknown experience. A good community, a living culture, will, because of this, not only make room for but actively encourage all and any

who can contribute to the advance in consciousness which is the common need. Wherever we have started from, we need to listen to others who started from a different position. We need to consider every attachment, every value, with our whole attention; for we do not know the future, we can never be certain of what may enrich it; we can only, now, listen to and consider whatever may be offered and take up what we can.[17]

The anger palpable in much of Datblygu's music presented an open challenge to the Welsh cultural establishment, and their resulting lack of exposure on Welsh radio did not improve relations between the band and media. But the act of cultural criticism is necessary to the health of a community. Dave Edwards illuminated the weaknesses in Welsh culture, and articulated the opinion of many contemporary musicians, that Welsh pop was deeply conservative, that it needed to change, and that 'marginalized' voices needed to be heard.

Yet Datblygu might have encountered a harsher reaction, were it not for the underlying humor in Edwards' lyrics. Though his songs may have been difficult for the 'establishment' to bear at times, the sophistication of Edwards' language and his lyrical subtleties provide for a strangely affective reassessment of the meaning of Wales and the possibilities of Welshness. This is not to say that Edwards' lyrics were met with universal acceptance; in a more general assessment of the state of Welsh pop in 1987 Dafydd Iwan was quoted as saying:

Mae byd grwpie'r ifainc y dyddie hyn yn mynd yn dipyn o jyngl i un fel fi, wrth gwrs, sy'n tynnu ymlaen mewn oed. Ac mae'n rhaid dweud, mae 'na bwyslais ar bethe traddodiadol fel petai nhw'n cael eu taflu allan drwy'r ffenest. Mae'r pwyslais ar alaw yn mynd. Mae'r pwyslais ar eirie, i raddau, yn mynd. Yn sicr, does 'na ddim ymgais i sgrifennu geirie yn farddonol mewn unrhyw ffordd. Mae geirie yn cael eu taflu o gwmpas ac yn cael eu hailadrodd lawer ac mae'r holl beth braidd yn undonog. Ond dw i hefyd yn sylweddoli fod yn rhaid i gerddoriaeth newid. A mae'n rhaid i fiwsig yr ifainc fynd drwy gyfnod o newid. Ond y peth sy'n fy mlino i fwyaf ynglyn â llawer iawn o gerddoriaeth y grwpiau heddiw ydi agwedd negyddol, nihilistaidd braidd at y byd. Mae eisie newid, mae eisie chwyldro, mae eisie dileu yr hen drefn. Ond dyw hi ddim yn glir iawn beth maen nhw eisie'i roi yn ei le fe.

[The world of young groups these days is turning into a bit of a jungle for someone like me, of course, who's getting on in years. And it must be said, there's an emphasis on traditional things as though they're being thrown out the window. The emphasis on melody is going. The emphasis on words, to some extent, is going. There's certainly no effort taken to write words in any kind of poetic manner. Words are being thrown around and being repeated a lot and the whole thing is fairly monotonous. But I also realize that music has to change. And the music of youth has to go through a period of change. But the thing that troubles me most about so much of the music of today's groups is the negative, almost nihilistic attitude toward the world. They want change, they want revolution, they want to delete the old order. But it's not very clear what they want to put in its place.][18]

---

17 Raymond Williams, *Culture and Society: 1780–1950*, p. 334.

18 Quoted in Lyn Ebenezer, *Radio Cymru 21* (Llandysul: Gwasg Gomer, 1998), p. 113; translation mine.

Edwards' symbolic relationship with Dafydd Iwan deserves a brief mention here. Edwards' disdain for 'popular' Welsh culture found its outlet in song titles such as 'Dafydd Iwan yn y Glaw' (Dafydd Iwan in the Rain) and 'Sgorio Dafydd Iwan Dyn Eira' (Snowman Dafydd Iwan's Scoring), as well as in textual references to other 'mainstream' Welsh artists. The underlying ironic humor in much of Datblygu's music is important to note, for it suggests a turning point in the process of Welsh identity.

> Cultures struggling for recognition cannot usually afford to be intricate or self-ironizing, and the responsibility for this should be laid at the door of those who suppress them. But intricacy and self-irony are virtues even so. That someone in the process of being lowered into a snakepit cannot be ironic is a critical comment on his situation, not on irony. The fact that Culture can afford such virtues, whereas culture often cannot, makes no difference to this fact. We would know if a cultural identity had been securely established by its ability to engage in irony and self-criticism.[19]

Of the many examples of Edwards' ironic cultural criticism, 'Cân i Gymru' (Song for Wales),[20] is worth isolating. It is an obvious reference to the Wales-based Eurovision-style contest of the same name, and itemizes a number of truths about an 'older' generation of Welsh-language 'activists':

Gradd dda yn y Gymraeg	A good degree in Welsh
Ar y Volvo bathodyn Tafod y Ddraig	On the Volvo a *Tafod y Ddraig* sticker
Hoff o fynychu pwyllgorau blinedig	Fond of attending tiresome committee meetings
Am ddyfodol yr iaith yn enwedig	About the future of the language in particular
Meistroli iaith lleiafrifol fel hobi	Mastering a minority language as a hobby
Platiau dwyieithog i helpu'r gyrru	Bilingual plates to help the driving
Agwedd cwbl addas ar gyfer cynllun cartre	A perfectly appropriate attitude for a home plan
sydd mas o set *Dinas*	straight out of the *Dinas* set[21]
Wastad yn mynd i Lydaw,	Always going to Brittany,
byth yn mynd i Ffrainc	never going to France
Wastad yn mynd i Wlad y Basg,	Always going to the Basque Country,
byth yn mynd i Sbaen	never going to Spain
Fin nos yn mynychu bwytai	Frequenting restaurants of an evening
wedi dydd ar y prosesydd geiriau	after a day at the word processor
Mewn swydd sy'n talu'r morgaits	In a job that pays the mortgage

---

19 Terry Eagleton, *The Idea of Culture* (Oxford: Blackwell, 2000), p. 65–6.

20 'Cân i Gymru', from *Datblygu 1985–1995*. Lyrics reprinted by permission; translation mine. Dave Edwards' lyrical performances often vary from one recording to the next, and his delivery can present certain hindrances to the successful negotiation of the Welsh language. I am therefore indebted to Dilwyn Roberts-Young and Jon Gower for their native Welsh ears.

21 *Dinas* (City), was a contemporary drama series on S4C, based in Cardiff.

i'ch gwyneb person cwbl cwrtais

for your perfectly courteous person's face

O'r ysgol feithrin i brifysgol Cymru

From the Welsh nursery to the University of Wales

Tocyn oes ar y trên grefi
Byddai'n well da fi fod yn jynci
na bod mor wyrdd â phoster Plaid Cymru

A lifetime ticket on the gravy train
I would rather be a junkie
than be as green as a *Plaid Cymru* poster

Darnau gosod yr Ŵyl Gerdd Dant

Rules for penillion at the *Cerdd Dant* Festival

A holl broblemau'r ddau o blant

And all the troubles of the two children

Gwersi telyn Llinos Wyn
a phroblem acne Llywarch Glyn
Heb anghofio codi stŵr
am straen angheuol job y gŵr

Llinos Wyn's harp lessons
and Llywarch Glyn's acne problem
Not forgetting to raise a fuss
about the deadly strain of the husband's job

Mae'n gorfod gweithio 1:00 tan 3:00
yn gynhyrchydd BBC

He has to work from 1:00 to 3:00
as a producer at the BBC

Llosgwch eich tafodau ar eich panedi piwritanaidd
Collwch eich dynoliaeth mewn economeg academaidd
Enwch gyfeillion sy'n enwogion i gyd o Seiri Rhyddion
Trafodwch tapiau corau meibion
a'r eitemau sydd ar *Hel Straeon*
Rhifau cynulleidfa'r oedfa

Burning your tongues on your puritan cups
Losing your humanity in academic economics
Naming your friends, all famous, from the Freemasons
Discussing male voice choir tapes
and items on *Hel Straeon*[22]
The numbers in the congregation at the chapel service

pha liw lenni'r lolfa
Tiwtoriaid preifat i helpu'r plant yn Neuadd Dewi Sant

what color for the lounge curtains
Private tutors to help the children in St. David's Hall

Digon o wyliau i gynnal lliw haul
Digon wrth Brydeinig i swnio fel *Sieg Heil*
Meistroli iaith lleiafrifol fel hobi

Enough holiday to keep a suntan
Anti-British enough to sound like *Sieg Heil*
Mastering a minority language as a hobby

Dweud fod Cymru'n cael ei orthrymu
Er fod eich ceir â'r sticyrs Tafod y Ddraig
Achos gradd dda yn y Gymraeg

Say that Wales is being oppressed
Despite your cars and their *Tafod y Ddraig* stickers
Because of a good degree in Welsh

22 A contemporary, topical magazine program on S4C.

The outward symbols of Welshness – *Cymdeithas yr Iaith* stickers on cars, participation in policy meetings about the future of the language – and the cultivation of Welshness – Welsh-language nursery schools, the University of Wales, a degree in Welsh, harp lessons for the children, contributions to the *cerdd dant* festival – are lampooned in 'Cân i Gymru', not for the sake of those fulfilling the stereotype, but for Edwards' own generation. The reality of language activism, and the political context within which it operated, was much different for college-aged students in the 1980s than it was for the 1960s and 1970s generation. The symbolic show of solidarity with the contemporary campaigns for property law in Wales, *Deddf Eiddo*, for example, rang false when expressed by middle-class members of the 'establishment' – the BBC, the Freemasons. Again, this song could only have been written in the context of Thatcherite Britain, and only at a particular point of crisis in the process of Welsh identity. That 'Cân i Gymru' succeeds at criticizing the complacency of a 'middle-aged' construction of Welshness, and the separation between that world and the reality of contemporary Wales, is indication that the younger generation, represented here by Datblygu, had already established an ideology by which to negotiate a modern, collective cultural identity. A new structure of feeling had emerged in the 1980s, which had chosen its ancestors – language activism, politicized popular music – and developed its infrastructure – Recordiau Ofn, Recordiau Ankst. Most importantly, at this moment in the development of Welsh pop the possibility for opening the musical utterance to the physical as well as the political was the decisive factor which contemporized it.

Datblygu and the Sexualization of Welsh Pop

[Expression] is carried not by dramatic inflections, subtle stresses, sympathetic accents, but by the *grain* of the voice, which is an erotic mixture of timbre and language, and can therefore also be, along with diction, the substance of an art: the art of guiding one's body.... Due allowance being made for the sounds of the language, *writing aloud* is not phonological but phonetic; its aim is not the clarity of messages, the theater of emotions; what it searches for (in a perspective of bliss) are the pulsional incidents, the language lined with flesh, a text where we can hear the grain of the throat, the patina of consonants, the voluptuousness of vowels, a whole carnal stereophony; the articulation of the body, of the tongue, not that of meaning, of language. A certain art of singing can give an idea of this vocal writing; but since melody is dead, we may find it more easily today at the cinema. In fact ... the cinema capture[s] the sound of speech *close up* ... and make[s] us hear in their materiality, their sensuality, the breath, the gutturals, the fleshiness of the lips, a whole presence of the human muzzle (that the voice, that writing, be as fresh, supple, lubricated, delicately granular and vibrant as an animal's muzzle), to succeed in shifting the signified a great distance and in throwing, so to speak, the anonymous body of the actor into my ear: it granulates, it crackles, it caresses, it grates, it cuts, it comes: that is bliss.[23]

---

23 Roland Barthes, from *The Pleasure of the Text*, translated by Richard Miller and extracted in Susan Sontag, ed., *A Roland Barthes Reader* (London: Vintage, 1983), pp. 413–14. Some problem is encountered in the above passage with the term 'bliss' and the distinction between Barthes' original *plaisir* and *jouissance*. In the Translator's Note to

The 'embodiment' of Welsh popular music in the 1960s and 1970s was informed by a kind of singing cultivated in the chapel, in competitions at the Eisteddfod, and in communal singing at *Urdd* camps. While a gross generalization, this nonetheless enables an understanding of the vocal delivery of early Welsh pop and, to some extent, the relatively slow development of Welsh pop from the acoustic to the electric. The recordings of Dafydd Iwan illustrate this point: the clarity of his diction, the purity and sweetness of his vocal inflection, the use of *vibrato*, were much more closely associated with the formality of the chapel and Welsh folk tradition than with the Anglo-American folk singers whose songs influenced his work. There was a roughness to the way in which Woody Guthrie and Bob Dylan sang their protest songs, and the lyricism which infused Dafydd Iwan's performance of 'Mae'n Wlad i Mi', for example, is decidedly antithetical to it. The general absence of drums in Welsh pop until the early 1970s is similarly indicative of the conservative nature of its parent culture. The reggae beat which was introduced to Welsh pop via the music of Geraint Jarman was radical in its inherent physicality; but Jarman's voice, though different in its delivery to the established Welsh pop sound, was a thin instrument, almost always treated in final production by multiple-tracking or reverberation. Jarman's voice was disembodied, as in 'Fflamau'r Ddraig' and therefore not associated with the corporeal nature of the music which supported it.

Dave Edwards' voice has a presence unlike almost all other Welsh pop, and Datblygu's recordings exploited it to great effect. Due in part to the nature of his lyrics, his vocal delivery is less concerned with an accurate melodic rendering than an affecting recitation of the words. Edwards' vocal timbre is resonant not only of his own physicality, but of his separation from his immediate environment. That is to say, his marginality from the Welsh establishment infuses his voice with an undeniable anger, while replacing the urgency of community with the confident knowledge of a subjective identity. Divorced from a larger social context the 'grain' of Edwards' voice carries the burden of cultural meaning.

> The 'grain' is the body in the voice as it sings, the hand as it writes, the limb as it performs.
> If I perceive the 'grain' in a piece of music and accord this 'grain' a theoretical value (the

---

Roland Barthes' *Image – Music – Text* (New York: Hill and Wang, 1977), Stephen Heath writes that 'English lacks a word able to carry the range of meaning in the term *jouissance* which includes enjoyment in the sense of a legal or social possession…, pleasure, and, crucially, the pleasure of sexual climax. The problem would be less acute were it not that *jouissance* is specifically contrasted to *plaisir* by Barthes in his *Le Plaisir du texte*: on the one hand a pleasure (*plaisir*) linked to cultural enjoyment and identity, to the cultural enjoyment of identity, to a homogenizing movement of the ego; on the other a radically violent pleasure (*jouissance*) which shatters – dissipates, loses – that cultural identity, that ego. The American translation of *Le Plaisir du texte* … uses the word "bliss" for *jouissance*; the success of this is dubious, however, since not only does "bliss" lack an effective verbal form (to render the French *jouir*), it also brings with it connotations of religious and social contentment ("heavenly bliss", "blissfully happy") which damagingly weaken the force of the original French term' (p. 9). Such terms would be equally awkward to translate into Welsh; but wherever invoked in the above, 'bliss' should be inferred as meaning '*jouissance*' with all the sexual connotations therein.

emergence of the text in the work), I inevitably set up a new scheme of evaluation which will certainly be individual – I am determined to listen to my relation with the body of the man or woman singing or playing and that relation is erotic – but in no way 'subjective' (it is not the psychological 'subject' in me who is listening; the climactic pleasure hoped for is not going to reinforce – to express – that subject but, on the contrary, to lose it).[24]

It is more than just the register of Edwards' voice which resonates with his physicality. The manner in which his voice is recorded – 'Gwlad ar Fy Nghefn' is one such example – foregrounds his voice and, by inference, the physical action of his enunciation, 'the whole carnal stereophony'. The explosion of consonants and the harshness of the guttural elements of spoken Welsh in some of Datblygu's recordings highlight the emotional investment in the words, but more importantly 'throw Edwards' (displaced) body' into the ear of the listener. In this way the experience of listening to Datblygu is unlike the experience of listening to any Welsh pop which preceded it, and it is an experience which can only be described as visceral.

The wider Anglo-American musical context within which Datblygu were active was developing from the 'New Wave' of the early part of the 1980s into the type of synthesized dance music typical of the latter part of the decade. The musical structure which supported Dave Edwards' performances was modeled very closely on the contemporary Anglo-American popular style; Dave Edwards' vocal stylings, so far removed from the music of Dafydd Iwan and Geraint Jarman, was much more closely allied with vocalists such as Mark E. Smith of The Fall and Ian Curtis of Joy Division. Significantly, the roughly-sung, largely declaimed nature of David Edwards' delivery provided a transitional stage between the Welsh 'pop' voice and the Welsh 'rap' voice. The emphasis on words is the same, though the latter generally explores a greater physicality with the backing music. There is not the same sense of driving beat in the music of Datblygu as in some contemporary Anglo-American pop;[25] but in its defiance of structural norms the lyrics are given textural precedence, and this again contributes to the exposure of the 'human muzzle'.

When Dave Edwards trawls the realm of sexual experience the results can be alarming:

Rwy am rannu dy gorff o dy ben i dy draed	I want to share your body from your head to your feet
Gamblo gyda AIDS a rhannu dy waed	Gamble with AIDS and share your blood
Rhanna fy ngwaed	Share my blood[26]

---

24 Roland Barthes, 'The Grain of the Voice', translated by Stephen Heath, in *Image – Music – Text*, p. 188.

25 It should be mentioned that other Ankst and Crai artists were developing Welsh dance music, which represents a parallel strain of contemporary Welsh pop. Though not cited specifically here, bands such as Tŷ Gwydr and Llwybr Llaethog should be understood as representing that pattern.

26 Datblygu, 'Slebog Bywydeg' (Biology Slut), from *BBC Peel Sessions*. Lyrics reprinted by permission; translation mine.

The ensuing effect is significant, and it should be stressed that very little Welsh popular music had been recorded which displayed any kind of sexual overtones. In the new structure of feeling which emerged in Wales in the 1980s, the Welsh language became a forum for the release of the morality which had shaped much of its expressive culture;[27] the result was a music reflective of its immediate context, continuing to look inward at Wales, but aware of the position of Wales on the margins of Anglo-American culture.

One final example serves to summarize the development of Welsh popular music in the 1980s. 'Maes E' (E Field), recorded in 1992,[28] is a distillation of the wider political and social climates of the 1980s. In it the former sense of community unification – within Wales, within the United Kingdom – is irretrievable but for the physical unification of the speaker and the object of his desire.

Pan oedd yr heddlu'n curo'r glowyr	When the police were beating the miners[29]
ro'n i ond yn aros amdanat ti	I was only waiting for you
Pan rhoddodd Bob Geldof ei law yn ein poced	When Bob Geldof put his hand in our pockets[30]
o'n i ond yn chwarae hebddot ti	I was only playing without you
A phan oedd hi'n gwadu ein bod yn gymuned	And when she denied we were a community[31]
o'n i ond am gymuno gyda ti	I only wanted to commune with you
A phan gorchuddiwyd Irac o dan garped	And when Iraq was covered by a carpet[32]
o'n i am y dillad gwely drosom ni	I only wanted the bedclothes over us
Ar Maes E	On E Field[33]

---

27 The publication of the first (and apparently only) pornographic novel in the Welsh language, Androw Bennett's *Dirmyg Cyfforddus* (Talybont: Y Lolfa, 1994) was roughly contemporaneous.

28 Datblygu, 'Maes E', from *Datblygu 1985–1995*. Lyrics reprinted by permission; translation mine. I am deeply grateful to David R. Edwards for clarifying some of the lyrics of 'Maes E', and for elaborating on the more personal aspects of his work.

29 The miners' strike took place in Wales from 1984 to 1985.

30 Band Aid released the single, 'Do They Know It's Christmas?' in 1984 to raise money for African famine relief; Live Aid took place in London and Philadelphia on 13 July 1985.

31 Margaret Thatcher once claimed that 'there is no society, only individuals'.

32 A carpet of fire, presumably, courtesy of the US and British forces.

33 Reference to the National Eisteddfod; 'Maes B', the alternative, youth-oriented rock field, was the subject of the sole recording of Y Blew (1967), long before Maes B became a reality. Significantly, the pronunciation of 'E' in the Datblygu recording is the anglicized 'ee', rather than the Welsh 'eh'; it is at once a sonic reference to the Blew recording ('Maes B', pronounced 'bee' rather than 'buh') and a reference to ecstasy, the social narcotic associated with rave culture in the 1980s and 1990s. The judgment and competitions which constitute cultural activities at the National Eisteddfod are here forgotten in the chemically-induced euphoria associated with the drug. 'E' was also the first initial of Edwards' then-girlfriend, making 'E field' an explicitly sexual reference.

heb y barnu na'r cystadlu	with neither the judgment nor the competing

Pan penderfynon nhw ddechrau'r rhyfel — When they decided to start the war

mi welais dy ddelwedd mewn rhîmau o ffilm — I saw your image in film strips

Saethon nhw i fwydo y Hollywood newydd — They shot to feed the New Hollywood[34]

a syllais i arno cyn symud i hyn — and I stared at it before moving to this

Unwaith mi wisgodd Hitler fel menyw — Once Hitler dressed as a woman[35]

priododd feddwyn oedd yn yfed cymaint â ni — she married a drunk[36] who drank as much as we did

Arhosodd e'n ddall ond dest ti â'r eli, — He stayed blind but you brought the ointment,

tynnu'r hoelion o fy nhraed ac yna eu golchi — pulled the nails from my feet and then washed them[37]

Ar Maes E — On E Field

heb y barnu na'r cystadlu — with neither the judgment nor the competing

Rhai amlwg yn gi ar linyn Barbara Woodhouse — Some are obviously dogs on Barbara Woodhouse's string[38]

a sa i'n mynd i ddawnsio fel Ian C. — and I'm not going to dance like Ian C.[39]

Ond condemnio'r ffordd yr adeiladwyd — But condemn the way

y wal Berlin sy rhyngddom ni — this Berlin Wall was built between us

Sa i am agor lan fel hen glwyf — I'm not going to open up like an old wound

i waedu dagrau am addewidion ffug — to bleed tears over false promises

Am beth waeth mae dy gofio'n felys ond — For what's worse, remembering you is sweet but

---

34 *Hedd Wyn* (dir. Paul Turner), was released in 1992, and nominated for an Academy Award for best foreign-language feature film in 1994.

35 Again, a reference to Thatcher.

36 Dennis Thatcher, Margaret's husband, was apparently fond of gin.

37 When asked to clarify this line, Dave Edwards said simply, 'Thatcherism crucified me. Not just me, but my whole generation.' (Telephone conversation with the author, 16 March, 2002.) This point is clearly deserving of greater mention than is possible in a footnote, and should be inferred as the overall subtext to 'Maes E' and, indeed, to much of Datblygu's recorded work.

38 A dog-training television personality.

39 A reference to the unique dancing style of Ian Curtis, lead singer of Joy Division, who committed suicide in 1980.

| heno mae'r cofio'n dristach na chig | Tonight the memory is sadder than meat.[40] |

| Ar Maes E | On E Field |
| heb y barnu na'r cystadlu | with neither the judgment nor the competing. |

Though clearly a love song, the most intimate element of 'Maes E' is Dave Edwards' voice. There is an intensity in the performance which permeates the recording, despite – or perhaps because of – the dynamic level of the voice in the overall texture.[41] Most importantly, the relative lack of inflection in Edwards' voice – the absence of obvious rage or tension, so present in the other songs discussed above – allows for the Barthesian *jouissance*. The meaning of the text, the *plaisir* associated with the understanding of and identifying with the textual message, is subverted by the 'erotic mixture of timbre and language', the 'voluptuousness' of the delivery – the grain of Edwards' voice.

The sexualization of Welsh pop was not a wholly conscious process. It was a side-effect of the increasingly close relationship between Welsh pop and its Anglo-American counterpart. The efforts to modernize the Welsh language and Welsh pop in the 1980s were reflected in the anti-establishment stance taken by Welsh 'punk' bands such as Anhrefn, the founding of independent record labels and the general interest in establishing relationships between Welsh bands and central British cultural figures such as John Peel. Individual utterances of these attempts were simply reflections of the emergence of an alternative ideology – a musical ideology divorced from its closest familial relations, a political ideology in open revolt against the powers imposed upon it. I have invested the music of Datblygu with the responsibility of representing this ideology, not because they were universally recognized as central components of it, but because the music which followed could not have developed in the same way without the fearlessness with which Dave Edwards and Datblygu expounded their philosophy of modern Welsh existence.

In the same way that Geraint Jarman served as a symbolic middleground between the early Welsh pop of Dafydd Iwan and the music of the 1980s, so does Datblygu serve as a symbolic middleground between all Welsh pop which preceded it and the Welsh pop of the final decade of the twentieth century. The omnipresence of Anglo-American popular music in modern Welsh life would suggest that Welsh rap might

---

40   One of the more obtuse lines in the song, this is a reference to Edwards' vegetarianism, and might be inferred as a reference to the Smiths' *Meat Is Murder* (Rough Trade, 1985). I am grateful to Emyr Glyn Williams of ankst*musik* for mentioning Edwards' eating habits.

41   The relationship of performance intensity and dynamic level is explored by Serge Lacasse in 'Technological Musical Parameters in Recorded Popular Music', in Kimi Kärki, Rebecca Leydon and Henri Terho, eds., *Looking Back, Looking Ahead: Popular Music Studies 20 Years Later* (IASPM-Norden, Turku, 2002). Phonographic staging is an idea he explores further in 'Interpretation of Vocal Staging by Popular Music Listeners: A Reception Test', *Psychomusicology* 17 (spring/autumn 2001): 56–76, and 'La musique populaire comme discours phonographique : fondements d'une approche analytique', *Musicologies*, no 2 (printemps 2005): 23–39.

have emerged at some point in the 1990s; but the indigenous example of Datblygu enabled 'underground' Welsh pop to flourish in unexpected locations, and infused it with a cultural self-confidence unrealized in the previous decades.

Chapter Thirteen

Y Tystion: Wales Joins the Hip Hop Nation

Figure 13.1 MC Gruff and MC Sleifar

In 1998 the music pages of *Golwg* and *Y Cymro* announced the formation of the first Welsh-language hip hop group.[1] Y Tystion (The Witnesses) were the product of an evening spent by MC Sleifar and MC Gruff in a bar in Aberystwyth in 1996, and they went on to release three albums and two EPs over the next four years. While the novelty value of Welsh rap was rather high at the time of their first EP, *Brewer Spinks*,[2] rap and hip hop had already established themselves in the mainstream of Anglo-American popular culture, and had been adopted by innumerable other cultures and adapted into innumerable other languages. There had been groups in Wales who dabbled in rap as a type of fictitious identity (Diffiniad, Hanner Pei), utilizing a certain style of vocal delivery unrelated to their general output; but there had not been a group solely devoted to creating, as Tystion put it, 'hip hop poetry in motion in the mother tongue'.[3] Tystion stressed from the outset the importance of their poetry; it is important now to explore the musical and poetic roots of Welsh hip hop, for they lie not only in international hip-hop, 'the hip hop nation', but in the music of earlier Welsh groups, notably Datblygu and Llwybr Llaethog.

The Roots of Rap

It is generally agreed that rap began on the streets of New York in the late 1970s.[4] Associated with street parties, graffiti art, breakdancing, and dj-ing, rap grew to define a particular mix of past and present in a 'found' cultural product; and in its approach to music-making rap continued the DIY trajectory established by skiffle a quarter of a century earlier and punk in the mid-1970s. The cultural need may have been different, but the motivation was the same: creating a musical product relevant to the contemporary social climate of a given locality.

The roots of rap can generally be traced to two different sources: the 'toasting' tradition in Jamaican music, and the emergence of the Black Power movement in the United States in the late-1960s. Though neither of these roots would appear to be immediately relevant to the Welsh experience, they were both indigenized into the Welsh language, and the results serve as a twin inspiration for the development of Y Tystion's Welsh hip hop. But the most important subtext here is that the international nature of hip hop today – its indigenization into the vernaculars of cultures throughout the world – has served to create a network of 'families of resemblance', of which Y Tystion serve as the Welsh agents.

In his article, 'The State of Rap: Time and Place in Hip Hop Nationalism', Jeffrey Louis Decker distinguishes between two types of black nationalism in contemporary

---

1   See the review of Y Tystion's *Brewer Spinks* EP in *Y Cymro* 26 August, 1998, p. 18.

2   Tystion released their first album, *Rhaid i Rywbeth Ddigwydd...* ('Something's Got to Happen') on their own label, Fitamin Un (Fit 004, 1997) before being signed to Ankst, who collected three songs from the LP and one new song and released them as an EP.

3   See *Brewer Spinks* (ankst*musik* 083, 1998).

4   For a history of rap and hip hop see Tricia Rose, *Black Noise: Rap Music and Black Culture in Contemporary America* (Middletown, Connecticut: Wesleyan University Press, 1994), and David Toop, *Rap Attack 3: African Rap to Global Hip Hop* (London: Serpent's Tail, 2000).

rap and traces their roots to what he terms 'sixties-inspired hip hop nationalism' and 'Afrocentric hip hop nationalism'.[5] It is these two roots which serve as a connecting thread between Welsh hip hop and the international 'hip hop nation', as well as between Welsh hip hop and those earlier moments of crisis in the history of Welsh pop. More importantly, Decker explores the importance of nationalism, language, and myth in the motion toward cultural empowerment; the mobilization of the Welsh community in the second half of the twentieth century resonates with these very ideals.

Decker outlines two trajectories of rap: first, he traces 'sixties-inspired hip hop nationalism' back to the Black Aesthetic movement of the 1960s and 1970s,[6] and specifically to Gil Scott-Heron and The Last Poets. Scott-Heron's song, 'The Revolution Will Not Be Televised', is often cited as a seminal moment in the history of 'rap',[7] as its extended attack on the American media and its relationship to contemporary black America was recited over a jazz-based accompaniment. Though the free-form approach to lyrical and musical delivery is not one normally associated with rap as it is performed today, there are political and textual links between Scott-Heron and present-day rap which warrant further mention. Of the many threads of rap which have emerged since the late-1970s, the 'message rap'[8] is one most easily

---

5   Jeffrey Louis Decker, 'The State of Rap: Time and Place in Hip Hop Nationalism', *Social Text* 34 (1993): 53–84.

6   Decker describes 'hip hop nationalists' as organic intellectuals, which has a particular resonance with the idea of Welsh hip hop and families of resemblance. The term 'organic intellectual' is posited by Antonio Gramsci in 'Hegemony, Intellectuals and the State', in *Selection from Prison Notebooks*, trans. Quintin Hoare and Geoffrey Nowell-Smith (London: Lawrence & Wishart, 1971). He states that

> every social group, coming into existence on the original terrain of an essential function in the world of economic production, creates together with itself, organically, one or more strata of intellectuals which give it homogeneity and an awareness of its own function not only in the economic but also in the social and political fields. The capitalist entrepreneur creates alongside himself the industrial technician, the specialist in political economy, the organisers of a new culture, of a new legal system, etc. [...] [T]he 'organic' intellectuals which every new class creates alongside itself and elaborates in the course of its development are for the most part 'specialisations' of partial aspects of the primitive activity of the new social type which the new class has brought into prominence. [...] One of the most important characteristics of any group that is developing towards dominance is its struggle to assimilate and conquer 'ideologically' the traditional intellectuals, but this assimilation and conquest is made quicker and more efficacious the more the group in question succeeds in simultaneously elaborating its own organic intellectuals.

Quoted in John Storey in *Cultural Theory and the Study of Popular Culture*, pp. 212–13.

7   Mention should be made here of the distinctions between 'rap' and 'hip hop'. 'Hip hop' is a general cultural category encompassing graffiti art, dress, musical style, dance, etc.; 'rap' refers solely to a particular musical style. For a more detailed account of the differences and contestations between 'rap' and 'hip hop' see Adam Krims, *Rap Music and the Poetics of Identity* (Cambridge: Cambridge University Press, 2000).

8   David Toop uses the term 'message rap' in his discussion of the Last Poets and Gil Scott-Heron; I will use 'message rap' as a broad categorical term, as it has been used in other studies of rap and hip hop.

traced back to the Last Poets and Gil Scott-Heron in the late-1960s: it can be traced through Grandmaster Flash and the Furious Five's 1982 single 'The Message', right through to Public Enemy's 1990 album, *Fear of a Black Planet*. The message was and is intended as a commentary on black contemporary life, and aimed at the communities neglected or misunderstood by mainstream mass media. The 'message rap' project is essentially to create a black mass media, disseminating political ideals and unifying imagined communities into a more powerful network. As Decker suggests, the connection between Public Enemy and the Last Poets is based in radical black politics of the 1960s. Public Enemy have revisited the militant imagery of the Black Panthers in a hip hop context,[9] and samples of the voices of 1960s black radical politics and the civil rights movement are used for a similar, aural effect, re-contextualizing a radical politics to suit the needs of contemporary society.

The second trajectory of rap outlined by Decker is that of 'Afrocentric hip hop nationalism'. This places at the center of its philosophy an African value system, in an attempt, as Decker says, 'to find – through spiritual and psychological transcendence – freedom from Western oppression'.[10] This Afrocentrism finds spiritual basis in the Nation of Islam, which states that 'the black man must strive to regain his original religion (Islam), language (Arabic), and culture (astronomy and mathematics)'.[11] Afrocentric nationalism has led some to locate ancient Egypt as the original civilization, claiming that Egypt is 'not only the origin of the black nation to come, but also the cradle of all civilization, [empowering] hip hop nationalists in their struggle against a history of white supremacy.'[12] Decker suggests that a more potent argument for the cradle of the black nation would be the precolonial, African sub-Sahara and its empires dating back to 700AD; the western notion of 'civilization' and its implications of inherent slave culture do not preclude Egypt, but rather include it, thereby positioning the black nation 'to come' in the contradictory position of embracing a history, itself riddled with the very problems against which contemporary black society has fought.

Decker's is a fascinating argument, one which refers on a basic level to the possible implications of inventing new traditions, and of community-building based on nostalgia for the distant past. These are not issues restricted to the black community and the network united in the 'hip hop nation', but are rather issues common to any marginalized community – racial, religious, linguistic – located within a dominant culture. In this way the hip hop nation is international. The universality of the problems facing black Americans is similarly reflected in the experience of West Africans in France, Maoris in New Zealand, French-speakers in Québec, and Welsh-speakers in Wales, to note but four examples.[13] The individuality of the messages of each of

---

9   Notably by re-staging a familiar photograph of Black Panthers leader Huey Newton while dressed in contemporary hip hop 'street' fashion, thereby visually updating a radical 1960s philosophy for the 1990s.

10 Decker, 'The State of Rap', p. 73.

11 Ibid., p. 75.

12 Ibid., p. 77.

13 For studies of the international appropriation of rap see Tony Mitchell, *Popular Music and Local Identity: Rock, Pop and Rap in Europe and Oceania* (London and New York:

these communities, and many more besides, service different political needs, but their commonality expands the notion of 'nation' in unexpected ways, forging a type of sympathetic network of marginalized communities, or families of resemblance.

The Roots of Welsh Rap

There is an important pattern in the history of Welsh popular music which involves the appropriation of Anglo-American popular songs into the Welsh vernacular. If American rap can be traced back to the Black Power movement in the 1960s and the music of the Last Poets and Gil Scott-Heron, so can Welsh rap be traced back to the indigenization of Gil Scott-Heron's most famous song. 'The Revolution Will Not Be Televised'[14] is a three-minute distillation of a particular moment in history and of a particular political ideology. It is accusatory, implicating American media in both ignoring the needs of the black community and in perpetuating fear and ignorance in the minds of the American public. The superficiality of (white American) television shows ('*Green Acres*, *The Beverly Hillbillies* and *Hooterville Junction* will no longer be so damned relevant / And women will not care if Dick finally got down with Jane on *Search for Tomorrow* / Because black people will be in the street looking for a brighter day') is punctuated with 'reality' footage of black people caught in moments of criminal activity or staged acts of unity ('There will be no pictures of you and Willie Mays pushing that shopping cart down the block on the dead run / Or trying to slide that color tv into a stolen ambulance'). 'The Revolution Will Not Be Televised' is early 'message rap', designed to challenge the establishment and inspire a community into greater political awareness.

Given the very specific cultural and historical associations of 'The Revolution Will Not Be Televised' it might seem an inappropriate choice for incorporation into an unrelated context; yet in 1992 the Welsh performance poet Ifor ap Glyn used it as a template for an assessment of the Welsh language media, which he recorded with Llwybr Llaethog (Milky Way) in a techno-dub context.[15] The implications of this song to a sense of Welshness in the 1990s are enormous. The musical accompaniment

---

Leicester University Press, 1996) and Tony Mitchell, ed., *Global Noise: Rap and Hip-Hop Outside the USA* (Middletown, Connecticut: Wesleyan University Press, 2001).

14 Gil Scott-Heron, 'The Revolution Will Not Be Televised', from *Pieces of a Man* (RCA 07863 66627-2, 1971).

15 Llwybr Llaethog and Ifor ap Glyn, 'Fydd y Chwyldro Ddim ar y Teledu, Gyfaill', on *Ap Elvis* (Ankst 038, 1993). Poem published in Ifor ap Glyn, *Golchi Llestri Mewn Bar Mitzvah* (Llanrwst: Gwasg Carreg Gwalch, 1998). Lyrics reprinted by kind permission of Gwasg Carreg Gwalch; translation mine. I am deeply indebted to Ifor ap Glyn for his comments on, and corrections to, the translation above. Though the published lyric inhabits the entire width of the page, I have had to break individual lines for the purpose of side-by-side translation. This should not distract from the stream-of-consciousness feel to the poem or to its fluid declamation.

suggests an urban context, yet the lyrics are firmly rooted in the experience of an intelligent cultural commentator living in a small, rural country.[16]

Fydd ddim modd i chdi aros adra, gyfaill,	You won't be able to stay home, friend,
Fydd ddim modd i chdi diwnio mewn,	You won't be able to tune in,
troi ffwrdd, nac aros ar y ffens,	turn away or stay on the fence,
Fydd ddim modd i chdi ymgolli mewn lagyr ffrenzi,	You won't be able to lose yourself in a lager frenzy
na phicio allan am banad yn ystod yr hysbysebion,	or pop out for a cup of tea during the adverts
Achos fydd y chwyldro ddim ar y teledu, gyfaill.	Because the revolution will not be on television, friend.
Chaiff y chwyldro mo'i ddangos ar S4C, gyfaill,	The revolution won't be shown on S4C, friend,
Ddim hyd yn oed wsnos ar ôl iddo ymddangos	Not even a week after it's shown
ar Sianel 4, hefo cyflwyniad gan Melfyn Bragg.	on Channel 4, presented by Melvyn Bragg.
Fydd y chwyldro ddim yn cael ei noddi	The revolution won't be sponsored
gan y Cyngor Celfyddydau,	by the Arts Council,
Na'i gyflwyno gan Wasg Gregynog	Or presented by Gregynog Press[17]
mewn rhwymiad arbennig o groen Aardvark anorecsig.	in a special binding of anorexic aardvark hide.
Fydd y chwyldro ddim yn dangos lluniau o Neil Kinnock	The revolution won't show pictures of Neil Kinnock
yn canu pennill fwyn i'w nain	singing flattering verses to his grandmother
Ac yn arwain y lemming ffyddloniaid	And leading the lemming faithful
yn erbyn pwerau'r Fall a phwerau disgyrchiant.	against the powers of darkness, and gravity.
Chaiff y chwyldro mo'i ddangos ar y teledu, gyfaill.	The revolution won't be shown on television, friend.
Fydd y chwyldro ddim yn cael ei gyflwyno	The revolution won't be presented

---

16 It should be mentioned that Ifor ap Glyn was raised in London, though his use of the patronymic and mastery of Welsh poetic meters refutes the suggestion of any national affiliation other than Welsh. Similarly the two members of Llwybr Llaethog were born in England, moved to Wales and learned Welsh as young adults. I am grateful to John Griffiths of Llwybr Llaethog for making this latter point.

17 Gregynog Press specializes in the production of limited-edition, hand-crafted volumes.

ar ôl y pwdin Dolig gan Ffilm Cymru mewn cydweithrediad
ag o leia' tri chwmni Ewropeaidd

after Christmas pudding by Film Wales in co-operation
with at least three European companies.

Fydd Dafydd Hywel na John Ogwen
ddim yn y prif rannau
Na Bryn Fôn fel Che Guevara
yn mynd i'r capel mewn Levis
ac yn gwisgo beret yn y sêt fawr. chwaith

Dafydd Hywel and John Ogwen
won't be taking the leading roles
Or Bryn Fôn[18] as Che Guevara
going to chapel in Levis[19]
and wearing a beret in the front pew, either.

Fydd y chwyldro ddim yn helpu i chdi swsio'n well
Fydd y chwyldro ddim yn clirio plorod
Fydd y chwyldro ddim yn gwneud i chdi edrach
hanner stôn yn sgafnach
Achos fydd y chwyldro ddim ar y teledu, gyfaill.

The revolution won't help you kiss better
The revolution won't clear pimples
The revolution won't make you look
half a stone thinner
Because the revolution won't be on television, friend.

Fydd 'na ddim llunia ohonot ti a Sulwyn Tomos
yn gwthio troli siopa trwy ffenast Woolworth
Ac yn stwffio'r teledu lliw i gefn y car heddlu
'dach chi newydd ei ddwyn.
Fydd Dewi Llwyd ddim yn gallu amcangyfrif
y canlyniad terfunol am bum munud i naw ar ei ben
ar sail ad-ro-ddia-dau ein go-he-bydd ar-be-nnig.

There won't be any pictures of you and Sulwyn Tomos[20]
pushing a shopping cart through Woolworth's window
And stuffing a color tv in the back of a police car
you've just stolen.
Dewi Llwyd[21] won't be able to predict

the final results at five minutes to nine
on the dot
on the basis of re-ports by our spe-cial cor-res-pon-dent.

Fydd Angharad Mair ddim yn gallu rhoi recipe
ar gyfer lobsgows hefo dau soffa,

Angharad Mair[22] won't be able to give a recipe
for soup with two sofas

---

18 Actor and lead singer of Sobin a'r Smaeliaid, one of the more popular Welsh groups of the late-1980s and early 1990s.

19 Reference to 'Mynd i'r Capel Mewn Levis' ('Going to Chapel in Levis'), the lightly subversive late-1970s hit by Y Trwynau Coch.

20 Host of *Stondin Sulwyn*, a long-running daily current affairs program on Radio Cymru.

21 Anchor of *Newyddion*, the BBC nightly news for S4C.

22 Broadcaster, athlete and host of magazine programs on S4C.

Na mynd yn fyw at Glynnog
yng nghlwb fferets Cwmllynfell.
Fydd 'na ddim lluniau o'r slobs yn
clobio pobol LA,
na phobol Brynsiencyn,
Fydd neb yn gofyn – 'dach chi newydd
golli
eich unig ferch – sut 'dach chi'n
teimlo?'
Fydd y chwyldro ddim ar y teledu,
gyfaill.

Or go live to Glynnog
in the Cwmllynfell Ferrets' Club.
There won't be pictures of cops
clubbing people of LA
or people of Brynsiencyn,
No one will ask – 'you've just lost
your only daughter – how do you
feel?'
The revolution won't be on television,
friend.

Fydd 'na ddim lluniau lloeren o Hywel
Gwynfryn
yn cerdded trwy Drelai, Penrhys,
Glyncoch,
na Maesgeirchen mewn siwt loncian
coch-gwyn-a-gwyrdd-Mistar-Urdd
y bu'n 'i chadw'n ôl
ar gyfer achlysur arbennig fel hwn.

There will be no satellite pictures of
Hywel Gwynfryn
walking through Ely, Penrhys,
Glyncoch,
or Maesgeirchen in a
red-white-and-green-Mr-Urdd suit that
he's been saving
for a special occasion like this.

Bydd safon iaith, *Stondin Sulwyn*,
ac amseroedd darlledu *Dechrau Canu
Dechrau Canmol*
yn peidio bod mor ddiflas a
hollbwysig,
A fydd neb yn becso os fydd Magi
wedi ffeirio Tush
am Ford Fiesta a gwerthu'r Post i'w
ailddatblygu
fel ffatri Anthrax ar *Pobol y Cwm*,

Linguistic standards, *Stondin Sulwyn*,
and viewing times of *Dechrau Canu
Dechrau Canmol*[23]
will cease to be so boringly all-
important,
And no one will care if Magi swapped
Tush
for a Ford Fiesta and sold the Post
Office for
redevelopment as an anthrax factory
on *Pobol y Cwm*[24]

Achos fydd pobol pob cwm allan ar
y strydoedd
yn ceisio gwell yfory.

Because people of all valleys will be
out on the streets
seeking a better tomorrow.

Bydd yr Heddlu Iaith a'r Securetate
Camdreiglo

The Language Police and the Mis-
mutation Securitate[25]

---

23 Welsh equivalent of *Songs of Praise*.

24 'People of the Valley', long-running nightly Welsh-language soap opera on S4C.

25 The more militant language activists, those who monitor the Welsh content in the media, are sometimes referred to as 'language police'; the more militant Welsh learners occasionally revel in the unfortunate habit of informing other people – notably native Welsh speakers – of the correct application of the system of Welsh mutations.

yn cael eu cloi fyny hefo llond
    stafell o fwncwns ar asid
A gorfod eu gwylio nhw yn trio
    ail-greu
gwaith Alan Llwyd ar hap
efo teipiadur a pheiriant cynganeddu.

will be locked up with a full room of
    monkeys on acid
And forced to watch them trying to
    re-create
the words of Alan Llwyd[26] at random
with a typewriter and cynghanedd
    machine.

Fydd yna ddim pigion ar *Post
    Prynhawn*
na *Wales at Six* am gampau diweddara'

y Bwrdd Iaith, Cadeiriau Iaith,

Nag unrhyw ddodrefnyn amherthnasol
    arall o'r un casgliad
sydd byth yn clasho efo dim byd ...
    GLAS!

There will be no highlights on *Post
    Prynhawn*[27]
or *Wales at Six* describing the latest
    feats
of the Language Board, Language
    Chairs
Or any other irrelevant furniture from
    the same
collection that never clashes with
    anything ... BLUE![28]

Fydd y gerddoriaeth ar gyfer y
    chwyldro ddim yn cael
ei chyfansoddi gan Huw Chiswell
    na Chas and Dave
Na'i chanu gan Margaret Williams,
    Dennis O'Neill
na Wyn Roberts a'i crypt kicker five

OND mi fydd hi'n cael ei chyhoeddi
    ar label ANKST!

The music for the revolution won't be

composed by Huw Chiswell or Chas
    and Dave
Or sung by Margaret Williams, Dennis
    O'Neill
or Wyn Roberts[29] and his crypt kicker
    five

BUT it will be released on ANKST!

Fydd y chwyldro ddim yn ôl ar ôl yr
    egwyl
Fydd y chwyldro ddim ar y teledu,
    gyfaill
Fydd y chwyldro ddim yn
    ailddarllediad,
Fydd y chwyldro ddim yn
    ailddarllediad,
Fydd y chwyldro ddim yn
    ailddarllediad, cyfieithiad,

The revolution won't be back after the
    break
The revolution won't be on television,
    friend
The revolution won't be a re-run,

The revolution won't be a re-run,

The revolution won't be a re-run,
    translation,

---

26 Winner of the Bardic Chair, National Eisteddfod 1973 and 1976.

27 'Afternoon Post', daily afternoon news summary on Radio Cymru.

28 Reference to the Conservative Party, still in power at the time of the recording.

29 Wyn Roberts was a Minister in the Welsh Office during Thatcher's tenure. A native Welsh-speaker, he argued, along with others, for the creation of S4C.

nac addasiad o syniad gwael a aeth i fyn sbwriel

or adaptation of a lousy idea that went into the

Teledu Thames tua 1973

Thames Television trashbin around 1973

Fydd y chwyldro ddim angen is-deitlau achos

The revolution won't need subtitles because

fydd y chwyldro ddim ar y teledu, gyfaill

the revolution won't be on tv, friend

Fydd y chwyldro ddim ar y teledu, gyfaill

The revolution won't be on television, friend

Fydd y chwyldro yn hollol wreiddiol

The revolution will be completely original

Ac yn dod i chi yn FYW.

and will come to you LIVE.

In much the same way that Gil Scott-Heron derided the American mass media for its irrelevance to the black experience, here Ifor ap Glyn suggests the failure of the Welsh media to speak to the needs of the community which it seeks to represent. It must be remembered that the campaign to obtain a Welsh-language television station was long and culminated in a threatened hunger strike by Gwynfor Evans, the leader of *Plaid Cymru*. The political implications of a Welsh-language television station were surpassed only by the potential of the station to educate and inform a new generation of Welsh speakers, as well as those older generations whose daily experience of the Welsh language pre-dated the early *Cymdeithas yr Iaith* campaigns. The burden placed on S4C was therefore enormous. Just as Radio Cymru exists to provide Welsh-language equivalents of all four BBC Radio services, so does S4C exist to provide a wide variety of services, during the limited number of daily Welsh-language broadcast hours. That programming on S4C therefore necessarily includes 'light entertainment' – soap operas, *Noson Lawen*, and magazine programs – alongside news, current affairs, and children's educational broadcasting, has led some to wonder how relevant the channel is to the continuing struggle for the future of the Welsh language.

A glance through the lyrics for 'Fydd y Chwyldro…' gives some indication of these concerns. Not only does S4C provide Welsh-language programming, they serve as the regional outlet for English-language Channel Four programming. The ideal bilingual S4C viewer would therefore watch an evening of prime-time Welsh entertainment followed by the generally delayed broadcast of Channel Four programming. The Anglophone S4C viewer, however, would need either the Teletext simultaneous translation service to understand Welsh programs, or an aerial powerful enough to receive Channel Four's western, English, signals. And the Welsh-speaking viewer whose prime-time interests do not extend to magazine programs or farming reports would find him- or herself in the awkward position of wishing to support Welsh programming, while wishing for programming more relevant to the changing nature of contemporary Wales. The all-encompassing mission of S4C broadcasting necessarily excludes some portion of the population of Wales at any given time; as can be inferred from 'Fydd y Chwyldro...', it is the younger generation of Welsh speakers whose lives are not reflected in S4C programming.

When Ifor ap Glyn derides the state of S4C – delayed Channel Four output, superficial entertainment and 'safe' news reporting – he is performing the same service to the Welsh community that Gil Scott-Heron did for the African-American community in 1971. In charging the Welsh media with irrelevance, he is also reminding the Welsh-speaking community that the struggle for the language did not end with the creation of S4C. Although many *Cymdeithas yr Iaith* members active in the campaign for Welsh-language broadcasting later found themselves pursuing careers in the media, their political drive was mellowed by employment in the 'establishment', and even prior membership in early Welsh pop groups is not enough to understand the importance of popular music to the lives of contemporary youth.[30] A preference for Welsh-language broadcasting over English may be a political act, but its reward should be material worthy of the consumer's time, and relevant to his or her own experience.

The moment at which Ifor ap Glyn connects his message to Gil Scott-Heron's, and to contemporary American rappers, is in the penultimate stanza:

> The music for the revolution won't be composed by Huw Chiswell or Chas and Dave
> Or sung by Margaret Williams, Dennis O'Neill or Wyn Roberts and his crypt kicker five
> BUT it will be released on ANKST!

By bemoaning the omnipresence of middle-of-the-road artists on S4C and Radio Cymru, Ifor ap Glyn is stressing the importance of popular music to the formation of contemporary political consciousness. That Ankst is named as the bastion of hope in an otherwise homogeneous culture is itself important.[31] Ankst was founded by two college students at Aberystwyth four years before 'Fydd y Chwyldro...' was recorded; one of the founders was imprisoned for his participation in *Cymdeithas yr Iaith* protests. From its inception in 1988, Ankst represented the 'cutting edge' of Welsh popular culture. Anti-establishment in its cultural and political remit, Ankst served as the axis upon which Welsh and Anglo-Welsh popular music sought a balance. Ifor ap Glyn and Llwybr Llaethog are celebrating Ankst and its anti-establishment ethos, in much the same way that contemporary rap labels served as an alternative to the mainstream. That rap had already infiltrated and changed the mainstream by the time Llwybr Llaethog and Ifor ap Glyn recorded 'Fydd y Chwyldro...' does not diminish the significance of the song to the development of Welsh pop, for the cultural time-lag evident throughout the history of Welsh pop had lessened by 1992, largely due to the founding of Ankst.

---

30 The obvious example is Huw Jones, 1960s singer-songwriter, whose single, 'Dŵr' was the first release on the Sain record label, which he founded with Dafydd Iwan. An early presenter of the seminal Welsh pop program, *Disg a Dawn*, Huw Jones was the head of S4C until late 2005.

31 Of course, this song was released on Ankst, investing this line with an element of ironic self-congratulation.

As I suggested in the previous chapter, the music of Datblygu exposed the state of contemporary Wales in a manner resonant with the 'message rap' aesthetic. Though not strictly rhymed, or delivered in the manner of 'rap', the music of Datblygu certainly created a divide in Welsh pop much as early rap did in American popular music. Similarly, 'Fydd y Chwyldro...' places Welsh poetry in contemporary Welsh youth culture, and together with the Ankst-recorded, inimitable vocal stylings and cultural commentary of Dave Edwards and Datblygu, serves as the root of Welsh-language 'message rap'.[32]

'Hip Hop Poetry in Motion in the Mother Tongue'

With the release in 1997 of *Rhaid i Rywbeth Ddigwydd...* ('Something's Got to Happen'), Y Tystion continued on the trajectory established by Datblygu and Llwybr Llaethog. The songs of Datblygu reflected the experience of a man on the fringes of Welsh society, speaking of the state of rural Wales in the Thatcher years and the societal problems hidden just below the surfaces around him. The techno-based music of Llwybr Llaethog, when paired with the poetry of Ifor ap Glyn, straddled the space between the dominant, urban culture and a minority community in a struggle with its history and its present. Y Tystion emerged to explore another idea of Welshness, within an urban soundscape, employing a vernacular which fluctuates haphazardly between English and Welsh, reflecting at once the influence of American speech on international popular culture, and a challenge to the notion of 'Welsh' popular music.

The message rap, or 'sixties-inspired hip hop nationalism' was traced by Decker back to Gil Scott-Heron and the Last Poets; 'Afro-centric hip hop nationalism' has at its core the desire to define and embrace an African value system in the hope of liberating black culture from western oppression. By emphasizing the importance and commonality of an ancient language, culture and religion, Afro-centric hip hop forms communities around shared ideals and an idealized future. Three songs by Y Tystion show the extent to which Welsh rap has adopted the ideals of American rap, and to what extent it is possible for Wales to join the hip hop nation.

The songs on Y Tystion's first album, *Rhaid i Rywbeth Ddigwydd...* vary from straightforward boasting to politically-tinged rap, and the backing music from drum and bass to funk. It is suggestive of a band 'coming to terms with their "routes"', in the words of Stuart Hall, and illustrating the ease with which Welsh speech may be grafted onto a familiar, dominant soundscape. Y Tystion received regular airplay on Radio Cymru's nighttime slot, *Gang Bangor*,[33] on the strength of their debut album and individual tracks such as 'Gwyddbwyll' (Chess), which has enjoyed an unusually

---

32 Dave Edwards participated in an Ankst recording, *Ll. Ll. vs. T.G.* (Llwybr Llaethog vs. Tŷ Gwydr [Glass House]), wherein he was billed as MC D.R.E. (Ankst 025, 1992). As I suggested earlier, the lyrical content and vocal delivery of much of Datblygu's music would suggest a natural progression into more straightforward rap.

33 Y Tystion were also offered studio time at the BBC to record a session for broadcast on the Radio Cymru afternoon and Saturday program *Ram Jam*.

long shelf-life.[34] When Y Tystion released their second album, *Shrug Off Ya Complex* their challenge to the Welsh media had long been accepted, and their lyrics reflected a much more politically-charged intent. Two songs from the album, 'Shrug Off the Complex' and 'Tryweryn' illustrate the type of Welshness being negotiated in mid-Wales in the last years of the twentieth century.[35]

Gonna shrug off the complex with help from my lyrics
not the result of a match or headlines we catch
a way forward, new century
figuring out how to be free
stop getting impeded, motivation's needed
it comes from within, so let us begin
shrugging off the complex
it's more than a reflex
not afraid to stand out or shout
not part of this British State so we're getting rid of our hate
our country's coming back to us
no bother, no mess, no fuss, no less than we expect
got to direct anger in a positive way
Tystion here join the fray
yeah bang bang beats and rhymes
we're moving ahead of our times

Ie camu 'mlaen byth sbio'n ôl

edrych ymlaen i'r dyfodol
c'mon amser bod yn benderfynol
shrug off the complex
ie hyn, llall, neb dim callach
gormod o leisiau, neb a ddyfeisiau,
eisiau bod yn gryf
a welwn y dydd?

Yeah, stepping forward, not looking back

looking forward to the future
come on, time to be decisive
shrug off the complex
yeah this, that, no one the wiser
too many voices, no one planning
want to be strong
will we ever see the day?

---

34 'Gwyddbwyll' was performed live on S4C on a number of occasions, most notably in the winter of 1997, for which the bassist wore a shirt emblazoned with the words 'Career Move' in hand-lettering, and MC Sleifar wore a similarly-emblazoned shirt bearing the sentiment, 'Media Whore'. In addition to providing a type of distance between Y Tystion and the 'mainstream' Welsh media establishment – a means of retaining Y Tystion's 'street credibility' – it is also evocative of the type of visible commentary employed by Manic Street Preachers to establish a new 'punk ethos' in the early years of their career. Since Y Tystion's S4C appearance in 1997, and since their personnel changes, Y Tystion notably performed 'Gwyddbwyll' for the documentary film *Beautiful Mistake* (Boda/Hummingbird, 2000), with John Cale on viola.

35 'Shrug Off Ya Complex' and 'Tryweryn' (Meredith/Cravos/Lloyd) ©ankst*musik*, from *Shrug Off Ya Complex* (ankst*musik* CD088, 1999). Lyrics reprinted by permission; translations mine.

angen asgwrn cefn Hwlffordd i Wrecsam	need backbone, Haverfordwest to Wrexham
anodd gwneud efo pawb ar y sgam	hard to say with everyone on the scam
dwi'n llwgu, llosgi, trosi a throsi	I'm starving, burning up, tossing and turning
ffili ymlacio cael ein crogi	I can't relax, we're being strangled
angen rheolau ni ein hun	we need our own rules
a ddim cael trin fel *machine*	and not be treated like a machine
angen torri, addysgu hunan hyder	we need to break, learn self-confidence
i ddod â ni allan o'r gwter	to bring us out of the gutter
codi lan nawr, off y llawr	rise up now, off the floor
1,2,3 pwy sy wir yn cyfri?	1,2,3, who's really counting?
hei *John Dough* wyt ti dal o ddifri?	Hey John Dough, are you still serious?
yn gwynebu pwerau mawr	facing major powers
da ni'n cael ein sathru	we're being trampled
fel malwen ar lawr	like a snail on the ground
da ni'n *slow* y'all	we're slow, y'all
sgen ti *blow*? sgen ti chwim?	got blow? got speed?
na! sgen a'i ddim	no! I've got none
cos dwi isio meddwl clir	cause I need a clear mind
i hawlio'n hyn,	to save our rights
mae'n ddigon blaen	it's clear enough
mae'n hollol blaen	it's totally obvious
annibynol, tanddaearol,	independent, underground,
llais chwyldro yn yr ardal	the voice of revolution in the area
yn darlledu i'r genedl	transmitting to the nation
ar donfedd gyfrinachol	on a secret wavelength
dyma Sleifar	here's Sleifar
Bygythiad i'r sefydliad	A threat to the establishment
rebel gweithgar cynllwynio'r chwyldro	a working rebel planning the revolution
fydd Cymru'n ffrwydro	Wales is going to explode
dwi'n aros am fy nghyfle	I'm waiting for my chance
i ymladd am fy hawlie	to fight for my right
dwi'n onest, onest	I'm honest, honest
dwi byth yn cysgu	I never sleep
dal methu cymysgu	I still can't mix it
gyda'r deyrnas	with the Kingdom
sy'n gwneud fi'n wan	that makes me weak
dwi isio gweiddi *damn*	I want to shout damn
dwi isio gwybod pam	I want to know why
rymblo, rymblo ar y stryd	rumble, rumble on the streets
cicio'r *crap* YO ar y cyd	kicking the crap YO together
i mewn i hyn da ni i gyd	we're all into this

| erbyn hyn dio ddim yn fater o gael gelyn | by now it's not a matter of having enemies |
| 'sdim byd *wrong* hefo chwarae'r delyn | there's nothing wrong with playing the harp |

Kick against the system
that's not the point
you'll never get any solace smoking a joint
what's the point
you sit in front of the telly
you sit still, that's when the enemy comes in for the kill
and the best form of defense is attack
and this conviction I will never lack
the people inside of me tire me
get a grip hold onto it
I don't give a shit what goes on inside of it
in the side, genocide
in the sights, suicide
on the bright side
inner sight moments like
shrug off the complex
yeah yeah coming on strong *gyda'r Tystion*
never gonna quit, never going legit
from the wrong side of the law
got a lotta rhymes in store
making the feet raw
making connections, major selections
time for a change in direction
what the hell give us a written constitution
further devolution
voice for the nation
shrug off the complex
everyday life politics over filthy guitar licks
watch out London
don't have to give a reason for keeping on
if our stance is treason
we ain't justifying aggression
we don't have to justify anything
hip hop poetry in motion
streets are in commotion
our mother tongue was stolen
the lies of lay men
they tried to crush the nation
Henry VIII destroyed our religion
burnt our books stole our faith
our history is a set of lies agreed upon

but some had another notion
and over the years planned revolution
shrug off the complex.

The most obvious element of 'Shrug Off the Complex' is its bilingualism. This free use of English raised some concerns when *Shrug Off Ya Complex* was released, that Y Tystion would be the next Welsh band to attempt to break through to the Anglo-American market. This in turn raised certain questions about the marketability of Y Tystion's message. If their original remit was to provide 'hip hop poetry in motion in the mother tongue', why rap in English? And if they sought to provide Welsh culture with its own indigenous hip hop, of what relevance would an exploration of contemporary Wales be to a market already over-saturated with all manner of rap, indigenous and otherwise?

The lyrics to 'Shrug Off the Complex' reveal a number of issues affecting the continuing process of Welshness. First, Wales was entering the new century with a newly-formed, devolved governmental body in Cardiff. The 'complex' in question derives in part from centuries of English rule, of enforced assimilation into English culture, and of the gradual disappearance of the native Welsh language. The lack of cultural self-confidence perceptible in Wales was reflected on a wider scale by the low voter participation in the referendum for the Welsh Assembly in 1997, and by the extremely close margin by which the campaign was won.[36] Y Tystion here are inciting the Welsh people to seize the opportunity to create a modern Wales in the new century, and to meet the challenges of her political future with confidence.

'Shrug Off the Complex' is a Welsh message rap for the turn of the century: mobilizing a community, stating alternative political ideals, utilizing anti-establishment rhetoric. But it is also something approaching a different kind of hip hop nationalism: where the template is Afrocentric, here it is pan-Welsh. First of all, there are the linguistic elements of the rap: English and Welsh, interchangeable, informal, peppered with slang, percussed with poetry. Second, there is the acknowledgment of a common history, before the linguistic divide – 'our mother tongue was stolen / the lies of laymen / they tried to crush the nation'; of a common religion – 'Henry VIII destroyed our religion / burnt our books stole our faith'; and the self-implication in the eradication of a common culture – 'our history is a set of lies agreed upon'. This is not defining a common history as nostalgic yearning, but rather the acknowledgement of a former strength of character and a nation once unified against the encroaching influence of a more powerful culture. Where ancient Egypt is the focus of Afrocentric hip hop nationalism, Wales before the Act of Union is here the focus of pan-Welsh hip hop nationalism. The effect is the same: seeking to instill in a community the sense of transcendence beyond oppression, and seeking to encourage within that community the strength to create a new future.

The song 'Tryweryn' continues in the same pan-Welsh vein, using a moment in history to negotiate a sense of contemporary Welshness.

---

36 The measure to create a National Assembly for Wales was passed by a margin of 50.3% to 49.7% (559,429 to 552, 698). The total voter turnout was estimated at 51.3% of the population.

Tystion unwaith eto'n glanio	Tystion landing again
cymryd bwell at *grand piano*	taking an axe to a grand piano
arllwys petrol drosto a'i danio	cover it in petrol and ignite
tân yw dy ffrind gore yn y byd	fire is your best friend in the world
pan yn dywyll ag oer mae'n dy gadw yn glud	when it's cold and dark it keeps you warm
pridd – rhaid ei barchu pan yn tyfu a phlannu	soil – got to respect it when you're growing and planting
neu yn codi dŷ arni	or building your house on it
dŵr yw rhodd y cymyle i dy gadw rhag syched	water is a gift from the clouds to keep you from thirst
a golchi dy gyhyrau	and to wash your muscles
ond weithiau mae'r elfennau yn gallu bod dy elyn	but sometimes the elements are your enemy
pan fod dŵr yn boddi'r dyffryn	when the water drowned the valley
o'n i heb fy ngeni ond dwi'n cofio Tryweryn	I wasn't even born but I remember Tryweryn
watsiwch allan	watch out
rhyddiaeth, llenyddiaeth	prose, literature
da ni'n bwydo'r arddull	we're feeding the style of
y dull ôl-foderniaeth	the post-modern condition
dim sylw academaidd	no academic observation
dim heddlu iaith ar daith	no language police in the area
sawl gwaith ma nhw'n myggio	how many times will they mug
ein rhaglenni teledu hollol amherthnasol	our totally irrelevant television programs
sdim angen bod yn glyfar medde Sleifar a fi	there's no need to be clever say Sleifar and me
jyst dod 'mlaen â'r busnes o greu gwlad newydd	just get on with the business of creating a new country
da ni ar agor rhywbryd	we're open some time
da ni'n cofio Tryweryn	we remember Tryweryn
mae na barch i Llywelyn	there's respect for Llywelyn
mae'r haf yn felyn	the summer is yellow
dwi'n clywed tannau'r delyn	I can hear harp strings
dim ond trwy gyfathrebu yr allwn ddehongli	only through communication can we understand
bob peth sy wedi digwydd	everything that's happened
a mwynhau agor drysau newydd	and enjoy opening new doors
trwy gwrando, rhesymu	by listening and reasoning
fe gawn wared o'r gorthrwm	we'll get rid of oppression
dysgwn, ennillwn	we'll learn, we'll win
diffaith fydd y pastwn	the club will be useless
mae'n hen bryd i hanes Cymru	it's high time that the history of Wales
gael y llwyfan mae hi'n ei haeddu	gets the platform it deserves
ie cofiwch Dryweryn	yeah, remember Tryweryn

gwrthsafiad gan y werin	resistance by the people
gweld y dyfodol mae'n gwella yn flynyddol	see the future improving every year
ein dwylo ar y llyw	our hands on the wheel
mae'n pobl ni yn driw	our people faithful
dim pennau yn y niwl	no heads in the clouds
ni 'di cyrraedd pen y rhiw	we've reached the summit
lawr yr allt o hyn ymlaen	it's downhill from now on
mae'r sgwennu ar y maen	it's written on the stone
ni angen craen	we need a crane
tyrd 'laen	come on
mae'r ffiws yn mynd yn fyr	the fuse is getting short
a dwi'n gweld trwy y triciau budr	and I see through the dirty tricks
fel haen o wydr	like a pane of glass
rhegi dan fy anadl	swearing under my breath
dwi'n benderfynol fel Saunders a DJ	I'm decisive like Saunders and D.J.
yn llosgi lawr yr hen ysgol	burning down the old school
mae'r hadau wedi hau	the seeds have been sown
sdim ffiniau i'n syniadau	our ideas know no bounds
rhwystrau i fewn i eiriau	turn hindrances into words
sianeli diffaith i fewn i odlau	channel devastation into rhymes
dwi'n cofio tre fechan yn '62	I remember a small town in '62
cofiwch Tryweryn, gwrthsafiad gan y werin.	remember Tryweryn, resistance from the people.

The 1957 Parliamentary bill to drown the valley of Tryweryn is used here by Y Tystion as a cautionary tale. The English decision to drown the valley was made without regard for the cultural implications of the loss of an entire community of Welsh speakers. The implications of such a loss should have been clear; but from the sense of powerlessness a more radical community was formed, and operated under the aegis of *Cymdeithas yr Iaith*. Tystion refer to another moment of radical change in Welsh political history, when in 1936 three leading members of *Plaid Cymru*, Saunders Lewis, Reverend Lewis Valentine, and D.J. Williams, set fire to an RAF bombing school in the Llŷn Peninsula, then approached the authorities and claimed responsibility for the action. The bombing school was seen as a threat to the Welsh farming community, though no amount of local protest would prevent its being built. The case was tried not in Wales, but in the Old Bailey, and the three *Plaid Cymru* members were imprisoned for nine months. Y Tystion cite this moment in Welsh history as the inspiration for contemporary radical Welsh politics and suggest a pattern of subversion: the bombing school fire presaged the campaign of *Meibion Glyndŵr* half a century later. The threat to Welsh communities in both instances was significantly linguistic: 'swearing to myself / I'm decisive like Saunders and D.J. / when they burnt down the old school / the seeds have been sown / our ideas know no bounds / channel hindrances into words'.

The power of the Welsh community is in its words – in chapel, in schools, in literary and musical traditions. It is the ability to crystallize an otherwise disempowering event into words, scribbled or uttered in a language impenetrable by those whose actions intend damage, which re-empowers a minority community such as the Welsh. And when such a community recognizes similar struggles in the lived experience of other communities, a sympathetic network among them further increases the sense of self-empowerment, and of menace to the dominant order. For in much the same way that the black communities in the United States mobilized in the 1960s to demand civil rights, so did the Welsh communities mobilize to demand rights of their own. In the first four decades of Welsh popular music history, the sense of connection between Welsh people and aggrieved communities throughout the world has been nurtured and explored in the adaptation of a variety of musical styles and aesthetics.[37] George Lipsitz defines this type of network as a 'family of resemblance', a central idea to the discussion of Wales' place in the hip hop nation.

The Hip Hop Nation as Family of Resemblance

George Lipsitz introduced the idea of families of resemblance in his study of Hispanic musicians in Los Angeles: [38]

> In many areas of cultural production, but especially in popular music, organic intellectuals within the Los Angeles community pursued a strategy of self-presentation that brought their unique and distinctive cultural traditions into the mainstream of mass popular culture. Neither assimilationist nor separatist, they played on 'families of resemblance' – similarities to the experience and culture of other groups – to fashion a 'unity of disunity'. In that way, they sought to make alliances with other groups by cultivating the ways in which their particular experiences spoke with special authority about the ideas and alienations felt by others. They used the techniques and sensibilities of postmodernism to build a 'historical bloc' of oppositional groups united in ideas and intentions if not experience.[39]

The organic intellectuals in Lipsitz' study are much like the organic intellectuals Decker mentions in his study of hip hop nationalism. They are persons located in historically marginalized communities within a dominant culture, and they exploit their own marginalization as a means of self-empowerment. Numerous examples may be cited of Welsh musicians allying themselves with other 'alienated' musical communities through the appropriation of their musical styles: Geraint Jarman is one notable example, and Y Tystion are another.

---

37 In 1999, under the aegis of the Aberystwyth-based organization *Ein Gilydd* (Each Other), Y Tystion participated in a cultural exchange tour with popular musicians from the Basque Country. Ein Gilydd sought to connect Welsh musicians with those of smaller societies around the world. These exchanges were organized by Meic Llewellyn, whose article, 'Popular Music in the Welsh Language and the Affirmation of Youth Identities', *Popular Music* 19/3 (October 2000): 319–39, mentions Y Tystion and others with regard to counter-hegemonic strategies.

38 George Lipstiz, 'Cruising Around the Historical Bloc'.

39 Ibid., p. 160.

In the 1980s and 1990s the enormous variety of musical styles incorporated into the Welsh pop music scene was indicative of the omnipresence of Anglo-American popular culture, and it was also indicative of a continuing search for a Welsh musical and cultural identity.[40] The existence of Welsh-language radio and television provided the market for Welsh popular music, and it appeared at times that any song recorded in the Welsh language would be guaranteed an audience, regardless of the standard of musicianship. Yet if the Welsh media did not cater for their younger audiences, the younger audiences would turn to the English-language media for the type of music they wanted to consume. One subtext to the history of Welsh popular music has undoubtedly been the desire to create for the Welsh audience a Welsh-language equivalent of popular contemporary Anglo-American bands. The relative successes or failures of such endeavors have already been outlined; in the case of Y Tystion, though their music may have been an amalgamation of hip hop styles, their lyrics were clearly designed to encourage reflection, and it is the nature of their 'message rap' which links them to African-American hip hop, and the international hip hop nation.

The civil rights movement in the 1960s served as a symbolic inspiration for the Welsh Language Society, and contemporary music on both sides of the Atlantic was the vehicle for the expression of an international desire for social change. In the decades which followed, the political content of popular music in general may have become much more location-specific, but the messages could be adapted to suit cultural needs elsewhere. In the late-1980s and 1990s, the sound of a particular kind of rap became the signifier of the expression of cultural anger. Regardless of the language in which it was rapped, the message could be inferred and adopted into similarly aggrieved communities.

The effect of this kind of cross-cultural family of resemblance on the dominant Anglo-American popular culture is interesting to consider. As Lipsitz states:

> Inter-referentiality, inter-textuality, juxtaposition of multiple realities, and bifocality characterize the music of Chicano rock-and-roll musicians from Los Angeles, and explain much of its internal significance to the Mexican-American community. Yet this music was not intended solely as an internal form of expression. Its very identity as a part of mass popular culture, its uneasy dialogue between the Anglo and Chicano worlds, and its complicated system of codings and references express a desire to reach out to others to form a historical bloc capable of posing a counter-hegemony to the domination of today. One of the singular successes of this music has been its ability to build that alliance, to touch members of other groups on the strength of its families of resemblance to the alienation and oppressions of people outside the *barrio*.[41]

---

40 This is a topic which I explore in much greater detail in *Resemblances and Differences: Welsh Popular Music and the Postmodern Condition* (unpublished MA thesis, Cardiff University, 1998), an exploration of the variety of musical styles available in the Welsh market, and the implications of those styles on the development of a modern sense of 'Welshness'.

41 Lipsitz, 'Cruising Around the Historical Bloc', p. 173.

There are certain signifiers which would be of 'internal significance' to the Welsh-speaking audience – references to previous struggles, historical figures, cultural traditions. The 'uneasy dialogue' between Wales and the Anglo-American world has informed the majority of Welsh popular music of the last four decades, for the greatest threat to Welsh culture has been the English language. Playing on the margins of the Anglo-American mainstream while appropriating its most audible cultural referents, and relaying political messages through a language impenetrable by the cultural dominant, are all means by which Welsh popular music retains its political roots. This kind of 'complicated system of codings and references' can reach out most directly to members of other minority-language populations, and build alliances based on linguistic sympathies. It is this kind of family of resemblance which enables minority-language communities to enact counter-hegemonic strategies.

In their last recording, *Hen Gelwydd Prydain Newydd* (New Britain's Old Lie),[42] Y Tystion returned to their political roots and explored the position of Wales at the turn of the millennium. There is a palpable anger pervading *Hen Gelwydd Prydain Newydd*, from the cover photographs of Y Tystion carrying placards with various slogans drawn from the tracks within – 'Un Bobl, Dwy Iaith, Un Genedl' (One People, Two Languages, One Nation); 'Wales is Over – If You Want It'; 'Ddoe O'n I'n Brotestwr; Heddiw Dwi'n Derfysgwr' (Yesterday I was a Protester; Today I'm a Terrorist'). One track, 'Y Byd Hip Hop vs Y Byd Cymraeg' (The Hip Hop World vs the Welsh World)[43] serves as a final example of the uneasy dialogue between Wales and Anglo-American culture, and suggests a placement for Wales in the 'hip hop nation'.

Yo! Dwi'n byw ar y blaned *hip hop*	Yo! I'm living on planet hip hop
Ond paid galw fi'n *boyo*	But don't call me boyo
Cos dwi ishe'r ddau blaned wrthdaro	Cos I want the two planets to clash
Er mwyn cynnal unrhyw iaith	In order to support any language
Rhaid cyfoethogi ac ychwanegu at eu diwylliant	You must enrich and add to their culture
Dim jyst core, oedfa'r bore a cherdd dant	Not just choirs, morning meetings and *cerdd dant*
Dwi ishe gweld gwelliant	I want to see improvement
Dim cynhyrchwyr teledu di-dalent	No talentless television producers
Yn trin artistiaid fel bechgyn *rent*	Treating artists like rent boys
Ym mynwent diwydiant y byd adloniant	In the graveyard of the entertainment industry
Ra ra rant am gant punt wythdeg – *Stop!*	Ra ra ra rant for a hundred and eighty pounds – Stop!

---

42 Y Tystion, *Hen Gelwydd Prydain Newydd* (ankst*musik* CD093, 2000). Y Tystion's performance at the Pembrokeshire Eisteddfod of 2002 ended, somewhat abruptly, with the announcement that the band were breaking up.

43 'Y Byd Hip Hop vs Y Byd Gymraeg' (Cravos/Jenkins/Mackay/Pegg), recorded for the John Peel Show 10 February 2000, Maida Vale, London. Lyrics reprinted by permission; translation mine.

Dwi'n caru'r Gymraeg gymaint	I love Welsh so much
A dwi'n caru'r byd *hip hop*	And I love the world of hip hop
Heb anghofio be' dwi'n gwbod	Without forgetting what I know
Jyst yn dilyn fy nghydwybod.	Just following my conscience.
Yr iaith fain yn erbyn Tafod y Ddraig	The thin language[44] against *Tafod y Ddraig*[45]
Y Blaned Hip Hop yn erbyn y blaned Gymraeg	The Hip Hop Planet against the Welsh Planet
Cyfwelwyr yn cyfweld â chyfwelwyr	Interviewers interviewing interviewers
Brodyr a chwiorydd lle mae'r synnwyr?	Brothers and sisters, where's the sense?
I gynnal ein gwlad a'n iaith	To support our country and our language
Rhaid symud gyda'r rhaglen	We've got to move with the program
Dwi'n parchu ein hunaniaeth	I respect our identity
Ond dwi ishe popeth yn fy mamiaith	But I want everything in my mother tongue
Dwi'n wyn, mae'n ffaith,	I'm white, it's a fact,
Ond dyma neges i'r rhai sy'n meddwl	But here's a message to those who think
Na all dyn gwyn rapio –	A white man can't rap –
Dyma'r farn cul o feddwl	Here's a narrow way of thinking
Sy'n gyfystyr â na all ddyn du	That's the same as saying a black man
Ganu opera neu chware yn y byd roc,	Can't sing opera or play rock
Dwi'n wyn, dwi'n Gymraeg, *ad hoc*,	I'm white, I speak Welsh, *ad hoc*,
Ond ma gen i'r *skillz*,	But I've got the skills
Da ni'n symudiad ymarferol,	We're a practical movement,
Byddarol,	Deafening,
Ma nhw'n dweud bod ni'n herfeiddiol	They say we're defiant
Ond dwi wedi cael llond bol	But I've had enough
Ar anallu, apathi a diogi	Of inability, apathy and idleness
Er mwyn goroesi rhaid i ni gyfaddasu	In order to survive we've got to adapt
Er mwyn cynyddu a thyfu.	In order to increase and grow.
Ie, da ni'n arbrofol,	Yeah, we're experimental,
Hanfodol,	Essential,
Da ni'n ddigidol,	We're digital,
Reel to reel	Reel to reel
Dim strach – lawr gyda John Peel	No bother – down with John Peel
Reel to reel,	Reel to reel,

---

44 English.

45 *Tafod y Ddraig* (The Dragon's Tongue), the newsletter produced by *Cymdeithas yr Iaith Gymraeg*.

Bellach da ni'n lot cryfach,	Furthermore we're a lot stronger,
Yo G! Lle wyt ti?	Yo G! Where are you?
Allan o'r hen wlad fach	Out of the little old country
Dim strach.	No bother.

The fact that 'Y Byd Hip Hop vs Y Byd Cymraeg' was recorded for a national, British, audience presents an interesting paradox, for it is clearly a song addressed to the Welsh audience. It is a challenge to the Welsh media and the Welsh establishment to allow for a further modernization of the Welsh language, and it is a recognition of the power available to the Welsh-language community via the adaptation of a dominant cultural form. A general audience interest in hip hop would suggest an acceptance of the form in the medium of any language; the message behind 'Y Byd Hip Hop vs Y Byd Cymraeg' is that the purveyors of Welsh culture should be similarly open-minded in their acceptance of an expression of Welshness within a 'black', urban musical context.

Samples play an obviously central role in the construction of rap. In the case of Public Enemy, samples from speeches by Malcolm X and Martin Luther King serve to ground their music in an immediately-identifiable political ideology; Y Tystion take samples from Radio Cymru and Saunders Lewis broadcasts, and musical support from prominent folk musicians such as Ceri Rhys Matthews (pipes) and Julie Murphy (voice) similarly ground them in an immediately-identifiable 'Welshness'.[46] That Welshness can be inferred in this context is understandable; an interesting question to ask is how Welshness could be inferred from a context in which an immediately-identifiable sample from another culture were woven into the rap fabric. Without some reference to Wales or the Welsh language, this would be a difficult task, which leads us to another problem addressed by Lipsitz:

Chicano musicians had to assume a bifocal perspective as a matter of self-respect. The dominant culture already imposed an identity on them. Regardless of their personal characteristics, Anglo stereotypes about Chicanos and their culture influenced the ways in which Mexican-Americans were received outside of the *barrio*, and they had to be aware of the limits imposed upon them by that cultural domination. But simply to accept the stereotypes would necessitate denying one's own vision. Prevented from defining themselves because of pervasive discrimination and prejudice, but unwilling to leave the work of definition to others, they adopted a bifocal perspective that acknowledged but did not accept the majority culture's images of Chicanos. They sought outside recognition and success, but on their own terms.[47]

---

46 Julie Murphy is the lead singer of the folk band Fernhill; Ceri Rhys Matthews is their guitarist/piper. While they have been enormously successful in international folk terms, it is important to note that Murphy – and indeed three-fifths of Fernhill – is English. Fernhill presents the most recent example of a group of prominent musicians who adopted the Welsh language for artistic expression.

47 Lipsitz, 'Cruising Around the Historical Bloc', p. 165. This issue of bifocality is of particular relevance in the following chapter on Welsh musicians in the Anglo-American market.

In both 'Shrug Off the Complex' and 'Tryweryn', there is reference to a Welsh cultural stereotype: 'there's nothing wrong with playing the harp'; and 'I can hear harp strings'. It is at once an acknowledgment of a particular preconception of Welsh musical life, and a common cultural referent. Y Tystion accept the stereotype and play with it.[48] The desire of a dominant culture to maintain control over its peripheries is suggested by Lipsitz in the passage above; here Y Tystion are negating any preconceived notion of Welsh music simply through the use of a non-indigenous urban musical construction. By so doing, they are aligning themselves with the sounds of urban change throughout the world, and are bringing Wales into a larger family of resemblance, the hip hop nation.

There is a delicate balance in Welsh pop between urban and rural; even more precarious is the balance between Welsh and English. Y Tystion's use of English reflects at once the natural flow of spoken language in some parts of Wales and the lack of vernacular terminology for certain aspects of contemporary youth culture, such as sex and drugs. An attempt at creating a modern vernacular in the Welsh language is a continuation of the political process begun by *Cymdeithas yr Iaith* in the 1960s; the close relationship between the *Cymdeithas* and popular music continues to provide contemporary Welsh society with the tools it needs to nurture younger generations of Welsh speakers. The omnipresence of the hip hop nation cannot be ignored. Y Tystion are claiming that Welsh culture needs to adapt and domesticate hip hop, thereby growing beyond the musical boundaries which have constrained the expression of political and social urgency in contemporary Wales.

---

48 It is significant also that the more recent Welsh hip-hop collective, Pep le Pew, used a sample of the harp to ground their song, 'Dysgwch am y Doethion', from their debut album *Y Da, Y Drwg ac yr Hyll* (The Good, The Bad and the Ugly) (MPLP 002, 2001), in an ironic Welshness. Their juxtaposition of the arcadian (harp), the urban (hip hop) and the rural (Pep le Pew hail from the area around Porthmadog) represents a distillation of the process of Welsh popular music from the 1960s to the present day.

Chapter Fourteen

Dis-Located: Welsh Musicians in the Anglo-American Market

Figure 14.1   Gruff Rhys and Dafydd Ieuan of Super Furry Animals

The previous four case studies were concerned with expressions of Welshness at distinct moments in the temporal arc of Welsh pop. Those expressions of Welshness were articulated from within the geographical boundaries of Wales, at the heart of the 'location' of Welsh popular music. The subtext to the previous four case studies, and to the overall cultural history of Welsh popular music, has been one of self-definition – a community's self-definition based on a sense of 'home', of belonging, of entitlement, of territoriality. This case study considers the negotiations of Welshness at the close of the twentieth century, as expressed through the medium of the English language, from within the heart of the Anglo-American cultural dominant. This challenges that subtext to Welsh popular music, as well as the (linguistic) expressions of Welshness examined earlier.

The linguistic border-crossings mentioned in previous chapters have provided another subtext to the cultural history of Welsh pop. Politically and culturally, the symbolic motion from the Welsh margins to the Anglophone center has contested the very formation of Welsh identity negotiated through popular music in the past fifty years. Because this Welshness has been determined in opposition to Englishness – because this Welshness has in part celebrated its 'otherness' to the Anglo-American mainstream culture – a shift in linguistic loyalty reveals fissures in the identity construction. Two bilingual Welsh bands from the 1990s, Catatonia and Super Furry Animals, challenged these assumptions: in their linguistic remits, in their relationship to the Welsh popular music tradition, and for their contributions to mainstream Anglo-American popular culture.

'Cool Cymru'

It was a chronological coincidence that the mainstream success of the bilingual bands Catatonia and Super Furry Animals coincided with that of Anglo-Welsh bands Manic Street Preachers and Stereophonics. Nevertheless the Anglo-American (English) marketing machine needed to explain it and control it, and the term 'Cool Cymru' found its way into the press as an umbrella image describing the sudden and almost simultaneous emergence of four popular bands from Wales.[1] That this coincided rather neatly with the Labour government's movement toward devolution – ultimately resulting in National Assemblies for Wales and Northern Ireland, and the Scottish Parliament – was a matter of no little convenience. But more importantly, these four bands, two from the Welsh tradition and two from the Anglo-American tradition, were defined, from outside their community, as collaborators in a single cultural phenomenon. In previous decades they would have been defined, from within their community, as representing different traditions, and from outside their community, grudgingly if at all.

As recently as 1996 the idea of 'Welsh culture' was discussed in the general British press as nonexistent, as exemplified in the following article in *Scotland on Sunday*:

> ... And what about singers? The Welsh love music, but who have they shared with the wider world? Tom Jones – a tax exile with a tight perm and tighter trousers. Writing? Dylan Thomas, perhaps, and he died in 1953. Film? *How Green Was My Valley*, a tremendous example of Hollywood schmaltz.
>
> Such is the dismal fate of all Welsh culture. Everything from comedy to literature is at best ridiculed and at worst ignored. Even at a time when all things Celtic are cool and Scotland and Ireland are enjoying a cultural renaissance, Wales cowers without a shred of credibility. [...]
>
> 'The Welsh have never made any significant contribution to any branch of knowledge, culture or entertainment,' spat the novelist and critic A.N. Wilson in the *London Evening Standard*. 'They have no architecture, no gastronomic tradition and, since the Middle Ages, no literature worthy of the name. Even their religion, Calvinistic Methodism, is boring.

---

1   The term 'Cool Britannia' was coined at the beginning of Tony Blair's administration, as a 'rebranding of Britain'. This coincided with the rise of 'Britpop', discussed below. For more on Blair and the rise and fall of Britpop, see John Harris, *The Last Party* (London: Fourth Estate, 2003).

'The thing about Welsh culture,' says the (Irish) television producer, 'is that there isn't one. Wales is suffering from the same problem as the Ulster Unionists. It is a culture in retreat, scrambling around to find an identity and failing.'[2]

This passage illustrates that the impenetrability of the Welsh language has been an insurmountable obstacle to the British public's understanding of the organic development of Welsh culture. Anglophone Welsh culture was derided largely because of its geographic marginality to the center of British culture, and out of ignorance of the longer, parallel Welsh-language literary and poetic traditions.

Although Manic Street Preachers had, by the time this article was published, already released four albums,[3] their output was not enough to suggest to the media that Wales was in the process of any kind of cultural revival.[4] After Stereophonics released *Word Gets Around* (V2 Music, 1997) the mention of 'Wales' in the same sentence as 'pop music' became less a cause for bemusement than for genuine surprise. When formerly Welsh-language bands signed major label contracts – Gorky's Zygotic Mynci with Mercury (subsequently dropped); Catatonia with Blanco y Negro (a subsidiary of Warner Brothers); and Super Furry Animals with Creation (influential home of Oasis) – Wales' two little-acknowledged cultural traditions came to the attention of the British mainstream press. Although Welsh-language bands had been championed by John Peel on Radio One since the 1970s, it was not until three of the more popular Welsh bands of the 1990s emerged in the Anglophone market that the existence of Welsh popular music was ever given any serious notice.

Of course, there was an English precedent for Cool Cymru. 'Britpop' was a similarly media-contrived term denoting a kind of 'rebirth' of British (English) popular music, heralded by a kind of postmodern plundering of 1960s British pop by bands such as Oasis, whose *Definitely Maybe* (Creation, 1994) and *(What's the Story) Morning Glory* (Creation, 1995) signalled a return to melody-based pop tunes (and an antidote to American grunge); and Blur, whose *Modern Life Is Rubbish* (Food, 1993) and *Parklife* (Food, 1994) encapsulated a particular kind of Englishness through the incorporation of knowing references to contemporary popular culture.[5] The first years of Blair's New Labour government, and the palpable sense of social

---

2   Gillian Harris, 'Little to Harp On About', *Scotland on Sunday*, 11 August, 1996.

3   *Generation Terrorists* (Columbia, 1992), *Gold Against the Soul* (Columbia, 1993), *The Holy Bible* (Columbia, 1994), *Everything Must Go* (Epic, 1996).

4   Indeed, the disappearance (and presumed death) of Manic Street Preachers lyricist Richey Edwards on 1 February 1995 provoked some worry that Wales was about to lose the only band which showed any promise of dispelling the 'Welsh culture' myth. After the band returned to the studio as a trio, however, to record *Everything Must Go,* they were rewarded with three Brit Awards, for Best Live Act, Best Single ('A Design for Life') and Best Album.

5   For further references to Englishness and Britpop see Andy Bennett, '"Sitting in an English Garden": Representations of "Britishness" in the Songs of the Beatles and 1990s Britpop Groups', in Ian Englis, ed., *The Beatles, Popular Music and Society: A Thousand Voices* (Houndmills, Basingstoke and London: Macmillan Press, 2000): 189–206; Martin Cloonan, 'State of the Nation: "Englishness", Pop, and Politics in the 1990s', *Popular Music and Society* 21/2 (1997): 47–69; and Allan Moore, *Rock: The Primary Text* (Aldershot: Ashgate, 2001).

change which accompanied the change in administration, inspired references to 'Cool Britannia'.[6] In a symbolic gesture toward acknowledging the distinction between Welsh and English cultures, 'Cool Cymru' was also meant to inspire a certain sense of national pride; but the term itself is problematic, and raises certain questions about the presumed homogeneity of Welsh and Anglophone musical traditions.

This question of 'traditions' must be re-addressed, for it seems to lie at the heart of the moniker 'Cool Cymru'. If a mainstream marketing technique was created in order to categorize a particular trend in 'Welsh' popular music, is there any substance to the suggestion that the four bands in question are in some way similar? Do they share any common roots or any common, 'Welsh', cultural referents? Is there something inherently 'Welsh' in the music of Stereophonics, Manic Street Preachers, Catatonia and Super Furry Animals? Given that Anglo-Welsh popular music did not need to go through a period of translation and adaptation, of indigenization, as did Welsh-language popular music, Anglo-Welsh popular music was, generally speaking, historically more contemporaneous with Anglo-American popular music, and indeed was part of the same cultural process. Welsh-language popular music, though adapting and translating Anglo-American styles, followed its own trajectory, intersecting at certain points with Anglo-American popular music, but generally developing at a different cultural pace. Catatonia and Super Furry Animals are two examples of such a cultural collision, and their relationship to Stereophonics and Manic Street Preachers suggests a kind of fluidity to the idea of 'Welshness'.

Manic Street Preachers and Stereophonics emerged from the guitar-rock tradition of British popular music. Sterophonics' musical aesthetic is somewhat more mainstream than that of Manic Street Preachers, but both groups share a particular political agenda forged in the mining communities of the South Wales valleys. The Stereophonics do not comment about specific moments in Welsh history, but they ally themselves with Anglo-Welsh culture and draw attention to their roots in Cwmaman, most notably by dedicating their album *Word Gets Around* to their home village,[7] and through their collaboration with local hero Tom Jones.[8] But a type of Welshness permeates the Manic Street Preachers' 'breakthrough' album, *This Is My Truth Tell Me Yours* (1998).[9] The record title is taken from a quote by Aneurin Bevan, the Welsh Labour politician and architect of the British National Health system; the single, 'If

---

    6   And certainly the appearance of Noel Gallagher from Oasis at a party at 10 Downing Street was an endorsement of Blair's 'street credibility'.

    7   Stereophonics, *Word Gets Around* (V2 Music, 1997). The liner notes include the message 'this record is dedicated to the people of Cwmaman – "keep the village alive"'.

    8   Tom Jones, *Reload* (Gut Records, 1999) includes collaborations with Stereophonics ('Mama Told Me Not to Come'), James Dean Bradfield of Manic Street Preachers ('I'm Left, You're Right, She's Gone'), and Cerys Matthews from Catatonia ('Baby, It's Cold Outside').

    9   By 'breakthrough' I refer primarily to commercial marketability. The popularity of *This Is My Truth Tell Me Yours* is due in large part to its accessibility; but this 'accessibility' prompted Manic Street Preachers to all but disown the album in the period immediately preceding the release of their subsequent album, *Know Your Enemy* (2001). The title of the latter album is self-reflexive, suggesting that the band were aware that they were in some way 'selling out', pandering to public taste and neglecting their more 'post-punk' aesthetic. Their political dedication, however, remained unchanged.

You Tolerate This Your Children Will Be Next', concerns the volunteers from Wales who fought against Franco in the International Brigade; 'Ready for Drowning' refers to the village of Tryweryn; and, more visibly, the album sleeve features a poem by Anglo-Welsh poet, R.S. Thomas.[10] The Manics comment on the history and politics of their country without drawing attention to her linguistic divide, yet draw on Welsh politics to locate themselves culturally in Anglo-Welsh South Wales. There is thus an inherent political agenda in the music of Sterophonics and Manic Street Preachers, for they do not pretend to belong to any culture, or any community, other than Wales. Their Welshness is as much a fact of their music as the Welsh language is to the agents of Welsh pop. The division between the two traditions, Anglo-Welsh and Welsh, is one grafted from within the habitus which these traditions share.

The response by the Welsh media to Cool Cymru presents a number of interesting contradictions. Cool Cymru emerged at a time when Radio Cymru had relaxed its language policy, and began integrating English-language songs into certain youth-oriented programs throughout the day. This provided a platform for the inclusion of Anglophone Welsh bands such as Stereophonics and Manic Street Preachers, which in turn provided Radio Cymru with justification for playing them – namely, the fact that they are *Welsh* bands. The terminology introduced earlier – the label *Y Sîn Roc Gymraeg* (the Welsh-language Rock Scene) – was soon replaced in the media by the more all-encompassing *Sîn Roc Cymru* (Wales' Rock Scene), to negate any linguistic exclusion, and to lay equal claim to the successes of bands active in both English and Welsh. This is in one sense a negation of the cultural and political 'roots' which spawned the 'scene' in the 1960s; but it is also an acknowledgment of the difficulties inherent in maintaining linguistic purity in the context of a global cultural marketplace. The desire to support 'local' talent (defining Wales as the locality) superceded the desire to insist on linguistic difference.

The acceptance into the Anglo-American mainstream of bands such as Gorky's Zygotic Mynci, Catatonia and Super Furry Animals also presented the Welsh establishment with a number of difficulties. Though there was a desire to showcase young talent at annual events such as the Cnapan Festival and the National Eisteddfod, the linguistic basis for the founding of such festivals was impossible to ignore. The Welsh weekly papers of the time provide a catalogue of debates and public arguments over the right of Radio Cymru and S4C to include Anglophone Welsh bands in their entertainment. The furore surrounding Super Furry Animals' appearance at the National Eisteddfod at Llandeilo in 1996 was similarly charted in the weekly and

---

10 R.S. Thomas, 'Reflections', from *No Truce with the Furies* (Tarset: Bloodaxe Books, 1995), p. 31, quoted in The Manic Street Preachers, *This Is My Truth Tell Me Yours* (Epic, 1998):

The furies are at home / in the mirror; it is their address. / Even the clearest water, / if deep enough can drown.

Never think to surprise them. / Your face approaching ever / so friendly is the white flag / they ignore. There is no truce

with the furies. A mirror's temperature / is always at zero. It is ice / in the veins. Its camera / is an x-ray. It is a chalice

held out to you in / silent communion, where gaspingly / you partake of a shifting / identity never your own.

monthly Welsh press. Following their appearance at Cnapan, where they angered a number of audience members by singing in English, Super Furry Animals were told that they could not sing in English on the *maes*, in keeping with the language rules of the National Eisteddfod. The group therefore whistled all their English songs, having provided for the audience lyric sheets with the songs' words in Welsh, English and Japanese, encouraging the audience to sing in whichever language they chose.[11] 'Welsh' bands such as Stereophonics and Manic Street Preachers would never have been invited to perform at the Cnapan or the Eisteddfod; the expectation that Catatonia and Super Furry Animals would perform for a Welsh-language audience stems from their prior engagement with the Welsh musical community. The fact that their current incarnation was focused more on contributing to the Anglo-American musical community is what created the difficulty for the Welsh media during the height of the 'Cool Cymru' period. Catatonia and Super Furry Animals emerged from within the Welsh musical community, and negotiate their Welshness from the other side of their cultural borders.

Y Cyrff into Catatonia

One of the more popular and influential groups on the Ankst roster was Y Cyrff (The Bodies), a quartet from Llanrwst. Theirs was a sound influenced by The Clash, The Fall and Echo and the Bunnymen, and their lyrics were informed by life in North Wales during the Thatcher years. They enjoyed a brief period of extensive television exposure, European concerts, and a dedicated, mixed-language, following. By the time they disbanded in 1992 they had recorded some of the most powerful pop songs in the Welsh language,[12] though mainstream interest had eluded them until the release of their first and final full-length recording, *Llawenydd Heb Ddiwedd* (Endless Joy).[13] Though perhaps biased, the Welsh-language press viewed Y Cyrff as the source of hope for a struggling Welsh pop scene, and their recordings were generally heralded as landmarks in Welsh cultural production:

> Does yna ddim (a fuodd yna erioed) grwp tebyg i'r Cyrff yn Gymraeg. Weithiau mae eu hannibyniaeth yn edrych fel styfnigrwydd, eu hymddygiad ar lwyfan yn gyfuniad peryglus o drais ac angerdd, a'u hyder yn gallu hudo a gelyniaethu am yn ail. Ond, yn wahanol i'r grwpiau eraill, mae'r caneuon wastad wedi bod yn *fyw*, yn ddatganiadau cig a gwaed yn herio'r difaterwch o'u cwmpas….
>
> Fel pob record bwysig arall ym myd canu cyfoes, mae'r cyfan [o *Lawenydd Heb Ddiwedd*] yn gymysgedd o hyder, gweledigaeth, crefft a ffydd. Tair cân ar ddeg yn ymdrin â serch, blinder, gwendid, colled a'r brwydro diddiwedd yn erbyn y gorffennol; i gyd yn treiddio'n unigol i'r isymwybod fel cyffur trwy'r gwythiennau. Rhai o'r caneuon yn gaddo cysur, eraill yn bygwth poenydio ond i gyd yn llwyddo i gyffroi. Mae trefniant yr

---

11 I am grateful to Super Furry Gruff Rhys for making this point.

12 Y Cyrff's lyrics are considered in Damian Walford Davies, '"Rewriting the Law Books"'.

13 Y Cyrff, *Llawenydd Heb Ddiwedd* (Ankst 016, 1991). Y Cyrff had recorded a number of EPs for independent labels and for Sain, before moving to Ankst.

offerynnau yn annisgwyl, does yna ddim byd wedi'i guddio, mae pob melodi yn lân, yn glir ac yn onest. Mae'r cynhyrchu spartan yma'n sicrhau fod pob sŵn yn hanfodol. [...]

Mae'r cyfan yn oes mewn eiliad – profwch.

[There isn't now (nor shall there ever be) another Welsh-language group like Y Cyrff. Sometimes their independence looks like snobbery, their onstage behavior a dangerous combination of violence and passion, and their confidence capable of charming and antagonizing at the same time. But, in contrast to other groups, the songs have always been alive, rendering flesh and blood and challenging the indifference around them....

Like every other important record in the world of popular song, the whole [of *Llawenydd Heb Ddiwedd*] is a mixture of confidence, vision, craft and faith. Thirteen songs dealing with love, weariness, weakness, loss and the endless fight against the past; all penetrating the subconscious like a drug through the veins. Some of the songs promise comfort, others threaten to torment, but all succeed in thrilling. The instrumental arrangement is unexpected, there's nothing hidden, every melody is clean, clear and honest. The spartan production ensures that every sound is essential.

The whole is an age in a moment – experience it.][14]

When two members of Y Cyrff recruited the drummer of Ffa Coffi Pawb (Everybody's Coffee Beans), and a keyboard player and singer from Cardiff,[15] the general concern was that the new group, Catatonia, would be unable to reach the same kind of lyrical and musical sophistication as Y Cyrff. Because the music of Y Cyrff was deemed of central importance to Welsh-language popular culture it would have been inconceivable to expect that English would be the medium of their new incarnation; more inconceivable still that their first two extended play recordings would be the first bilingual releases on Crai, Sain's sister-label.[16] Though the issue of bilingualism in Welsh pop had been a point of contention for a number of years, this marked the beginning of an extended language debate in the Welsh print media, Welsh radio and television, and the National Eisteddfod. Catatonia and Super Furry Animals, formed as they were from two of the more popular Welsh-language groups (Y Cyrff and Ffa Coffi Pawb), were at the center of the debate.

The primary distinction between Y Cyrff and Catatonia is a vocal one. Cerys Matthews formed Catatonia with her songwriting partner and Cyrff guitarist Mark Roberts, and it is her distinctive vocal style which is at the heart of the 'Catatonia sound'. Given the bilingual nature of the group, it is particularly interesting to

---

14 Emyr Glyn Williams, 'Oes Mewn Eiliad: Adolygiad *Llawenydd Heb Ddiwedd*', in *Golwg* 3/33 (2 May, 1991), p. 16; translation mine.

15 The early days of Y Cyrff and Ffa Coffi Pawb, and their respective transitions into Catatonia and Super Furry Animals, are documented briefly in David Owens, *Cerys, Catatonia and the Rise of Welsh Pop* (London: Ebury Press, 2000).

16 Catatonia released two EPs on the Crai label, *For Tinkerbell* (1993) and *Hooked* (1994), which were then re-released as a compilation compact disc, *Catatonia 1993/1994* (Crai CD064). This compact disc, released in the wake of Catatonia's mainstream (UK) success, was met with some hostility by Warner Brothers, Catatonia's new label. Representatives of Warner Brothers sent a number of letters to Rhys Mwyn of Crai Records, threatening legal action, but his decision to ignore them resulted in no litigation, and a rather well-received (and well-sold) record in the Crai catalogue.

compare the quality of Matthews' voice in recordings of English and Welsh versions of the same song, notably 'New Mercurial Heights' and 'Gyda Gwên' (With a Smile), from *For Tinkerbell* (1993).[17] Though the melody remains unchanged, there is a palpable sense that the Welsh version sits more comfortably in her range, and the Welsh words are also much more clearly enunciated than the English. This might suggest that Cerys Matthews is more comfortable singing in Welsh than in English, but it seems also to suggest that the development of an Anglophone Welsh 'rock' voice was not an effortless process.

There are very few precedents for women 'pop' singers in the Welsh language, which places Cerys Matthews in very exclusive – and not closely related – company. There are examples of the female Welsh pop voice in the 1960s, for example, in groups such as Perlau Tâf (Taff Pearls), Y Diliau (The Honeycombs) and Y Pelydrau (The Rays); in the popular duet Tony ac Aloma; and the solo voices of Mary Hopkin and Heather Jones. With the exception of the latter, the Welsh female pop voice in the 1960s was rooted in the acoustic folk tradition, and was rarely, if ever, utilized in a forceful, or 'non-feminine' manner.[18] In the 1970s Heather Jones made the difficult transition from folk to rock, Caryl Parry Jones adopted different vocal styles to suit different genres such as folk, rock, and disco; and finally, in the 1980s Rhiannon Tomos emerged as the first natural female rock voice in the Welsh language. Because she had not been a member of an earlier group, and therefore was not associated with a particular sound or style of singing, she was viewed as a type of Welsh pop vanguard, although by that time the 'forceful' female voice was a central and uncontested component of notable Anglo-American pop groups such as Blondie and The Pretenders. In other words, though Rhiannon Tomos did not emerge from any obvious Welsh 'pop' background, the distinct influence on her own vocal delivery of American singers such as Janis Joplin, allies Tomos much more closely with the Anglo-American tradition than with the Welsh.

When Cerys Matthews began recording with Catatonia there were a number of female vocalists in other Welsh pop groups – Fflaps, Ectogram, Melys – whose music could not be easily categorized. Because Catatonia's music has a straightforward 'pop' sensibility the tendency in the mainstream press was to associate Cerys Matthews' voice with those of Anglo-American singers such as Debbie Harry and Chrissie Hynde, although it in fact bears little resemblance to either. Cerys Matthews' voice seems to seek a balance between the sweetness and innocence of her Welsh

---

17 Dai Griffiths discusses vocal production in Welsh popular music in 'Kelly, Cerys and James Dean Bradfield', in Trevor Herbert and Peter Stead, eds., *Hymns and Arias: Great Welsh Voices* (Cardiff: University of Wales Press, 2001), pp. 209–22. The language shift in Catatonia's music is also mentioned in his 'Ffordd Eingl-Gymreig Grêt o Fyw?', *Golwg* 9/33 (1 May, 1997).

18 That the range of (white) women vocalists in the 1960s Anglo-American mainstream culture spanned the folk – Joan Baez, Joni Mitchell – to the rock – Grace Slick, Janis Joplin – should be further indication of the conservative nature of contemporary Welsh popular music. Gender politics and the development of the female Welsh pop voice are issues which I pursue further in a separate study, 'Mary Hopkin and the Deep Throat of Culture', in Laurie Stras, ed., *She's So Fine: Whiteness, Femininity, Adolescence, and Class in 1960s Music* (Duke University Press, forthcoming).

antecedents and the more dynamic style of her Anglo-American contemporaries. This kind of playful search for an Anglo-Welsh female 'rock' voice can be interpreted as a metaphor for the search for an Anglo-Welsh identity. Significantly, Cerys Matthews became a kind of icon of heightened 'Welshness' in the British press. This created a convenient female counterpart to the Britpop 'lad' culture arising from the antics of the Gallagher brothers of Oasis and Damon Albarn of Blur. Their type of masculine posturing and excessive alcohol consumption documented in the popular and daily press was matched by Cerys Matthews, who was to be seen in the music press, with great regularity, in varying degrees of inebriation, both on-stage and off. What this suggests is at once a need to justify the appeal of Catatonia – the sexualized central character – and to highlight the stereotype of the drunken Welsh person.[19] For her part, Cerys Matthews embraced the 'lad' culture of the South Wales valleys and it was merely that 'otherness' which she enacted for the media.

Given access to the reward structure of mainstream popular culture, the (bilingual) Welsh band has either to assimilate or to retreat to the periphery. This returns us to questions of power negotiation, hegemony and counter-hegemony, but also suggests the term 'mimicry', used by Homi Bhabha in his post-colonial theory of culture.

> ...[C]olonial mimicry is the desire for a reformed, recognizable Other, *as a subject of a difference that is almost the same, but not quite*. Which is to say, that the discourse of mimicry is constructed around an *ambivalence*; in order to be effective, mimicry must continually produce its slippage, its excess, its difference. The authority of that mode of colonial discourse that I have called mimicry is therefore stricken by an indeterminacy: mimicry emerges as the representation of a difference that is itself a process of disavowal. Mimicry is thus the sign of a double articulation; a complex strategy of reform, regulation and discipline, which 'appropriates' the Other as it visualizes power. Mimicry is also the sign of the inappropriate, however, a difference or recalcitrance which coheres the dominant strategic function of colonial power, intensifies surveillance, and poses an immanent threat to both 'normalized' knowledges and disciplinary powers.[20]

Bhabha mentions 'the *ambivalence* of mimicry (almost the same, *but not quite*)';[21] Catatonia represent a Welsh musical equivalent. While their music adheres to a kind of British guitar-based rock style – a contemporary style typified by a group such as Sterophonics – yet it is ironic, one of many possible guises Catatonia could have adopted for admission into the mainstream culture. Again, this suggests a conscious play with industry and public expectations, and a calculated effort at appealing to the widest possible fanbase. There are certainly residual elements in Catatonia's sound which define it as 'other'. One such element is Cerys Matthews' voice, recognizable as 'other' by its betrayal of both Welsh and 'British' roots, by Matthews' insistence on magnifying her natural west Wales accent in her English delivery. This lends the

---

19 Dylan Thomas is responsible in no small part for the perpetuation of this myth, of course, effectively drinking himself to death at the age of 39.

20 Homi Bhabha, 'Of Mimicry and Man', in *The Location of Culture* (London: Routledge, 1994), p. 86.

21 Ibid.

impression of Catatonia as being *almost* the same as other British bands, but not quite; *almost* English, *almost* English-speaking, but not quite.

Another, less subtle element of Catatonia's 'otherness' is lyrical, which is one other obvious distinction to be made between Y Cyrff and Catatonia. Y Cyrff recorded exclusively Welsh-language music; while Catatonia recorded in Wales they were bilingual, only turning exclusively to the English language once they were signed to a contractual agreement with Warner Brothers. Though comprised of former agents in the development of Welsh-language pop, Catatonia immersed themselves in Anglo-American mainstream culture in an attempt at world-wide recognition, which necessitated the use of the English language. How, then, to maintain a sense of Welshness? One way is to emphasize natural Welsh vocal inflections. Another, lyrical, means of asserting 'otherness' is to engage in the 'new' culture, while somehow maintaining a distance from it.

The title song from their first album with Blanco y Negro, *International Velvet*,[22] suggests a type of compromise between their Welshness and their current placement at the centre of mainstream British cultural production. Written in an ironic, vaulted Welsh, it is at once a concession to their Welsh roots, a series of cultural referents for their Welsh-speaking audience, and an obvious statement of difference.

Deffrwch Cymry cysglyd gwlad y gân	Wake up sleepy Welshmen of the land of song
Dwfn yw'r gwendid, bychan yw'r fflâm	Deep is the weakness, small is the flame
Creulon yw'r cynhaeaf ond pêr yw'r dôn	Cruel is the harvest, but sweet is the tune
'Da alaw'r alarch unig yn fy mron	With the lonely swan's song in my breast

Every day when I wake up I thank the Lord I'm Welsh

That *International Velvet* reached Number One in the UK album charts, its singles remained in constant rotation on British (and Welsh) radio, and it included the title track without offering a translation or explanation of the lyrics, suggests a number of interpretations: that Catatonia intend to play in the mainstream culture, but on their own terms; that they do not intend to conform to the British notion of what Welshness is; and that their bilingualism is a statement of fact which needs no justification. That is, 'English', but not quite.[23]

Catatonia's subsequent release, *Equally Cursed and Blessed*,[24] contained no Welsh of any kind, but they continued a sort of subversive attack on the culture into which they had already insinuated themselves, for example in the song 'Londinium':

---

22 Catatonia, 'International Velvet' (Catatonia, Matthews, Roberts), from the album *International Velvet* (Blanco y Negro, 1998); translation mine.

23 The possibility of an English audience joining in during the undeniably singable chorus of 'International Velvet' carries endless ramifications for the notion of community identity and the consumption of popular music. Though space prevents further exploration of this idea, it should be understood as a subtext to the present discussion.

24 Catatonia, *Equally Cursed and Blessed* (Blanco y Negro, 1999).

London never sleeps, it just sucks
The life out of me.[25]

This returns to the issue of mimicry. Though their music may adhere to a certain musical aesthetic, though Catatonia were undoubtedly made aware of certain industry expectations regarding their musical production, their disinterest in succumbing to a more generic 'British' identity is made evident in their lyrics. A comparison between the bands united under the Cool Cymru umbrella may reveal certain such similarities: a desire to maintain distance from the centre of British culture – London – while reaping the financial rewards of contributing to that culture, or of mimicking it. The kind of hybridity evident in the music of Catatonia – not quite Welsh, not quite English[26] – is one form of expressing 'otherness'. Another, perhaps more successful, 'projection of otherness'[27] may be interpreted in the music of Super Furry Animals.

Ffa Coffi Pawb into Super Furry Animals

The dissolution of Ffa Coffi Pawb was announced in 1993.[28] The drummer, Dafydd Ieuan, had already begun performing with both Anhrefn and Catatonia,[29] and the other members of Ffa Coffi Pawb had begun pursuing other projects. Along with

---

25 'Londinium' (Catatonia/Roberts).

26 Though not mentioned explicitly, the implication of Catatonia's hybridity is that it is specifically Anglo (British), and not Anglo-American. There is a particular *Britishness* in their music which did not transfer well to American culture, and as a result Catatonia were never able to break through to the American market, as had been expected of them. Similar problems were encountered by bands categorized as 'Britpop', specifically Oasis, whose Englishness was never really understood as relevant to the contemporary American experience.

27 This is a term used by Homi Bhabha in *The Location of Culture*, in which he states that '[t]he study of world literature might be the study of the way in which cultures recognize themselves through their *projections of "otherness"*. Where, once, the transmission of national traditions was the major theme of a world literature, perhaps we can now suggest that transnational histories of migrants, the colonized, or political refugees – these border and frontier countries – may be the terrains of world literature' (p. 12, italics mine). This has particular resonance, given the popularity of 'world music'; for the purposes of the present discussion, the interpretation of Wales as a 'colonized' nation lends credence to the suggestion that Welsh musicians are at once always 'other' and aware of their otherness. For a comprehensive study of the 'colonization' of Wales see Michael Hechter, *Internal Colonialism* (London: Routledge, 1975). Though subsequently criticized in later Welsh historical studies, Hechter's work does present an argument for the interpretation of the political and economic subjugation of the Welsh people by the English state as colonization. Dai Griffiths and I explore the idea of a post-colonial Welsh music in 'Postcolonial Music in Contemporary Wales: Hybridities and Weird Geographies', in Aaron and Williams, eds., *Postcolonial Wales*.

28 See 'Ffarwel Ffa Coffi' in *Golwg* 6/11 (11 November 1993), p. 25.

29 Shortly after the official announcement of the break-up of Ffa Coffi Pawb, the debut single by Catatonia, 'For Tinkerbell', was voted 'record of the week' by *New Musical Express*, which called it 'a rollicking rollercoaster that will leave you shagged and gasping and screaming for more'. The review is reproduced in its entirety in David Owens, *Cerys, Catatonia and the Rise of Welsh Pop*, p. 56.

Y Cyrff, Ffa Coffi Pawb were one of the more popular bands on the Ankst roster, and contributed to the Welsh pop aesthetic of the late-1980s and early-1990s. Two former members of Ffa Coffi Pawb (singer Gruff Rhys and drummer Dafydd Ieuan) joined with former members of Welsh groups U Thant (guitarist Huw Bunford and bassist Guto Pryce) and Wwzz (keyboard player Cian Ciaran) to create Super Furry Animals in 1994, and signed a recording contract with Creation Records in 1995. One of the stipulations of their contract was that they be allowed to record in both Welsh and English.[30] With the official sanction of their bilingualism, Super Furry Animals have been able to negotiate a type of hybrid identity of their own, and have subsequently proven to be the most successful Welsh export into the Anglo-American dominant culture.

Homi Bhabha's notion of 'hybridity' might suggest a 'place' for Super Furry Animals within the dominant Anglo-American culture:

> Strategies of hybridization reveal an estranging movement in the 'authoritative', even authoritarian inscription of the cultural sign. At the point at which the precept attempts to objectify itself as a generalized knowledge or a normalizing, hegemonic practice, the hybrid strategy or discourse opens up a space of negotiation where power is unequal but its articulation may be equivocal. Such negotiation is neither assimilation nor collaboration. It makes possible the emergence of an 'interstitial' agency that refuses the binary representation of social antagonism. Hybrid agencies find their voice in a dialectic that does not seek cultural supremacy or sovereignty. They deploy the partial culture from which they emerge to construct visions of community, and versions of historic memory, that give narrative form to the minority positions they occupy; the outside of the inside: the part in the whole.[31]

I mentioned Catatonia as representing a type of mimicry – a hybrid identity, neither Welsh nor English – *challenging* cultural dominance by the adherence to residual elements of their 'home' culture – speech inflections, vocal quality, 'distance' from the dominant culture. Super Furry Animals represent a different kind of hybridity: a *negotiation* of power, a negotiation of identity. Though Welsh is the first language of the band, and the language of inter-band communication, they sing in English; by embracing the binary opposition between Welsh and English they are able to draw from the traditions of both cultures – seeking 'neither supremacy nor sovereignty', privileging neither one language nor the other, thus refusing 'the binary representation of social antagonism'. The historic memory which Super Furry Animals recall in their music is inclusive of the entire repertory of popular music; not exclusively English, not particularly Welsh. They have created for themselves a unique perspective, occupying both the inside (major label support) and the outside (minority Welsh community support); the part (Wales) in the whole (Anglo-American culture).

Because Super Furry Animals embody a type of negotiation between English and Welsh cultures, they recall Doreen Masey's notion of a progressive sense of place:

---

30 Another stipulation was that they be given the First of March, St David's Day, off.

31 Homi Bhabha, 'Culture's In-Between', in Hall and Du Gay, eds., *Questions of Cultural Identity*, p. 58.

articulated movements in networks of social relations and understandings ... [allowing] a sense of place which is extroverted, which includes a consciousness of its links with the wider world, which integrates in a positive way the global and the local.[32]

That is to say, Super Furry Animals play with the *idea* of Wales within the larger Anglo-American culture, and they play with the *idea* of Anglo-American culture with a particularly Welsh outlook, thus integrating the global and the local. What is important here is the articulation of this negotiation. In what way does the music of Super Furry Animals suggest a mobile Welshness? What are the implications of a negotiated Welshness?

Musically, Super Furry Animals defy categorization. In much the same way as contemporary Welsh bands such as Gorky's Zygotic Mynci and Rheinallt H. Rowlands exploit their marginality through the appropriation of innumerable styles and genres, so Super Furry Animals pilfer cultural referents from throughout the history of popular music. But rather than considering Super Furry Animals as agents in the 'postmodern condition', it is helpful to think of their work as creating a *new* sense of cultural place. In Homi Bhabha's words:

> The borderline work of culture demands an encounter with 'newness' that is not part of the continuum of past and present. It creates a sense of the new as an insurgent act of cultural translation. Such art does not merely recall the past as social cause or aesthetic precedent; it renews the past, refiguring it as a contingent 'in-between' space, that innovates and interrupts the performance of the present. The 'past-present' becomes part of the necessity, not the nostalgia, of living.[33]

There are several key terms to illuminate in this passage. First, Bhabha's use of the term 'borderline work'. The notion of 'borders' has been central to the construction of Welsh identity in the postwar years. Borders invoke linguistic, geographical, and cultural boundaries, which then imply a distinction between center and periphery. Bhabha's mention of 'cultural translation' is important in both its literal and figurative senses. The translation, or transference, of one culture into another suggests processes of assimilation and incorporation. Such assimilation can work both ways, from the center to the periphery, and vice versa. The incorporation of elements of 'Welshness' into a mainstream cultural product – popular music – is such a process of assimilation; residual elements of one form of cultural expression inform the emergence of a new one. The literal translation of one culture into another, in purely linguistic terms, has been one subtext to the cultural history of Welsh popular music, and must be recalled as such. But the term of primary importance here is the 'contingent "in-between" space', for it is the essence of the hybridity embodied by Super Furry Animals, and expressed in their song, 'The International Language of Screaming':[34]

---

32 Doreen Massey, 'A Global Sense of Place', p. 239.

33 Bhabha, *The Location of Culture*, p. 7.

34 'The International Language of Screaming', words and music by Super Furry Animals, © Universal Music Publishing Ltd., on *Radiator* (Creation Records, 1997); lyrics reprinted by permission.

It's not where you're from
It's not where you're at
It's not where you've been
It's where you're between
It's not what you've been
It's not what you've seen
It's where you're between

From A to Bee then onto Cee
Don't stop the journey 'til you get to Zee
There's nothing to see 'til you get to Zee
Don't stop the journey

Every time I look around me everything seems so stationary
It just sends me the impulse to become reactionary
Spell it out rip it up rearrange it on the contrary
If I scream it I mean it
I hope you will understand me

The 'in between' of 'The International Language of Screaming' is geographical, linguistic, and temporal.[35] Super Furry Animals occupy that space between Wales and England, between Welsh and English, and between the past and the present. The title itself, 'The International Language of Screaming' can be interpreted as a reference to the language debate in Wales in the mid-1990s, and a reference to their own place at the center of it. The type of compromise implied here is that *no* language is being privileged; screaming, whether for ease of communication or out of sheer frustration, is not a coded linguistic signifier of either Welsh *or* English, or of either culture.

'The International Language of Screaming' is about motion. 'Where you're from' and 'where you've been' carry both geographical and temporal implications. 'Where you're from' generally refers to cultural place, a relationship to a tradition and to a community; 'where you've been' is more suggestive of life experience. 'Where you're at' challenges the 'past–present' continuum – as Bhabha calls it, 'part of the necessity, not the nostalgia, of living'. That is to say, a grounding in tradition may inform the present, but it should not hinder the process of cultural development. The line 'don't stop the journey' may suggest a motion away from a geographical center, from an historical grounding in a particular culture, or simply as the process of culture itself. This motion away from one thing and toward another – a transition or a translation – is another means of placing Super Furry Animals in an in-between space – 'the Third Space' – between Welsh and Anglo-American, Welsh and English, past and present.

---

35 'Blerwytirhwng?' ('Whereareyoubetween?'), the Super Furry Animals single, is mentioned here again as a reminder of the structural question at the heart of the development of Welsh popular music.

...[I]f ... the act of cultural translation (both as representation and as reproduction) denies the essentialism of a prior given original or originary culture, then we see that all forms of culture are continually in a process of hybridity. But for me the importance of hybridity is not to be able to trace two original moments from which the third emerges, rather hybridity to me is the 'third space' which enables other positions to emerge. This third space displaces the histories that constitute it, and sets up new structures of authority, new political initiatives, which are inadequately understood through received wisdom.[36]

It is only when we understand that all cultural statements and systems are constructed in this contradictory and ambivalent space of enunciation, that we begin to understand why hierarchical claims to the inherent originality or 'purity' of cultures are untenable, even before we resort to empirical historical instances that demonstrate their hybridity. [...] It is that Third Space, though unrepresentable in itself, which constitutes the discursive conditions of enunciation that ensure that the meaning and symbols of culture have no primordial unity or fixity; that even the same signs can be appropriated, translated, rehistoricized and read anew.[37]

Re-Located: *Mwng*

If Super Furry Animals inhabited the 'third space' between cultures and temporalities, their position was further complicated by the release in the year 2000 of their album, *Mwng* (Mane).[38] As I noted earlier, a stipulation of Super Furry Animals' contract with Sony Music was that they would be allowed to record in Welsh and in English. Though several of their B-sides were Welsh songs,[39] their full-length recordings were monoglot English. When Creation Records folded in 1999 Super Furry Animals were left with a backlog of music which they had not recorded, and decided to release an album on their own label, comprised entirely of those Welsh songs they had accumulated over the years. With no contractual or financial obligations to satisfy, *Mwng* might have been received as a vanity project; but the reputation that Super Furry Animals had built over their five-year career had ensured that it be given mainstream press notice. The Welsh press were uniformly ecstatic that Super Furry Animals were returning to record in their native tongue. The implications of *Mwng* to contemporary Welsh popular music were considerable; but the language debate had still not quieted. In the months before the release of *Mwng*, the recording was mentioned as emblematic of the difficult relationship between Welsh popular culture and the Anglo-American dominant. One summary report of the state of contemporary Welsh popular culture is quoted here at length:

[...] Wrth i gyd-fandiau Cymraeg ddechrau cael llwyddiant yn y byd roc rhyngwladol, mae yna ddadlau wedi bod ynglŷn â phenderfyniad rhai i ganolbwyntio ar ganu yn Saesneg. Nid dewis canu mewn iaith arall oedd y broblem, ond rhoi'r gorau i ganu yn Gymraeg.

36 Jonathan Rutherford, 'Interview with Homi Bhabha: "The Third Space"', in Rutherford, ed., *Identity: Community, Culture, Difference* (London: Lawrence & Wishart, 1998), p. 211.
37 Homi Bhabha, *The Location of Culture*, p. 37.
38 Super Furry Animals, *Mwng* (Placid Casual, 2000).
39 See *Outspaced* (Creation, 1998).

Nid dangos ei bod hi'n bosib i siaradwyr Cymraeg lwyddo yr oedden nhw, ond awgrymu fod anghofio'r iaith yn rhan o'r broses honno.

Mae'r rhan fwya' o bawb ohonon ni yn defnyddio'r Saesneg yn ein gwaith a llawer yn ennill arian trwy berfformio neu sgrifennu ynddi. Rhagrith ydi beio neb arall am wneud yr un peth.

Mi roeddan ni'n falch o lwyddiant y grwpiau ac mi roedd yna les yn dod o gynnwys ambell bennill Cymraeg – ond mi fyddai'r lles seicolegol yn llawer mwy pebaen nhw hefyd yn cynnal gig Cymraeg.

Y broblem efo rhai o'r grwpiau oedd eu bod nhw – fel y mae un o ganeuon diweddar Steve Eaves yn awgrymu – fel petaen nhw'n ymorchestu yn y Saesneg ac wedi diflannu o ddigwyddiadau mawr Cymraeg fel yr Eisteddfod.

Y canlyniad oedd fod y rhan fwya' o grwpiau Cymraeg newydd hefyd yn dechrau canu caneuon Saesneg, heb fawr ddim gobaith o wneud unrhyw argraff ar y byd rhyngwladol. Roedd y diwylliant ei hun yn troi'n Saesneg.

Roedd yna wendid yn rhai o'r dadleuon hefyd, yn enwedig mewn dwy:

• Os oedd cerddoriaeth yn 'iaith ryngwladol', pam oedd angen troi i unrhyw iaith ond y Gymraeg?

• Os ydi pawb bellach yn hyderus yn yr iaith, pam nad ydan ni'n ddigon hyderus i fynd â hi efo ni i'r byd y tu allan?

[...] Efo ymchwil [Aitchison a Carter] hefyd yn awgrymu na fedr yr iaith bellach ddibynnu ar garreg yr aelwyd nac ar gael ei gweld yn brif gostrel ein Cymreictod ni, mae'n rhaid ffeindio peiriannau grymus eraill i'w chynnal hi.

Un o'r rheiny ydi diwylliant modern. Petai ein cerddorion ifanc ni yn dweud nad oes pwynt creu trwy'r Gymraeg, mi fyddai'n amser chwilio am yr amdo.

[As other Welsh (language) bands begin to succeed in the international world of rock, there have been arguments about the decision of some to concentrate on singing in English. The problem wasn't deciding to sing in another language, but to give up singing in Welsh. They weren't showing that it was possible for Welsh speakers to succeed, but rather suggesting that forgetting the language was part of the process.

The great majority of all of us use English in our work and many earn money through performing or writing in it. It's hypocrisy to blame others for doing the same thing.

We were proud of the groups' success and it was beneficial to see the occasional Welsh verse – but the psychological benefit would have been much greater had they also held a Welsh gig.

The problem with some of the groups – as one of Steve Eaves' recent songs suggests – was that they seemed to have worn themselves out in English and disappeared from big Welsh events like the Eisteddfod.

The result was that the majority of new Welsh groups are also beginning to sing English songs, without much hope of making any kind of impression on the international world. The culture itself was becoming English.

There are weaknesses in some of these arguments, especially two:

• If music is an 'international language', why was it necessary to turn to any other language than Welsh?

• If everyone is confident in the language, why aren't we confident enough to take it to the outside world?

[...] With [Aitchison and Carter's] research also suggesting that the language shouldn't rely on a hearthstone nor be seen as the primary bottle of our Welshness, we have to find other strong machines to maintain it.

> One of those is modern culture. If our young musicians say there's no point creating through the medium of Welsh, it will be time to search for the shroud.][40]

Clearly these concerns would not have been voiced in the mainstream press. A review in the English press of a Welsh-language recording would have been unimaginable in the years before 'Cool Cymru'; but at a time when mainstream interest in Super Furry Animals' counterparts were beginning to wane,[41] *Mwng* was met with almost unanimous praise:

> Super Furry Animals are delicately poised on the board game that is the modern music industry. They're probably only one hit single away from climbing several ladders, but it's not yet clear how they will survive the disappearance of their record label, Creation – a great big snake down which other artists have already tumbled. How wilful, then, to choose this moment to release an album in Welsh. How self-indulgent can you get? Except, of course, how can it possibly be self-indulgent to record in your own language? *Mwng* ... marks a shift away from their recent psychedelic sound; but the band remain fixated on the music of the years 1966–74. Much of *Mwng* draws on the gentler music of that time – the Beach Boys, the Byrds and Nick Drake are all referenced...; but some of it also borrows from the trashy, glam sound of Bowie, early Roxy Music and the Velvet Underground. The heart of the album, however, lies in the rawest recordings here.... But the language issue isn't really a hindrance; in fact, on tracks such as Gwreiddiau Dwfn (Deep Roots) the inability to follow the lyrics leaves you more time to ponder the fact that the Super Furrys are rapidly approaching the melodic sophistication of old-school songwriters such as Burt Bacharach. Career-wise, who knows what this will do to the band; but musically, they've made exactly the right move. This is a delicate, organic, melancholic, utterly charming record.[42]

Super Furry Animals had thus achieved the one thing which was deemed impossible in the early days of Welsh popular music: succeeding in the Anglo-American market while singing in the Welsh language. That they could succeed in some small way at this kind of project proves that Welsh pop culture had finally developed the capacity to coexist with English pop culture, unapologetically and without fear of implosion. The release of *Mwng* did not alter their hybridity, however. On the contrary, their adherence to their own unique musical philosophy strengthened their position in the 'third space' – occupying 'the outside of the inside, the part in the whole'. It is therefore interesting to note the variety of influences identified, without irony, in the above passage. The combination of quintessentially American bands such as The Byrds and The Beach Boys with a quintessentially English musician such as Nick Drake does not seem unusual in any way; rather it endorses the earlier suggestion that style is a freely-adopted signifier of a particular historical identity. Catatonia

---

40 Editorial, 'Roc yn yr Iaith' ('Rock in the Language'), in *Golwg* 12/16 (9 March, 2000); translation mine. Reference is made to Aitchison and Carter, *A Geography of the Welsh Language 1961–1991*.

41 Catatonia's *Equally Cursed and Blessed* did not create the same excitement as its predecessor; and the overexposure of bands such as Manic Street Preachers and Stereophonics threatened to lessen the impact of their projects.

42 'Record of the Week: Super Furry Animals, *Mwng*', in *The Sunday Times* (14 May, 2000).

adopted British guitar-rock as one such style; Super Furry Animals prefer to play with a multiplicity of identities, remaining in some way unidentifiable – always familiar, but always distinctive.

One other song from *Mwng* serves as a final example of the negotiation of Welshness at the turn of the century. Super Furry Animals described 'Ymaelodi â'r Ymylon' (Joining the Periphery) on the *Mwng* website as follows:

> There's an old idiom in Welsh, 'y cythraul canu', which is about the demon in music, which creates friction between people. It's an old idiom. It's partly about our experiences of doing taboo moves like singing in English. It's about being banished from a musical scene but it could also be about being banished from a group of friends. Musically it's a celebration of our love of the Beach Boys and Love and Morricone. It's the first time we've used the harmonium, and if there's a song that sums up the album in terms of mood in under three minutes perhaps it's this one.[43]

Maen nhw'n dweud	Well, they say
Bo' ni ar yr ymylon	we're peripheral people
Yn weision bach ffyddlon	Spineless and feeble[44]
Yn arw ac estron	Roughneck and evil[45]
Ac mae hi'n llugoer yn llygad y ffynnon	And it's so cool in the eye of the fountain
Ond ar yr ymylon	But the peripheries sustain
Mae'r danadl poethion	The hottest nettle.
Ymaelodi â'r ymylon	Joining the periphery
(Cosb pob un sydd yn anffyddlon)	(the price to pay for all who stray)
Mae 'na sôn am y cythraul canu	And there's talk of the demon in music
Sy'n arwahanu	That divides and rules us
Yn hollti a rhannu	In musical envy
Ac mae hi'n unig ar yr ymylon	And it's so lonely on the periphery
Yn edrych o hirbell ar rywbeth sydd nepell	As if looking from afar at something that's near.

The periphery here is not only geographical, but political and cultural. 'Ymaelodi â'r Ymylon' is as much about the inner fractures in the Welsh community as it is about the placement of Wales as a culture in uneasy relation with the Anglo-American world. The political reliance of Wales on England is invoked, not in terms of passive subjugation, but of hidden strength: 'the peripheries sustain / the hottest nettle': at

---

43 Notes on 'Song/Cân 2: Ymaelodi â'r Ymylon ('Joining the Periphery', or it could mean 'Banished to the Periphery')', on 'Ymaelodi â'r Ymylon', words and lyrics Super Furry Animals, © Universal Music Publishing Ltd.. Lyrics reprinted by permission. The translations provided here are taken from the website, though I note alternate translations where appropriate.

44 Literally, 'faithful little servants'.

45 Or 'rough and foreign'.

once a reference to the heated debate surrounding Welsh culture and Welshness, and an acknowledgment of the powerlessness of the cultural center to quell it. 'The devil in music / that divides and rules us' is somewhat more complicated. The antagonism expressed by some members of the Welsh audience at the anglicization of the Welsh-language media is one example of an external force dividing a community; but the Anglo-American cultural dominant defines the trajectory taken by Welsh popular music – it *rules* Welsh popular culture. Agents in Welsh popular culture are therefore 'peripheral people', at once divided and ruled by a 'central' cultural force. But there is an inverse way of interpreting the center/periphery opposition: the 'price to pay for all who stray' from the Welsh-language rule is to be relegated to the periphery of a peripheral culture; an in-between space, neither Welsh nor English.

Super Furry Animals play with the idea of the place of Welsh popular music as well as with their own place in both Welsh and Anglo-American cultures. This brings to mind John Street's notion of locality as political experience; but rather than expressing a discontent for the larger political structure, Super Furry Animals are here exploiting the tensions of their geographical home, illuminating for audiences outside her borders the types of negotiation necessary to express belonging to such a contested cultural space. In that sense they have succeeded at articulating Welshness in a way their contemporaries have not, and it is through inhabiting the periphery of *both* cultures, Welsh and Anglo-American, and understanding each as the margin of the other. As Homi Bhabha suggests:

> For a willingness to descend into that alien territory – where I have led you – may reveal that the theoretical recognition of the split-space of enunciation may open the way to conceptualizing an *inter*national culture, based not on the exoticism of multiculturalism or the *diversity* of cultures, but on the inscription and articulation of culture's *hybridity*. To that end we should remember that it is the 'inter' – the cutting edge of translation and negotiation, the *in-between* space – that carries the burden of the meaning of culture. It makes it possible to begin envisaging national, anti-nationalist histories of the 'people'. And by exploring this Third Space, we may elude the politics of polarity and emerge as the others of our selves.[46]

Conclusions

The development of Welsh popular music provides a microcosm of the larger Anglo-American model. The movements outlined in the preceding chapters showed the progression from light entertainment to folk, from folk to rock, from mainstream to underground, and a general progression from the rural to the urban. These stylistic shifts may be interpreted as the emergences of new structures of feeling, or as articulations of larger societal concerns. In either case, they were represented in this study by the first expression of Welsh popular culture in 1945, the skiffle craze in the mid-1950s, the first folk recordings by Dafydd Iwan in 1966, the development of urban Welsh pop music in the mid-1970s, the anti-establishment underground pop

---

46 Homi Bhabha, *The Location of Culture*, pp. 38–9.

of the late-1980s, and the emergence of Welsh rap in 1997: articulations at moments of crisis in the process of Welsh identity.

These stylistic shifts are as much a means of forcing changes in the structure of the Welsh musical establishment as they are the adoption of emergent ideologies by the younger generations of Welsh musicians. That identifiable shifts occur with greater regularity in the latter part of this temporal arc is indicative of a greater cultural self-awareness and self-confidence. By the end of the 1990s Welsh popular music had assumed an autonomous existence, in mutual support of, but not sole relationship with, *Cymdeithas yr Iaith*. This is not to suggest that Welsh pop was not politicized in the 1990s, or that the struggle for the survival of the Welsh language was over; merely that the continuation of Welsh popular culture was associated with larger issues and the quest for greater financial reward. The separation of the cultural product from the political community for which it was adapted, signalled a decisive change in the needs of the larger Welsh community and, again, a self-confidence resulting from forty years of cultural process.

The release of *Mwng* by the Super Furry Animals serves as a symbolic end to the cultural history outlined here, and one of their early Welsh songs serves as the structural question upon which this study has been built. But in the years since the release of *Mwng* there have been other suggestions that Welsh pop is entering a phase of unusual creativity. Groups such as Anweledig, from Blaenau Ffestiniog, are continuing on the Tebot Piws/Dyniadon Ynfyd Hirfelyn Tesog trajectory; urban hip hop is slowly spreading across Wales, and in the wake of Y Tystion and MC Mabon (themselves reaping the rewards of their forerunners, Llwybr Llaethog) groups such as Pep Le Pew, from Porthmadog, are exploring the position of the Welsh language in an international community formation, and the continued popularity of Radio Cymru's night-time program ensures the platform, audience, and recording facilities for newer Welsh bands.

Welsh pop is still a minority cultural product, but it has survived forty years of linguistic and political trials, inspired the establishment of an indigenous music industry, fed the developing Welsh-language media, and provided the forum for the unification of a community. The relationship of Welsh pop with its Anglo-American 'other' is a difficult, familial one; but without a dominant constitutive outside, the Welsh pop musical culture would never have developed. It certainly would not have inspired the type of assertions of identity noted in the preceding pages. And if the answer to the structural question, *'Blerwytirhwng?'* is 'that in-between space', it is not an admission of weakness or defeat; it is a suggestion that negotiations of Welshness are being enacted in fertile ground.

Appendix

A Brief Timeline

1950s   Yr Hogia, Y Bois – roots of Welsh 'pop'
Shirley Bassey records her debut single, 'The Banana Boat Song' (1957)
Cardiff becomes capital city (1955)
Measure passed to drown Tryweryn (1957)

1960   Bridging gap between Noson lawen and pop scene

1961   Welsh speakers number 26% (656,002); monoglot 1%
First vote for Sunday pub openings

1962   Saunders Lewis' broadcast, *Tynged yr Iaith* (13 February) leads to
        creation of *Cymdeithas yr Iaith* Gymraeg (4 August)
First issue of *Barn*

1963   First public protest by *Cymdeithas yr Iaith*, Pont Trefechan
First Eisteddfod presence for Cymdeithas yr Iaith

1964   Shirley Bassey, 'Goldfinger'
BBC establishes national television service for Wales
Recordiau'r Dryw (Wren)
TWW weekly show, *Y Dydd*

1965   Group Sgiffl Llandegai become Hogia Llandegai, biggest-selling Welsh
        pop band so far
'Diolch i'r Iôr', religious song by Gwyn Jones, voted best original Welsh
        pop song
Meic Stevens releases first single, 'Did I Dream' (Decca)
Dafydd Iwan begins regular appearances on Y Dydd
Hob y Deri Dando first broadcast
300 language activists protest at Post Office, Dolgellau
Brewer-Spinks fires two factory workers for disobeying no-Welsh rule
Formation of Free Wales Army

1966   Tom Jones: 'The Green Green Grass of Home'
First Welsh pop TV show, *Disg a Dawn* first broadcast
Dafydd Iwan's first record, 'Wrth Feddwl am Fy Nghymru', sells 10,000
Geraint Jones first to be imprisoned for *Cymdeithas yr Iaith*

Cymdeithas yr Iaith begins campaign of painting over English road signs
   throughout Wales
Gwynfor Evans first *Plaid Cymru* candidate to be elected MP
Aberfan disaster

1967   Y Blew plug in at the National Eisteddfod, Y Bala
Tony ac Aloma form as duet, singing on *Y Dydd*
Eisteddfod yr Urdd holds competitions in new categories: Pop Soloist
   (Heather Jones) and Pop Group (Y Pelydrau)
First 'Deg Ucha'r *Cymro*'
BBC Llandaf opens; color studios. Movement begins for Welsh television
   channel

1968   Mary Hopkin appears on *Opportunity Knocks*
Y Dyniadon Ynfyd Hirfelyn Tesog formed for Eisteddfod Ryng-golegol
   (inter-collegiate)
Hogia'r Wyddfa: 'Siglo yn y Gwyn' ('Blowin' in the Wind')
Hywel Gwynfryn begins radio show, *Helo Sut Dach Chi?*
Dafydd Iwan elected chair of *Cymdeithas yr Iaith*
HTV, BBC showing six and a half hours of Welsh programming per week

1969   Mary Hopkin releases *Post Card*; the single, 'Those Were the Days' tops
   the UK pop charts
Dafydd Iwan: 'Carlo'
Huw Jones, 'Dŵr'
Y Bara Menyn, 'Caru Cymru'
Pinnacle Pop held in Pontrhydfendigaid to raise money for Eisteddfod yr
   Urdd; 2,000 people attend
Y Pelydrau appear on *Opportunity Knocks*; offered professional contract;
   decide to go to college instead
Sain record label founded
First Welsh pop magazine, *Asbri*
Investiture of, and protest against, the Prince of Wales, Caernarfon
Poster by Y Lolfa: If You're Welsh, You're Watched

1970   Mary Hopkin performs British Eurovision entry, 'Knock, Knock, Who's
   There'; places second
Y Tebot Piws release first recording
Meic Stevens, 'Y Brawd Houdini' single (Sain 04); *Outlander* LP (Warner
   Bros)
Gŵyl Werin Cymru (Folk Festival of Wales), Corwen
Dafydd Iwan goes to Cardiff prison for three months
Huw Jones releases 'Paid Digalonni' (Sain 03) to show support for
   Dafydd Iwan
First color television broadcast from Eisteddfod Rhydaman
First Welsh sit-com: *Fo a Fe*

1971   Hefin Elis: 'I'r Gad' (To the Battle)
       Endaf Emlyn signs five-year deal with EMI, who agree to release
           bilingual record
       Adfer buys first house; calls for members of *Cymdeithas yr Iaith* to come
           together for 'penwythnos gwaith' (a weekend of work)
       Adfer – Cymdeithas split
       Pop music given official recognition at the National Eisteddfod
       Early press notice that pop songs are being sung in Welsh

1972   Ac Eraill: 'Tua'r Gorllwein' (Toward the West)
       Mici Plwm sets up mobile discos
       Huw Ceredig and Hywel Gwynfryn start Nosweithiau Barbarella in
           Cardiff
       First issue of *Sŵn* (Sound), Welsh pop fanzine
       Cymdeithas yr Iaith publish first Maniffesto

1973   Edward H. Dafis debut at Tafodau Tân!, Corwen
       Hogia Llandegai release 'farewell' recording
       Huw Jones: 'Dwi Isio Bod yn Sais' (I Want to be an Englishman)
       Campaign against holiday homes, Caernarfon
       Welsh-language immersion course, Ulpan, taught in Cardiff

1974   Endaf Emlyn: *Salem*
       Edward H. Dafis: *Hen Ffordd Gymreig o Fyw*
       All-star cast perform first Welsh 'rock opera', *Nia Ben Aur*
       Formation of Mynediad am Ddim
       First episode of *Pobol y Cwm* broadcast
       Adfer now independent of *Cymdeithas yr Iaith*

1975   Edward H. Dafis, *Ffordd Newydd Eingl-Americanaidd Grêt o Fyw*
       Big gig: Twrw Tanllyd, Pontrhydfendigaid
       Sain open first studio in Gwernafalau, Llandwrog
       Dafydd Iwan goes on first tour
       Max Boyce releases first English-language record

1976   Hergest, *Ffrindiau Bore Oes*
       Edward H. Dafis split (temporarily)
       Ar Log form for folk festival in Brittany
       BBC Cymru broadcasting 337 hours of Welsh per year

1977   Tecwyn Ifan: *Y Dref Wen* (The White Town)
       Geraint Jarman: *Tacsi i'r Tywyllwch*
       Trwynau Coch form
       Welsh 'super-group', Injaroc: *Halen y Ddaear*
       'Steddfod Bop (Pop Eisteddfod), Dinbych
       First broadcast of *Helo Bobol*

First imprisonment for *Adfer*
Radio Cymru (FM) / Radio Wales (MW) established

1978   Y Trwynau Coch: 'Merched Dan 15' (Girls Under 15)
Geraint Jarman, *Hen Wlad Fy Nhadau*
Edward H. Dafis come back (temporarily)
'Rock Opera' *Dic Penderyn*
First issue of *Sgrech*, Welsh pop magazine
Sosban first broadcast on Radio Cymru
HTV broadcasts *Sêr* (Stars), hosted by Endaf Emlyn

1979   Geraint Jarman: *Gwesty Cymru*
New female-led bands: Rhiannon Tomos a'i Band; Bando
Dafydd Iwan tours to US; Ar Log tour worldwide
Hergest split
Twrw Tanllyd at the National Eisteddfod
Wales votes 'no' to a National Assembly
Gwynfor Evans loses his Parliamentary seat
Eight holiday homes burnt in December

1980   Cardigan Beat: Ail Symudiad, Malcolm Neon
Geraint Jarman: *Fflamau'r Ddraig*
Dafydd Iwan's 'Magi Thatcher' banned by BBC
Sain opens 24-track studio in Llandwrog
First Celtic Film Festival
Gwynfor Evans declares fast for S4C

1981   First Pabell Roc (Rock Tent) at the National Eisteddfod, Machynlleth
Premier of rock opera *Mab Darogan*
Y Trwynau Coch voted favorite band at Noson Sgrech
Edward H. Dafis split up for good
Dafydd Wigley leads *Plaid Cymru*

1982   Y Trwynau Coch split
Datblygu form
Meic Stevens, *Nos Du Nos Da*
Maffia Mr Huws, 'Gitar yn y To'
Dafydd Iwan and Ar Log on Taith 700 tour
Radio Cymru launch *Sosban*: youth-oriented late show
S4C first broadcast on 2 November

1983   Dafydd Iwan and Ar Log: 'Yma o Hyd' (Still Here); go on Taith Macsen
tour
'Ysbryd y Nos' (Spirit of the Night) by Edward H. Dafis voted song of the
year
Maffia Mr Huws voted favorite band, Noson *Sgrech*

1984   Steve Eaves: "¡Viva la Revolucion Galesa!"
       Steve Eaves edits *Y Trên Olaf Adref*, first Welsh pop lyrics anthology
       First Cnapan festival held
       Last Twrw Tanllyd until 1997
       Gŵyl Roc y Tâf (The Taff Rock Festival) held at St. David's Hall, Cardiff
       Anhrefn start their own record label

1985   'Dwylo Dros y Môr' (Hands Across the Water), Cyngerdd Arian Byw
          (Life Money Concert) raise money for Ethiopian famine relief
       Edward H. Dafis, *Breuddwyd Roc a Rol*
       'Underground' concert held at National Eisteddfod, Rhyl
       Radio Cymru launches *Cadw Reiat*

1986   Datblygu, 'Hwgrgrawthog'
       Geraint Jarman & Maffia Mr Huws: Taith y Carcharorion
       Llwybr Llaethog, 'Di-Drais'
       BBC Broadcasting in Welsh from 6:30a.m. to 6:30p.m.

1987   Roc Corwen held to welcome Ffred Ffransis, Cymdeithas yr Iaith activist,
          out of prison
       Cadw Reiat replaced by *Bambŵ*
       Datblygu record first session for the John Peel Show
       S4C broadcasting 25.5 hours of Welsh per week

1988   Datblygu: *Wyau*
       Jess: *Jess* EP
       Sobin a'r Smaeliaid: *Sobin a'r Smaeliaid*
       Ankst founded
       Crai established
       First issue of *Golwg*
       Jess tour to Prague

1989   Y Cyrff: *Cymru Lloegr a Llanrwst* EP
       Anhrefn the most successful Welsh group of the year
       Radio Cymru launches *Hwyrach*

1990   Ankst artists re-record Jarman's *Hen Wlad Fy Nhadau*
       Y Cyrff: *Awdl o Anobaith*
       Bob Delyn: *Sgwarnogod Bach Bob*
       Anhrefn tour Czech Republic

1991   Y Cyrff: *Llawenydd Heb Ddiwedd*
       Ffa Coffi Pawb: *Clymhalio*
       Tŷ Gwydr: *Effeithiol*
       Manic Street Preachers form
       The Alarm release Welsh album, *Tân* (Fire)

Sain release *Goreuon Hogia'r Wyddfa* (Hogia'r Wyddfa's Greatest Hits)

1992   Catatonia form
Ffa Coffi Pawb: *Hei Vidal!*
Bob Delyn: *Gedon*
Llwybr Llaethog v. Tŷ Gwydr: MC D.R.E.
Manic Street Preachers: *Generation Terrorists*
Hogia Llandegai: *Goreuon Hogia Llandegai* (Hogia Llandegai'r Greatest Hits)

1993   Super Furry Animals form
Llwybr Llaethog and Ifor ap Glyn record 'Fydd y Chwyldro Ddim ar y Teledu, Gyfaill'
Datblygu: *Libertino*

1994   Gorky's Zygotic Mynci: *Patio*
Manic Street Preachers: *The Holy Bible*

1995   Gorky's Zygotic Mynci: *Bwyd Time*
Welsh folk/dub/techno fusion Hen Wlad Fy Mamau
Richey Edwards from Manic Street Preachers disappears on 1 February

1996   Super Furry Animals: *Fuzzy Logic*
Catatonia: *Way Beyond Blue*
Gorky's Zygotic Mynci: *Amber Gambler*
Rheinallt H. Rowlands: *Bukowski*
Manic Street Preachers: *Everything Must Go*
Sain releases *Mary Hopkin: Y Caneuon Cynnar – The Early Recordings*

1997   'Cool Cymru'
Super Furry Animals: *Radiator*
Catatonia: *International Velvet*
Gorky's Zygotic Mynci: *Barafundle* (Mercury Records)
Y Tystion: *Rhaid i Rybeth Ddigwydd...*
Stereophonics: *Word Gets Around*
Urdd Gobaith Cymru (Welsh League of Youth) celebrates its 75th anniversary
Devolution Referendum passes by narrow margin

1998   Gorky's Zygotic Mynci: *Gorky 5*
Anweledig: *Sombreros yn y Glaw*
Manic Street Preachers: *This Is My Truth Tell Me Yours*

1999   Super Furry Animals: *Guerrilla*
Catatonia: *Equally Cursed and Blessed*
Y Tystion: *Shrug Off Ya Complex*

Sain celebrates 30th birthday
Establishment of National Assembly for Wales

2000   Y Tystion: *Hen Gelwydd Prydain Newydd*
Super Furry Animals: *Mwng*

Bibliography

Aitchison, John and Harold Carter, *The Welsh Language 1961–1981: An Interpretative Atlas* (Cardiff: University of Wales Press, 1985).

——, *A Geography of the Welsh Language 1961–1991* (Cardiff: University of Wales Press, 1994).

Alleyne, Mike, 'Echoes of Dub: Spatiality, Assimilation and Invisibility', unpublished paper delivered at *Looking Back, Looking Ahead: Popular Music Studies 20 Years Later*, the Eleventh Conference of the International Association for the Study of Popular Music, Turku, Finland, 6–10 July 2001.

Anderson, Benedict, *Imagined Communities* (London: Verso, 1991).

ap Glyn, Ifor, *Golchi Llestri Mewn Bar Mitzvah* (Llanrwst: Gwasg Carreg Gwalch, 1998).

ap Siôn, Pwyll, 'Voices of Resistance: Geraint Jarman and the Roots of Reggae in Welsh Popular Music', *Welsh Music History*, 2 (Cardiff: University of Wales Press, 1997): 263–77.

Appiah, Kwame Anthony, 'Is the Post- in Postmodernism the Post- in Postcolonial?', *Critical Inquiry* 17 (Winter 1991): 336–57.

Arnold, Matthew, *Culture and Anarchy* (London: Cambridge University Press, 1932).

Balsom, Denis, 'The Three-Wales Model', in John Osmond (ed.), *The National Question Again: Welsh Political Identity in the 1980s* (Llandysul: Gomer Press, 1985): 1–17.

——, 'The Smoke Behind the Fires', *Planet* 73 (1989): 16–19.

Barnard, Stephen, *On the Radio: Music Radio in Britain* (Milton Keynes: Open University Press, 1989).

Barrett, James, 'World Music, Nation and Postcolonialism', *Cultural Studies* 10/2 (1996): 237–47.

Barrow, Steve and Peter Dalton, *The Rough Guide to Reggae* (London: Rough Guides, 2001).

Barthes, Roland, *Image – Music – Text* , translated by Stephen Heath (New York: Hill and Wang, 1977).

——, *The Responsibility of Forms*, translated by Richard Howard (Berkeley and Los Angeles: University of California Press, 1991).

Bennett, Andrew, *Dirmyg Cyfforddys* (Talybont: Y Lolfa, 1994).

Bennett, Andy, 'Rappin' on the Tyne: White Hip-Hop Culture in Northeast England – an Ethnographic Study', *The Sociological Review* 47/1 (February 1999): 1–24.

——, '"Sitting in an English Garden": Representations of "Britishness" in the Songs of the Beatles and 1990s Britpop Groups', in Ian Englis (ed.), *The Beatles, Popular Music and Society: A Thousand Voices* (Houndmills, Basingstoke and London: Macmillan Press, 2000a): 189–206.

——, *Popular Music and Youth Culture: Music, Identity and Place* (Basingstoke: Macmillan Press, 2000b).

Bennett, David (ed.), *Multicultural States; Rethinking Difference and Identity* (London: Routledge, 1998).

Bennett, Tony, Simon Frith, Lawrence Grossberg, John Shepherd and Graeme Turner (eds.), *Rock and Popular Music: Politics, Policies, Institutions* (London: Routledge, 1993).

——, Colins Mercer and Janet Woollacott (eds.), *Popular Culture and Social Relations* (Milton Keynes: Open University Press, 1986).

Berland, Jody, 'Placing Television', *New Formations* 4 (Spring 1988): 145–54.

——, 'Radio Space and Industrial Time: Music Formats, Local Narratives and Technological Mediation', *Popular Music* 9/2 (1990): 179–92.

Bertens, Hans and Douwe Fokkema (eds.), *International Postmodernism: Theory and Literary Practice* (Amsterdam: John Benjamins, 1997).

Bhabha, Homi K., 'Location, Intervention, Incommensurability: A Conversation with Homi Bhabha', *Emergences* 1/1 (1989): 63–88.

—— (ed.), *Nation and Narration* (London: Routledge, 1990).

——, *The Location of Culture* (London: Routledge, 1994).

Bird, Jon, Barry Curtis, Tim Putnam, George Robertson, and Lisa Tickner (eds.), *Mapping the Futures: Local Cultures, Global Change* (London and New York: Routledge, 1993).

Borland, John, Ralph Fevre and David Denney, 'Nationalism and Community in North West Wales', *The Sociological Review* 40/1 (February 1992): 49–71.

Born, Georgina and David Hesmondhalgh (eds.), *Western Music and Its Others: Difference, Representation, and Appropriation in Music* (Berkeley: University of California Press, 2000).

Bowman, Glenn, 'Tales of the Lost Land: Palestinian Identity and the Formation of Nationalist Consciousness', in Eric Carter,James Donald and Judith Squires (eds.), *Cultural Remix: Theories of Politics and the Popular* (London: Lawrence & Wishart, 1995): 73–100.

Brackett, David, *Interpreting Popular Music* (Cambridge: Cambridge University Press, 1995).

Bradley, Dick, *Understanding Rock'n'Roll: Popular Music in Britain 1955–1964* (Buckingham: Open University Press, 1992).

Brake, Mike, *The Sociology of Youth Culture and Youth Subcultures: Sex and Drugs and Rock'n'Roll?* (London: Routledge & Kegan Paul, 1980).

Breen, Marcus, 'The End of the World As We Know It: Popular Music's Cultural Mobility', *Cultural Studies* 9/3 (1995): 486–504.

Brooks, Simon, *Diwylliant Poblogaidd a'r Gymraeg, neu Yr ifanc a wyr, yr hen a dybia* . Cyfres y Cynulliad 2, pamphlet (Talybont: Y Lolfa, 1998).

——, 'Miss America: America a Diwylliant Poblogaidd Cymraeg ei Iaith', in M. Wynn Thomas (ed.), *Gweld Sêr* (Cardiff: University of Wales Press, 2001): 211–27.

Buchanan, Keith, 'The Revolt Against Satellization in Scotland and Wales', *Monthly Review* 19/10 (1968): 36–48.

Burnett, Robert, *The Global Jukebox: The International Music Industry* (London: Routledge, 1996).

Cale, John and Victor Bockris, *What's Welsh for Zen? The Autobiography of John Cale* (London: Bloomsbury Publishing, 1999).

Carter, Erica, James Donald and Judith Squires (eds.), *Space & Place: Theories of Identity and Location* (London: Lawrence & Wishart, 1993).

——, *Cultural Remix: Theories of Politics and the Popular* (London: Lawrence & Wishart, 1995).

Castells, Manuel, *The Power of Identity* (Oxford: Blackwell Publishers, 1997).

Chambers, Iain, *Urban Rhythms: Pop Music and Popular Culture* (Basingstoke: Macmillan, 1985).

——, *Popular Culture: The Metropolitan Experience* (London: Routledge, 1986).

——, 'Maps for the Metropolis: A Possible Guide to the Present', *Cultural Studies* 1/1 (1987): 1–21.

——, *Border Dialogues: Journeys in Postmodernity* (London: Routledge, 1990).

——, *Migrancy, Culture, Identity* (London: Routledge, 1994).

——, 'Narrative of Nationalism: Being "British"', in Erica Carter, James Donald and Judith Squires (eds.), *Cultural Remix: Theories of Politics and the Popular* (London: Lawrence & Wishart, 1995): 14–164.

Clarke, Donald, *The Rise and Fall of Popular Music* (London: Penguin, 1995).

Clews, Roy, *To Dream of Freedom* (Talybont: Y Lolfa, 1980).

Cloonan, Martin, 'State of the Nation: "Englishness", Pop, and Politics in the Mid-1990s', *Popular Music and Society* 21/2 (1997): 47–70.

Cohen, Anthony P. (ed.), *Belonging: Identity and Social Organisation in British Rural Cultures* (Manchester: Manchester University Press, 1982).

——, *The Symbolic Construction of Community* (Chichester: Ellis Horwood, 1985).

Cohen, Sara, *Rock Culture in Liverpool: Popular Music in the Making* (Oxford: Clarendon Press, 1991).

——, 'Popular Music and Urban Regeneration: The Music Industries of Merseyside', *Cultural Studies* 5/2 (1992): 332–46.

——, 'Localizing Sound', in Will Straw, Stacey Johnson, Rebecca Sullivan and Paul Friedlander (eds.), *Popular Music – Style and Identity* (Montreal: The Centre for Research on Canadian Cultural Industries and Institutions, 1995): 61–8.

Conner, Walker, 'When Is a Nation?', *Ethnic and Racial Studies* 13/1 (January 1990): 92–103.

Conversi, Daniele, 'Language or Race? The Choice of Core Values in the Development of Catalan and Basque Nationalisms', *Ethnic and Racial Studies* 13/1 (January 1990): 50–70.

Cowley, John, 'Cultural "Fusions": Aspects of British West Indian Music in the USA and Britain 1918–51', *Popular Music* 5 (1985): 81–96.

Crockett, Kate, *Y Sîn Roc: Hwylio 'Mlaen* (Talybont: Y Lolfa, 1995).

Cuthbert, Marlene, 'Cultural Autonomy and Popular Music: A Survey of Jamaican Youth', *Communication Research* 12/3 (1985): 381–93.

Davies, Cynog, trans. Harri Webb, 'Cymdeithas yr Iaith – The Manifesto', *Planet* 26/27 (Winter 1974/1975): 77–135.

Davies, Damian Walford, '"Rewriting the Law Books": The Poetry of Welsh Pop Music', *Welsh Music History* 1 (Cardiff: University of Wales Press, 1996): 206–40.

Davies, Janet, *The Welsh Language* (Cardiff: University of Wales Press, 1993).

——, 'The Welsh Language', in Trevor Herbert and Gareth Elwyn Jones (eds.), *Post-War Wales* (Cardiff: University of Wales Press, 1995): 55–77.

Davies, John, *Broadcasting and the BBC in Wales* (Cardiff: University of Wales Press, 1994).

——, *A History of Wales* (London: Penguin, 1993).

Davies, Pete, *Postmodernism and the Politics of Difference: Deconstruction, Resistance, Wales* (PhD dissertation, University of Wales, Cardiff, 1994).

Day, Graham, 'The Sociology of Wales: Issues and Prospects', *The Sociological Review* 27/3 (1979): 447–74.

—— and Jonathan Murdoch, 'Locality and Community: Coming to Terms with Place', *The Sociological Review* 41/1 (February, 1993): 82–111.

——, 'A Community of Communities? Similarity and Difference in Welsh Rural Community Studies', *The Economic and Social Review* 29/3 (July 1998): 233–57.

DeCurtis, Anthony (ed.), *Present Tense: Rock & Roll and Culture* (Durham: Duke University Press, 1992).

—— and James Henke (eds.), with Holly George-Warren, *The Rolling Stone Illustrated History of Rock & Roll* (New York: Random House, 1992).

Decker, Jeffrey Louis, 'The State of Rap: Time and Place in Hip Hop Nationalism', *Social Text* 34 (1993): 53–84.

Denisoff, R. Serge and Richard A.Peterson (eds.), *The Sounds of Social Change: Studies in Popular Culture* (Chicago: Rand McNally & Company, 1972).

Dewe, Mike, *The Skiffle Craze* (Aberystwyth: Planet, 1998).

Diani, Mario, 'The Concept of Social Movement', *The Sociological Review* 40/1 (February 1992): 1–25.

Dicks, Bella, *Heritage, Place and Community* (Cardiff: University of Wales Press, 2000).

Docker, John, *Postmodernism and Popular Culture: A Cultural History* (Cambridge: Cambridge University Press, 1996).

Donald, James, 'How English Is It? Popular Literature and National Culture', in Erica Carter, James Donald and Judith Squires (eds.), *Cultural Remix: Theories of Politics and the Popular* (London: Lawrence & Wishart, 1995): 165–86.

Dunkerley, David and Andrew Thompson (eds.), *Wales Today* (Cardiff: University of Wales Press, 1999).

Dworkin, Dennis L. and Leslie G. Roman (eds.), *Views Beyond the Border Country: Raymond Williams and Cultural Politics* (New York: Routledge, 1993).

Eagleton, Terry, *The Idea of Culture* (Oxford: Blackwell Publishers Ltd., 2000).

Easthope, Anthony and Kate McGowan (eds.), *A Critical and Cultural Theory Reader* (Buckingham: Open University Press, 1992).

Eaves, Steve, *Jazz yn y Nos* (Talybont: Y Lolfa, 1984a).

—— (ed.), *Y Trên Olaf Adref: Casgliad o Ganeuon Cyfoes* (Talybont: Y Lolfa, 1984b).

Ebenezer, Lyn, *Ar Log ers 20 Mlynedd* (Llanrwst: Gwasg Carreg Gwalch, 1996).

——, *Radio Cymru 21* (Llandysul: Gwasg Gomer, 1998).

Edgar, Andrew and Peter Sedgwick (eds.), *Key Concepts in Cultural Theory* (London: Routledge, 1999).

Edwards, David R., *Al, Mae'n Urdd Camp* (Talybont: Y Lolfa, 1992).

Emmett, Isobel, 'Blaenau Boys in the Mid-1960s', in Glyn Williams (ed.), *Social and Cultural Change in Contemporary Wales* (London: Routledge, 1978): 87–101.

Evans, Gwynfor, *Land of My Fathers* (Talybont: Y Lolfa, 1998).

——, *The Fight for Welsh Freedom* (Talybont: Y Lolfa, 2000).

Evans, Meredydd, *Caneuon Noson Lawen: Neuadd y Penrhyn, Bangor* (Llandebie: Llyfrau'r Dryw, 1948).

Eyerman, Ron and Andrew Jamison, *Music and Social Movements: Mobilizing Traditions in the Twentieth Century* (Cambridge: Cambridge University Press, 1998).

Fabbri, Franco, 'What Kind of Music?', in Richard Middleton and David Horn (eds.), *Popular Music* 2: *Theory and Method* (Cambridge: Cambridge University Press, 1982): 131–43.

Fanon, Frantz, *The Wretched of the Earth* (London: Penguin, 1990).

Featherstone, Mike, 'In Pursuit of the Postmodern: An Introduction', *Theory, Culture & Society* 5 (1988): 195–215.

Ferguson, Russell, Martha Gever, Trinh T. Minh-ha and Cornel West (eds.), *Out There: Marginalization and Contemporary Cultures* (New York: The New Museum of Contemporary Art and the MIT Press, 1990).

Fevre, Ralph and Andrew Thompson (eds.), *Nation, Identity and Social Theory: Perspectives from Wales* (Cardiff: University of Wales Press, 1999).

Fiske, John, 'The Culture of Everyday Life', in Lawrence Grossberg, Cary Nelson and Paula Triechler (eds.), *Cultural Studies* (New York: Routledge, 1992).

——, *Reading the Popular* (London: Routledge, 1995a).

——, *Understanding Popular Culture* (London: Routledge, 1995b).

Formations Editorial Collective (eds.), *Formations of Pleasure* (London: Routledge & Kegan Paul, 1983).

Fowler, Bridget, *Pierre Bourdieu and Cultural Theory: Critical Investigations* (London: Sage Publications, 1997).

——, (ed.) *Reading Bourdieu on Society and Culture* (Oxford: Blackwell Publishers, 2000).

Frith, Simon, '"The Magic That Can Set You Free": The Ideology of Folk and the Myth of the Rock Community', in Richard Middleton and David Horn (eds.), *Popular Music* 1: *Folk or Popular? Distinctions, Influences, Continuities* (Cambridge: Cambridge University Press, 1981): 159–68.

——, 'The Pleasures of the Hearth: The Making of BBC Light Entertainment', in Formations Editorial Collective (eds.), *Formations of Pleasure* (London: Routledge & Kegan Paul, 1983): 101–23.

——, *Sound Effects: Youth, Leisure, and the Politics of Rock'n'Roll* (London: Constable, 1987).

——, *Music for Pleasure* (Oxford: Basil Blackwell, 1988).

——, 'Anglo-America and Its Discontents', *Cultural Studies* 5/3 (1991): 263–9.

——, *Performing Rites: On the Value of Popular Music* (Oxford: Oxford University Press, 1996).

——, 'Music and Identity', in Stuart Hall and Paul du Gay (eds.), *Questions of Cultural Identity* (London: Sage Publications, 1997): 108–27.

—— and Andrew Goodwin (eds.), *On Record* (London: Routledge, 1990).

——, Andrew Goodwin and Lawrence Grossberg (eds.), *Sound and Vision: The Music Video Reader* (London and New York: Routledge, 1993).

——, Will Straw and John Street (eds.), *The Cambridge Companion to Pop and Rock* (Cambridge: Cambridge University Press, 2001).

Ganguly, Keya, 'Migrant Identities: Personal Memory and the Construction of Selfhood', *Cultural Studies* 6/1 (1992): 27–50.

Garofalo, Reebee, 'How Autonomous is Relative: Popular Music, the Social Formation and Cultural Struggle', *Popular Music* 6/1 (January 1987): 77–92.

—— (ed.), *Rockin' the Boat: Mass Music and Mass Movements* (Boston: South End Press, 1992).

——, 'Whose World, What Beat: The Transnational Music Industry, Identity, and Cultural Imperialism', *The World of Music* 35/2 (1993): 16–31.

Geary, Roger, '*Meibion Glyndŵr*: Folk-Devils or Folk-Heroes?', *Planet* 92 (April/May 1992): 39–44.

Geertz, Clifford, *The Interpretation of Cultures* (London: Fontana Press, 1993).

Giddens, Anthony, *The Consequences of Modernity* (Cambridge: Polity Press, 1997).

Gillett, Charlie, *The Sound of the City: The Rise of Rock and Roll* (New York: Da Capo Press, 1996).

—— and Simon Frith (eds.), *The Beat Goes On: The Rock File Reader* (London: Pluto Press, 1996).

Gilmore, Mikal, *Night Beat: A Shadow History of Rock & Roll* (New York: Doubleday, 1998).

Gilroy, Paul, 'Sounds Authentic: Black Music, Ethnicity, and the Challenge of a Changing Same', *Black Music Research Journal* 10/2 (1991): 111–37.

——, *The Black Atlantic: Modernity and Double Consciousness* (London: Verso, 1999).

——, *'There Ain't No Black in the Union Jack': The Cultural Politics of Race and Nation* (London: Routledge, 2000).

Gramsci, Antonio, 'Hegemony, Intellectuals and the State', in his *Selection from the Prison Notebooks*, trans. Quintin Hoare and Geoffrey Nowell-Smith (London: Lawrence & Wishart, 1971).

Gray, Ann and Jim McGuigan (eds.), *Studying Culture: An Introductory Reader* (London: Edward Arnold, 1993).

Gregory, Derek, *Geographical Imaginations* (Cambridge: Blackwell Publishers, 1994).

Grenier, Line, 'From "Diversity" to "Difference": The Case of Socio-Cultural Studies of Music', *New Formations* 9 (1989): 125–42.

—— and Jocelyne Guibault, '"Authority" Revisited: The "Other" in Anthropology and Popular Music Studies', *Ethnomusicology* 34/3 (Fall 1990): 381–97.

—— and Val Morrison, 'Quebec Sings "E Uassuian": The Coming of Age of a Local Music Industry', in Will Straw, Stacey Johnson, Rebecca Sullivan and Paul Friedlander (eds.), *Popular Music – Style and Identity* (Montreal: The Centre for Research on Canadian Cultural Industries and Institutions, 1995): 127–30.

Griffiths, Dai, 'Ffordd Eingl-Gymreig Grêt o Fyw?', *Golwg* 9/33 (1 May 1997).

——, 'Kelly, Cerys and James Dean Bradfield', in Trevor Herbert and Peter Stead (eds.), *Hymns and Arias: Great Welsh Voices* (Cardiff: University of Wales Press, 2001): 209–22.

—— and Sarah Hill, 'Postcolonial Music in Contemporary Wales: Hybridities and Weird Geographies', in Jane Aaron and Chris Williams (eds.), *Postcolonial Wales* (Cardiff: University of Wales Press, 2005): 215–33.

Grossberg, Lawrence, 'The Politics of Youth Culture: Some Observations on Rock and Roll in American Culture', *Social Text* 8 (1983): 104–26.

——, 'Another Boring Day in Paradise: Rock and Roll and the Empowerment of Everyday Life', in Richard Middleton and David Horn (eds.), *Popular Music 4: Performers & Audiences* (Cambridge: Cambridge University Press, 1984): 225–58.

——, 'Wandering Audiences, Nomadic Critics', *Cultural Studies* 2/3 (1988): 377–91.

——, *We Gotta Get Out of This Place: Popular Conservatism and Postmodern Culture* (New York: Routledge, 1992).

——, 'The Deconstruction of Youth', in John Storey (ed.), *Cultural Theory and Popular Culture* (Hemel Hempstead: Harvester Wheatsheaf, 1994): 183–90.

——, (ed.), 'On Postmodernism and Articulation: An Interview with Stuart Hall', in David Morley and Kuan-Hsing Chen (eds.), *Stuart Hall: Critical Dialogues in Cultural Studies* (London: Routledge, 1996).

——, *Dancing in Spite of Myself: Essays on Popular Culture* (Durham: Duke University Press, 1997).

——, Cary Nelson and Paula Treichler (eds.), *Cultural Studies* (New York: Routledge, 1992).

Gruffudd, Pyrs, 'Tradition, Modernity and the Countryside: The Imaginary Geography of Rural Wales', *Contemporary Wales* 6 (1994): 33–47.

Guilbault, Jocelyne, 'On Redefining the "Local" Through World Music', *The World of Music* 35/2 (1993): 33–47.

Gupta, Sunil (ed.), *Disrupted Borders: An Intervention in Definitions of Boundaries* (London: Rivers Oram Press, 1993).

—— and James Ferguson, 'Beyond "Culture": Space, Identity, and the Politics of Difference', *Cultural Anthropology* 7/1 (1992): 6–23.

Guralnick, Peter, *Sweet Sould Music: Rhythm and Blues and the Southern Dream of Freedom* (Boston: Back Bay Books, 1999).

Gusfield, Joseph R. (ed.), *Protest, Reform, and Revolt: A Reader in Social Movements* (New York: John Wiley & Sons, 1970).

Hael, Ifor, *Hael ar y Wlad* (Caernarfon: Cyhoeddiadau Mei, 1979).

Hall, Stuart, 'Cultural Identity and Diaspora', in Jonathan Rutherford (ed.), *Identity: Community, Culture, Difference* (London: Lawrence & Wishart, 1990).

—— and Paul du Gay (eds.), *Questions of Cultural Identity* (London: Sage Publications, 1997).

—— and Tony Jefferson (eds.), *Resistance Through Rituals: Youth Subcultures in Post-War Britain* (London: Routledge, 1976).

—— and Paddy Whannel, *The Popular Arts* (London: Pantheon Books, 1964).

——, Dorothy Hobson, Andrew Lowe and Paul Willis (eds.), *Culture, Media, Language: Working Papers in Cultural Studies, 1972–79* (London: Routledge, 1980).

Hargreaves, David J. and Adrian C. North, *The Social Psychology of Music* (Oxford: Oxford University Press, 1997).

Harris, John, *The Last Party* (London: Fouth Estate, 2003).

Hastings, Adrian, *The Construction of Nationhood: Ethnicity, Religion and Nationalism* (Cambridge: Cambridge University Press, 1997).

Hatch, David and Stephen Millward, *From Blues to Rock: An Analytical History of Pop Music* (Manchester: Manchester University Press, 1987).

Hawkins, Stan, *Setting the Pop Score: Pop Texts and Identity Politics* (Aldershot and Burlington: Ashgate, 2002).

Hayward, Philip (ed.), *Sound Alliances: Indigenous Peoples, Cultural Politics and Popular Music in the Pacific* (London: Cassell, 1998).

Hebdige, Dick, *Cut 'n Mix: Culture, Identity and Caribbean Music* (London, 1987).

—— 'Reggae, Rastas & Rudies', in Stuart Hall and Tony Jefferson (eds.), *Resistance Through Rituals: Youth Subcultures in Post-War Britain* (London: Routledge, 1998a).

——, *Subculture: The Meaning of Style* (London: Routledge, 1998b).

Hechter, Michael, 'Regional Inequality and National Integration: The Case of the British Isles', *Journal of Social History* 5/1 (1971): 96–117.

——*Internal Colonialism* (London: Routledge, 1975).

Herbert, Trevor and Gareth Elwyn Jones, *Post-War Wales* (Cardiff: University of Wales Press, 1995).

Herbert, Trevor and Peter Stead (eds.), *Hymns and Arias: Great Welsh Voices* (Cardiff: University of Wales Press, 2001).

Hill, Sarah, 'Mary Hopkin and the Deep Throat of Culture', in Laurie Stras (ed.), *She's So Fine: Whiteness, Femininity, Adolescence, and Class in the 1960s* (Durham: Duke University Press, forthcoming).

Hobsbawm, Eric, *Age of Extremes: The Short Twentieth Century 1914–1991* (London: Michael Joseph, 1994).

—— and T. Ranger (eds.), *The Invention of Tradition* (Cambridge: Cambridge University Press, 1983).

Hoggart, Richard, *The Uses of Literacy* (Oxford: Oxford University Press, 1958).

Hopwood, Mererid, *Singing in Chains: Listening to Welsh Verse* (Llandysul: Gomer, 2005).

Horn, David and Philip Tagg (eds.), *Popular Music Perspectives* (Göteborg and Exeter: International Association for the Study of Popular Music, 1982).

Horner, Bruce and Thomas Swiss (eds.), *Key Terms in Popular Music and Culture* (Oxford: Blackwell Publishers, 1999).

Howell, W.J., Jr, 'Minority-Language Broadcasting and the Continuation of Celtic Culture in Wales and Ireland', in Stephen Harold Riggins (ed.), *Ethnic Minority Media* (London: Sage, 1992).

Hume, I. and W.T.R. Pryce, *The Welsh and Their Country* (Llandysul: Gomer Press, 1986).

Humphreys, Emyr, *The Taliesin Tradition: A Quest for the Welsh Identity* (Bridgend: Seren, 1989).

Ifan, Tecwyn, *Caneuon Tecwyn Ifan* (Talybont: Y Lolfa, 1980).

Iwan, Dafydd, *Oriau Gyda Dafydd Iwan* (Talybont: Y Lolfa, 1969).

——, *Holl Ganeuon Dafydd Iwan* (Talybont: Y Lolfa, 1992).

——, 'Label y Chwyldro', *Barn* 434 (Mawrth 1999): 52–7.

Jameson, Fredric, *Postmodernism, or, the Cultural Logic of Late Capitalism* (London: Verso, 1991).

——, 'On "Cultural Studies"', *Social Text* 34 (1993): 17–52.

Jarman, Geraint, *Eira Cariad* (Llandybie: Christopher Davies, 1970).

——, *Cerddi Alfred St.* (Llandysul: Gwasg Gomer, 1976).

Jenkins, Richard, *Pierre Bourdieu* (London and New York: Routledge, 2002).

Johnson, Hazel, 'Local Forms of Resistance: Weapons of the Weak', in Tracey Skelton and Tim Allen (eds), *Culture and Global Change* (London: Routledge, 1999): 159–66.

Jones, Alun R. and Gwyn Thomas (eds.), *Presenting Saunders Lewis* (Cardiff: University of Wales Press, 1973).

Jones, Bobi, 'The Roots of Welsh Inferiority', *Planet* 22 (March 1974): 53–72.

Jones, Gareth Elwyn, *Modern Wales: A Concise History* (Cambridge: Cambridge University Press, 1994).

Jones, Simon, *Black Culture, White Youth: The Reggae Tradition from JA to UK* (Basingstoke: Macmillan Education, 1988).

Kahn, Karen, 'Land, Language and Community: A Symbolic Analysis of Welsh Nationalism', *Michigan Discussions in Anthropology* 7 (1984): 11–32.

Kaplan, Ann, *Rocking Around the Clock* (London and New York: Routledge, 1987).

Keyes, Cheryl L., 'At the Crossroads: Rap Music and Its African Nexus', *Ethnomusicology* 40/2 (Spring/Summer 1996): 223–48.

Khleif, Bud, 'Ethnic Awakening in the First World: The Case of Wales', in Glyn Williams (ed.), *Social and Cultural Change in Contemporary Wales* (London: Routledge, 1978): 102–19.

King, Anthony D. (ed.), *Culture, Globalization and the World-System* (Basingstoke: Macmillan Education, 1991).

Klein, Joe, *Woody Guthrie: A Life* (London: Faber and Faber, 1998).

Krader, Barbara, 'Slavic Folk Music: Forms of Singing and Self-Identity', *Ethnomusicology* 31 (1987): 9–17.

Krims, Adam, *Rap Music and the Poetics of Identity* (Cambridge: Cambridge University Press, 2000).

Lacasse, Serge, 'Interpretation of Vocal Staging by Popular Music Listeners: A Reception Test', *Psychomusicology* 17 (spring/autumn 2001): 56–76.

——, 'Technological Musical Parameters in Recorded Popular Music', in Kimi Kärki, Rebecca Leydon and Henri Terho (eds.), *Looking Back, Looking Ahead: Popular Music Studies 20 Years Later* (Turku: IASPM-Norden, 2002).

——, 'La musique populaire comme discours phonographique: fondements d'une approche analytique', *Musicologies* 2 (printemps 2005): 25–39.

Laclau, Ernesto (ed.) *The Making of Political Identities* (London: Verso, 1994).

Leavis, F.R., *Mass Civilisation and Minority Culture* (Cambridge: Minority Press, 1930).

Lefebvre, Henri, *The Production of Space*, trans. Donald Nicholson-Smith (Oxford: Blackwell Publishers, 1996).

Lewis, George H., 'Storm Blowing from Paradise: Social Protest and Oppositional Ideology in Popular Hawaiian Music', *Popular Music* 10/1 (1991): 53–67.

——, 'Who Do You Love? The Dimensions of Musical Taste', in James Lull (ed.), *Popular Music and Communication* (London: Sage Publications, 1992): 144.

Leonard, Deke, *Maybe I Should've Stayed in Bed?* (Bordon: Northdown Publishing, 2000).

——, *Rhinos, Winos & Lunatics: The Legend of Man – a Rock'n'roll Band* (Bordon: Northdown Publishing, 2001).

Leyshon, Andrew, David Matless and George Revill (eds.), *The Place of Music* (New York: The Guilford Press, 1998).

Lipsitz, George, 'Cruising Around the Historical Bloc – Postmodernism and Popular Music in East Los Angeles', *Cultural Critique*, 5 (1986–87): 157–77.

——, *Dangerous Crossroads: Popular Music, Postmodernism and the Poetics of Place* (London: Verso, 1994).

Llewellyn, Meic, 'Beyond the Transatlantic Model: A Look at Popular Music as if Small Societies Mattered', *Critical Musicology Journal* (available online at: www.leeds.ac.uk/music/Info/CMJ/Articles/1998/02/01.html).

——, 'Welsh – The Language of Rock!', *Planet*, 129 (June/July1998): 56–64.

——, 'Popular Music in the Welsh Language and the Affirmation of Youth Identities', *Popular Music* 19/3 (October 2000): 319–39.

Lloyd, Tecwyn, 'Wales – See England', *Planet* 34 (1976): 36–47.

Llywelyn, Emyr, 'Cynghanedd Gytbwys', *Sgrech* 9 (Nadolig 1979): 8.

Longhurst, Brian, *Popular Music and Society* (Cambridge: Polity Press, 1995).

Ludwig, Hans-Werner and Lothar Fietz (eds.), *Poetry in the British Isles: Non-Metropolitan Perspectives* (Cardiff: University of Wales Press, 1995).

MacDonald, Sharon (ed.), *Inside European Identities* (Oxford: Berg Publishers, 1997).

Manuel, Peter, 'Andalusian, Gypsy, and Class Identity in the Contemporary Flamenco Complex', *Ethnomusicology* 33/1 (Winter 1989): 47–65.

Marcus, Greil, *Mystery Train* (London: Omnibus Press, 1977).

Martin, Peter J., *Sounds & Society: Themes in the Sociology of Music* (Manchester: Manchester University Press, 1995).

Martin-Barbero, Jesus, 'Communication from Culture: The Crisis of the National and the Emergence of the Popular', *Media, Culture and Society* 10 (1988): 447–65.

Marwick, Arthur, *The Sixties* (Oxford: Oxford University Press, 1998).

Massey, Doreen, 'A Global Sense of Place', in Ann Gray and Jim McGuigan (eds.), *Studying Culture: An Introductory Reader* (London: Edward Arnold, 1993): 232–40.

Mattern, Mark, *Acting in Concert: Music, Community, and Political Action* (New Brunswick: Rutgers University Press, 1998).

Mei, Dafydd, *Y Tebot Piws* (Penygroes: Gwasg y Tir, 1974).

Middleton, Richard, 'Articulating Musical Meaning / Re-Constructing Musical History / Locating the "Popular"', *Popular Music* 5 (1985): 5–43.

——, 'In the Groove, or Blowing Your Mind? The Pleasures of Musical Repetition', in Tony Bennett, Colins Mercer and Janet Woollacott (eds.), *Popular Culture and Social Relations* (Milton Keynes: Open University Press, 1986): 139–76.

—— (ed.), *Reading Pop: Approaches to Textual Analysis in Popular Music* (Oxford: Oxford University Press, 2000).

——, *Studying Popular Music* (Milton Keynes: Open University Press, 2002).

—— and David Horn (eds.), *Popular Music 1: Folk or Popular? Distinctions, Influences, Continuities* (Cambridge: Cambridge University Press, 1981).

Mitchell, Tony, *Popular Music and Local Identity: Rock, Pop and Rap in Europe and Oceania* (London: Leicester University Press, 1996).

—— (ed.), *Global Noise: Rap and Hip-Hop Outside the USA* (Middletown, Connecticut: Wesleyan University Press, 2001).

Moore, Allan F., *Rock: The Primary Text* (Aldershot: Ashgate, 2001).

Morgan, Kenneth O., *Rebirth of a Nation: Wales 1880–1980* (Oxford University Press, 1990).

Morgan, Peter, 'My Patio's On Fire', *Planet,* 125 (1997): 31–40.

Morgan, Prys, 'From a Death to A View: The Hunt for the Welsh Past in the Romantic Period', Eric Hobsbawn and T. Ranger (eds.), *The Invention of Tradition* (Cambridge: Cambridge University Press, 1983): 43–100.

Morley, David and Kuan-Hsing Chen (eds.), *Stuart Hall: Critical Dialogues in Cultural Studies* (London: Routledge, 1996).

Morus, Elena (ed.), *Camau'r Chwarter Canrif: Hanes Cwmni Sain Recordiau Cyf. 1969–1994* (Llanrwst: Wasg Carreg Gwalch, 1994).

Mukerji, Chandra and Michael Schudso (eds.), *Rethinking Popular Culture: Contemporary Perspectives in Cultural Studies* (Oxford: University of California Press, 1991).

Murphy, Tim, 'The When, Where, and Who of Pop Lyrics: The Listener's Prerogative', *Popular Music* 8/2 (1989): 185–93.

Mynediad am Ddim, *Digon Hen i Yfed! Dathlu Deunaw Oed Mynediad am Ddim 1974–1992* (Llanrwst: Gwasg Carreg Gwalch, 1992).

Nairn, Tom, 'Scotland and Wales: Notes on Nationalist Pre-History', *Planet,* 34 (1976): 1–11.

——, *The Break-Up of Britain* (London: Verso, 1981).

Nelson, Cary and Lawrence Grossberg (eds.), *Marxism and the Interpretation of Culture* (Urbana and Chicago: University of Illinois Press, 1988).

Nowell-Smith, Geoffrey, 'Popular Culture', *New Formations* 2 (1987): 79–90.

Oliver, Paul (ed.), *Black Music in Britain: Essays on the Afro-Asian Contribution to Popular Music* (Buckingham: Open University Press, 1990).

Osmond, John, *The National Question Again: Welsh Political Identity in the 1980s* (Llandysul: Gomer Press, 1985).

Owens, David, *Cerys, Catatonia and the Rise of Welsh Pop* (London: Ebury Press, 2000).

Parekh, Bhikhu, 'Discourses on National Identity', *Political Studies* 42/3 (1994): 492–504.

Patterson, Tim, 'Notes on the Historical Application of Marxist Cultural Theory', *Science and Society* 39/3 (Fall 1975): 257–91.

Peterson, Richard A., 'Why 1955? Explaining the Advent of Rock Music', *Popular Music* 9/1 (1990): 97–116.

Philip, Alan Butt, *The Welsh Question: Nationalism in Welsh Politics 1945–1970* (Cardiff: University of Wales Press, 1975).

Phillips, Dylan, *Trwy Ddulliau Chwyldro...? Hanes Cymdeithas yr Iaith Gymraeg, 1962–1992* (Llandysul: Gwasg Gomer, 1998).

Poole, Richard, 'The Politics of Place', *Planet*, 119 (1996): 66–71.

Potash, Chris (ed.), *Reggae, Rasta, Revolution: Jamaican Music from Ska to Dub* (London: Books with Attitude, 1997).

Potter, Russell A., *Spectacular Vernaculars: Hip-Hop and the Politics of Postmodernism* (Albany: State University of New York Press, 1995).

Pratt, Ray, 'Popular Music, Free Space, and the Quest for Community', *Popular Music and Society* 13 (Winter 1989): 58–76.

Pulis, John W,, '"Up-full Sounds": Language, Identity, and the Worldview of Rastafari', in Chris Potash (ed.), *Reggae, Rasta, Revolution: Jamaican Music from Ska to Dub* (London: Books With Attitude, 1997): 25–6.

Puw, Guto Pryderi, 'Dwyieithrwydd a Cherddoriaeth Boblogaidd yng Nghymru', *Tu Chwith* 8 (Gaeaf, 1997): 27–32.

Radway, Janice, 'Reception Study: Ethnography and the Problems of Dispersed Audiences and Nomadic Subjects', *Cultural Studies* 2/3 (1987): 359–76.

Rawkins, Phillip M., 'Outsiders as Insiders: The Implications of Minority Nationalism in Scotland and Wales', *Comparative Politics* 10/4 (July 1978): 519–34.

——, 'An Approach to the Political Sociology of the Welsh Nationalist Movement', *Political Studies* 27 (1979): 440–57.

Redhead, Steve, *The End-of-the-Century Party: Youth and Pop Towards 2000* (Manchester: Manchester University Press, 1990).

_____ and John Street, 'Have I the Right? Legitimacy, Authenticity and Community in Folk's Politics', *Popular Music* 8/2 (1989): 177–84.

Rhys, Robert, 'Yn Erbyn y Graen', *Barn* 467/468 (Rhagfyr 2001/Ionawr 2002): 57–9.

Riggins, Stephen Harold (ed.), *Ethnic Minority Media: An International Perspective* (London: Sage Publications, 1992).

Robertson, Roland and Burkart Holzner (eds.), *Identity and Authority: Explorations in the Theory of Society* (Oxford: Basil Blackwell, 1980).

Robinson, Deanna Campbell, Elizabeth B. Buck and Marlene Cuthbert (eds.) and The International Communication and Youth Consortium, *Music at the Margins: Popular Music and Global Cultural Diversity* (London: Sage Publications, 1991).

Rose, Tricia, *Black Noise: Rap Music and Black Culture in Contemporary America* (Middletown, Connecticut: Wesleyan University Press, 1994).

Ross, Andrew, *No Respect: Intellectuals & Popular Culture* (New York: Routledge, 1989).

Rutherford, Jonathan, *Identity: Community, Culture, Difference* (London: Lawrence & Wishart, 1998).

Rutten, Paul, 'Local Popular Music on the National and International Markets', *Cultural Studies* 5/3 (1991): 294–305.

Sarup, Madan, *Identity, Culture and the Postmodern World* (Edinburgh University Press, 1996).

Schlesinger, Philip, 'On National Identity: Some Conceptions and Misconceptions Criticized', *Social Science Information* 26/2 (1987): 219–64.

Scott, Derek (ed.), *Music, Culture and Society: A Reader* (Oxford: Oxford University Press, 2000).

Shade, Ruth, 'Direct Activists: The Roots of Welsh Rock', *Planet* 145 (February/March 2001): 25–35.

Shepherd, John, 'A Theoretical Model for the Sociomusicological Analysis of Popular Musics', in Richard Middleton and David Horn (eds.), *Popular Music 2: Theory and Method* (Cambridge: Cambridge University Press, 1982): 145–77.

——, Phil Virden, Graham Vulliamy and Trevor Wishart (eds.), *Whose Music? A Sociology of Musical Languages* (London: Latimer New Dimensions, 1977).

Shuker, Roy, *Understanding Popular Music* (London: Routledge, 1994).

Skelton, Tracey and Tim Allen (eds.), *Culture and Global Change* (London: Routledge, 1999).

Slobin, Mark, *Subcultural Sounds: Micromusics of the West* (Hanover: Wesleyan University Press, 1993).

Smith, Anna Marie, 'Rastafari as Resistance and the Ambiguities of Essentialism in the "New Social Movements"', in Ernesto Laclau (ed.), *The Making of Political Identities* (London: Verso, 1994): 171–204.

Smith, Dai, 'Shirley Bassey', in Trevor Herbert and Peter Stead (eds.), *Hymns and Arias: Great Welsh Voices* (Cardiff: University of Wales Press, 2001): 195–208.

Sontag, Susan (ed.), *A Roland Barthes Reader* (London: Vintage, 1983).

Stevens, Meic, *I Adrodd yr Hanes*, cofnodwyd gan Lyn Ebenezer (Gwasg Carreg Gwalch, 1993).

Stokes, Martin (ed.), *Ethnicity, Identity and Music: The Musical Construction of Place* (Oxford: Brg Publishers, 1994).

Storey, John, *Cultural Studies and the Study of Popular Culture*, (Edinburgh: Edinburgh University Press, 1996).

—— (ed.), *Cultural Theory and Popular Culture: A Reader* (Hemel Hempstead: Harvester Wheatsheaf, 1998).

Straw, Will, 'Systems of Articulation, Logics of Change: Communities and Scenes in Popular Music', *Cultural Studies* 5 (1991): 368–88.

——, Stacey Johnson, Rebecca Sullivan and Paul Friedlander (eds.), *Popular Music – Style and Identity* , International Association for the Study of Popular Music Seventh International Conference on Popular Music Studies (Montreal: The Centre for Research on Canadian Cultural Industries and Institutions: 1995).

Stephens, Huw, 'Wedi Cŵl Cymru', *Barn* 467/468 (Rhagfyr 2001/Ionawr 2002): 60–61.

Street, John, *Rebel Rock* (Oxford: Basil Blackwell, 1986).

——, 'Local Differences? Popular Music and the Local State', *Popular Music* 12 (1993): 43–55.

——, '(Dis)located? Rhetoric, Politics, Meaning and the Locality', in Will Straw, Stacey Johnson, Rebecca Sullivan and Paul Friedlander (eds), *Popular Music – Style and Identity* (Montreal: The Centre for Research on Canadian Cultural Industries and Institutions, 1995): 255–64.

——, *Politics & Popular Culture* (Cambridge: Polity Press, 1997).

Strinati, Dominic, 'Postmodernism and Popular Culture', in John Storey (ed.), *Cultural Theory and Popular Culture* (Hemel Hempstead: Harvester Wheatsheaf, 1994): 428–38.

Swartz, David, *Culture & Power: The Sociology of Pierre Bourdieu* (Chicago: University of Chicago Press, 1997).

Swiss, Thomas, John Sloop and Andrew Herman (eds.), *Mapping the Beat: Popular Music and Contemporary Theory* (Malden: Blackwell Publishers, 1998).

Symon, Peter, 'Music and National Identity in Scotland: A Study of Jock Tamson's Bairns', *Popular Music* 16/2 (1997): 203–17.

Szatmary, David P., *A Time to Rock: A Social History of Rock and Roll* (Upper Saddle River: Prentice Hall, 1996).

Szemere, Anna, 'Some Institutional Aspects of Pop and Rock in Hungary', in Richard Middleton and David Horn (eds.), *Popular Music 3: Producers and Markets* (Cambridge: Cambridge University Press, 1983): 121–37.

Tagg, Philip, 'Analysing Popular Music: Theory, Method and Practice', *Popular Music* 2 (1982): 37–67.

——, 'Open Letter: "Black Music", "Afro-American Music" and "European Music"', *Popular Music* 8 (1989): 285–98.

Tanner, Roger, 'National Identity and the One-Wales Model', *Planet* 17 (April/May 1973): 31–4.

Taylor, Timothy D., *Global Pop: World Music, World Markets* (New York: Routledge, 1997).

Thomas, M. Wynn (ed.), *Gweld Sêr: Cymru a Chanrif America* (Cardiff: University of Wales Press, 2001).

Thomas, Ned, 'Culture, Community, Territory and Survival', *Planet* 17 (April/May 1973): 21–4.

——, *The Welsh Extremist* (Talybont: Y Lolfa, 1994).

Thomas, R.S., 'Reflections', from his *No Trace with the Furies* (Tarset: Bloodaxe Books, 1995).

Toop, David, *Rap Attack 3: African Rap to Global Hip Hop* (London: Serpent's Tail, 2000).

Tudur, Gwilym, *Wyt Ti'n Cofio?* (Talybont: Y Lolfa, 1989).

Wade, Peter, 'Music, Blackness and National Identity: Three Moments in Colombian History', *Popular Music* 17/1 (1998): 1–19.

Waites, Bernard, Tony Bennett and Graham Martin (eds.), *Popular Culture: Past and Present* (London: Routledge, 1993).

Wallis, Roger and Krister Malm, 'Sain Cymru: The Role of the Welsh Phonographic Industry in the Development of a Welsh Language Pop/Rock/Folk Scene', in Richard Middleton and Trevor Horn (eds.), *Popular Music* 3: *Producers and Markets* (Cambridge: Cambridge University Press, 1983): 77–105.

——, *Big Sounds from Small Peoples: The Music Industry in Small Countries* (New York: Pendragon Press, 1984).

Walser, Robert, 'Rhythm, Rhyme, and Rhetoric in the Music of Public Enemy', *Ethnomusicology* 39/2 (Spring/Summer 1995): 193–217.

Ward, Brian, *Just My Soul Responding: Rhythm and Blues, Black Consciousness, and Race Relations* (Berkeley: University of California Press, 1998).

Ward, Ed, Geoffrey Stokes and Ken Tucker, *Rock of Ages: The Rolling Stone History of Rock & Roll* (New York: Summit Books, 1986).

Whiteley, Sheila, *Women and Popular Music: Sexuality, Identity and Subjectivity* (London: Routledge, 2000).

Wicke, Peter, trans. Rachel Fogg, *Rock Music: Culture, Aesthetics and Sociology* (Cambridge: Cambridge University Press, 1990).

Williams, Charlotte, 'Passports to Wales? Race, Nation and Identity', in Ralph Fevre and Andrew Thompson (eds.), *National, Identity and Social Theory: Perspectives from Wales* (Cardiff: University of Wales Press, 1999).

——, *Sugar and Slate* (Aberystwyth: Planet, 2002).

Williams, Colin H. (ed.), 'Non-Violence and the Development of the Welsh Language Society, 1962—c. 1974', *Welsh History Review* 8/4 (1977): 426–55.

——, *Language Revitalization: Policy and Planning in Wales* (Cardiff: University of Wales Press, 2000).

Williams, Daniel (ed.), *Who Speaks for Wales? Nation, Culture and Identity* (Cardiff: University of Wales Press, 2003).

Williams, Emyr Glyn, 'Oes Mewn Eiliad: Adolygiad *Llawenydd Heb Ddiwedd*', *Golwg* (2 May 1991): 16.

Williams, Glyn (ed.), *Social and Cultural Change in Contemporary Wales* (London: Routledge, 1978).

—— (ed.), *Crisis of Economy and Ideology: Essays on Welsh Society, 1840–1980* (BSA Sociology of Wales Study Group, 1983).

Williams, Gwyn A., *When Was Wales?* (London: Penugin, 1985).

Williams, Kevin, 'Singing in the Rain: Music Making and the Media', *Planet* 103 (February/March 1994): 16–19.

Williams, Raymond, *The Long Revolution* (London: Chatto & Windus, 1961).

——, *The Country and the City* (New York: Oxford University Press, 1973).

——, *Marxism and Literature* (Oxford: Oxford University Press, 1977).

——, *The Sociology of Culture* (Chicago: University of Chicago Press, 1981).

——, *Culture & Society: 1780–1950* (New York: Columbia University Press, 1983).

——, *Keywords* (London: Fontana Press, 1988).

——, *Culture* (London: Fontana Press, 1989).

Willis, Paul, *Common Culture* (Milton Keynes: Open University Press, 1990).

Wilson, Clint C. II and Félix Gutiérrez (eds.), *Race, Multiculturalism, and the Media: From Mass to Class Communication*, Second Edition (Thousand Oaks: SAGE Publications, 1995).

Winick, Stephen D., 'Breton Folk Music, Breton Identity, and Alan Stivell's *Again*', *Journal of American Folklore* 108/429 (Summer 1995): 334–54.

Witmer, Robert, '"Local" and "Foreign": The Popular Music Culture of Kingston, Jamaica, Before Ska, Rock Steady and Reggae', *Latin American Music Review* 8/1 (1987): 1–25.

Wodak, Ruth, Rudolf de Cillia, Martin Reisigl and Karin Liebhart (eds.), trans. Angelika Hirsch and Richard Mitten, *The Discursive Construction of National Identity* (Edinburgh: Edinburgh University Press, 1999).

Wyn, Hefin, 'The Alternative Eisteddfod', *Arcade* (7 August 1981): 9.

——, *Be Bop-a Lula'r Delyn Aur* (Talybont: Y Lofla, 2003).

Y Lolfa (pub.), *Canwn!* (Talybont: Y Lolfa, 1990).

Zizek, Slavoj, *Tarrying with the Negative: Kant, Hegel and the Critique of Ideology* (Durham: Duke University Press, 1993).

Index